M000265712

BLAMED
AND
BROKEN

CURT PETROVICH

BLAMED
AND
BROKEN

The Mounties and the
Death of Robert Dziekanski

DUNDURN
TORONTO

Copyright © Curt Petrovich, 2019

All rights reserved. No part of this publication may be reproduced, stored in a retrieval system, or transmitted in any form or by any means, electronic, mechanical, photocopying, recording, or otherwise (except for brief passages for purpose of review) without the prior permission of Dundurn Press. Permission to photocopy should be requested from Access Copyright.

Cover image: istock.com/Carnegie42
Printer: Webcom, a division of Marquis Book Printing Inc.

Library and Archives Canada Cataloguing in Publication

Petrovich, Curt, author
    Blamed and broken : the Mounties and the death of Robert Dziekanski
/ Curt Petrovich.

Includes bibliographical references and index.
Issued in print and electronic formats.
ISBN 978-1-4597-4293-2 (softcover).--ISBN 978-1-4597-4294-9 (PDF).--
ISBN 978-1-4597-4295-6 (EPUB)

    1. Dziekanski, Robert. 2. Dziekanski, Robert--Death and burial. 3. Royal Canadian Mounted Police.
4. Police--Complaints against--Canada. 5. Police misconduct--Canada. 6. Police brutality--Canada.
7. Law enforcement--Canada. 8. Stun guns--Canada. 9. Governmental investigations--Canada. I. Title.

HV7936.C56P48 2019   363.2'32   C2018-905126-4
                                              C2018-905127-2

1 2 3 4 5   22 21 20 19 18

 Conseil des Arts du Canada   Canada Council for the Arts    Canadä    ONTARIO ARTS COUNCIL CONSEIL DES ARTS DE L'ONTARIO an Ontario government agency un organisme du gouvernement de l'Ontario

We acknowledge the support of the **Canada Council for the Arts**, which last year invested $153 million to bring the arts to Canadians throughout the country, and the **Ontario Arts Council** for our publishing program. We also acknowledge the financial support of the **Government of Ontario**, through the **Ontario Book Publishing Tax Credit** and **Ontario Creates**, and the **Government of Canada**.

Nous remercions le **Conseil des arts du Canada** de son soutien. L'an dernier, le Conseil a investi 153 millions de dollars pour mettre de l'art dans la vie des Canadiennes et des Canadiens de tout le pays.

Care has been taken to trace the ownership of copyright material used in this book. The author and the publisher welcome any information enabling them to rectify any references or credits in subsequent editions.
— *J. Kirk Howard, President*

The publisher is not responsible for websites or their content unless they are owned by the publisher.

Printed and bound in Canada.

VISIT US AT

 dundurn.com |  @dundurnpress | dundurnpress | dundurnpress

Dundurn
3 Church Street, Suite 500
Toronto, Ontario, Canada
M5E 1M2

For Yvette, Eliana, and Daniel,
who graciously, sometimes grudgingly,
but always selflessly indulged me with the time,
space, and support to finish what I started.

CONTENTS

FOREWORD

THE STORY THAT UNFOLDS in the pages ahead is a formidable reminder that things are not always as they seem or as they are reported. Daily life is fast moving. Reports of injustices and tragedies in cases such as the Vancouver Airport (YVR) incident in 2007 inhabit our minds for a few minutes. Then, we get back to our lives until the next report comes out. Most of us don't have the luxury of stopping time to learn what lies beyond the headlines. News reports rarely disclose the breadth of a story. Most assuredly, Mr. Dziekanski's death was a tragedy. But, this book will allow you to see the tragedy did not end there.

I know something of injustice and the tendency of police and governments to practise obfuscation and misdirection. For the better part of a decade ending in 2005, I lead the Commission for Public Complaints Against the RCMP. As chair and CEO of the civilian agency charged with holding the Mounties accountable, combating the dysfunction of the force was my job. In my years as a lawyer — especially those spent as an investigator with the Security Intelligence Review Committee, which oversees Canada's spy agency CSIS — I have been at the nexus between human rights and national security cases. For a dozen years I was an advisor to Abdullah Almalki, the Canadian who was detained and tortured for two years in Syria based on false information supplied by the RCMP. It was an unconscionable abuse made worse by the complicity of successive federal governments. Injustice — whether deliberate or symptomatic of bureaucracies — can occur in many ways. The author of *Blamed and Broken* has been a patient witness to that.

The most vivid recollection of my first encounter with Curt Petrovich was when I was chair of the Commission for Public Complaints against the RCMP. In 1998, I called an inquiry infamously known as "Peppergate." RCMP members were accused of a multitude of serious misconduct against demonstrators who protested against the presence of Indonesia's President Suharto, a cruel dictator who attended the Asia Pacific Economic Conference in Vancouver. Demonstrators and the media were very critical of Prime Minister Chrétien for inviting Suharto. A political frenzy developed and media labelled me a puppet of the Prime Minister because I made it clear that my legislative mandate was to oversee the RCMP and not the Prime Minister. It was my first encounter with "paparazzi-like" journalism. I was besieged daily by reporters levelling accusations, putting words in my mouth and asking questions that were irrelevant to my duties as civilian overseer of the RCMP. I was completely unaccustomed to dealing with the media. I felt like a deer in headlights as reporters followed me home, to my office and in airports. I resolved to stop giving interviews.

One late evening, alone in my Ottawa office, my phone rang and I instinctively answered it. The voice on the line introduced himself as Curt Petrovich, a CBC journalist. I really wanted to hang up immediately but my strict French-Catholic upbringing would not allow me to be so rude. Unlike numerous other journalists I had dealt with before him, Curt was courteous, respectful, and already well informed on the matter. He was looking for truth and accuracy. You may think — that's the job of every reporter — but that had not been my experience up to that point. His calm manner immediately made me feel comfortable. He was thoughtful, well-prepared, and meticulous. I never forgot it. It is that approach that produces a great story in the hands of a journalist like Curt, that has allowed him to uncover so much on the ongoing Dziekanski tragedy.

It takes time and patience for journalists to dig deep to report on the scope of such a story. In the more than ten years since the YVR tragedy, Curt has worked tirelessly investigating, researching, interviewing witnesses, meeting with sources, analyzing videos, attending court hearings, and documenting everything he uncovered from those involved and those who had knowledge of the circumstances at different times along the way. Many troubling questions arose — questions that challenged the concept of justice, as we know it. The weight of the truth you will find in this book is heart wrenching.

Curt exposes how flaws creep into some of our important institutions, and how we are fed information from the media and some of our leaders that is too often one dimensional. They are flaws most Canadians will never see unless they are unfortunate enough to have an adverse contact with the courts, the police, or the media. When it comes to the death of Robert Dziekanski and the role four Mounties played, there are undoubtedly many who find satisfaction and closure in the final report of Thomas Braidwood's public inquiry into what happened. Likewise, many people are unfazed by the contradictory conclusions of the officers' criminal trials. Curt was unwilling to stop asking questions after the gavels fell — the sign of a dedicated journalist. Carl Bernstein, who helped bring the Watergate scandal to light has often said that it is the job of journalists to pursue and present "the best obtainable version of the truth." *Blamed and Broken* is just that.

Shirley Heafey, B.A., LLB.
September 2018

PREFACE

WHEN MY PHONE RANG on a Sunday morning in October 2007, I had no way of knowing the call would be an assignment with a rolling deadline lasting more than a decade. As I grudgingly abandoned a day off and went to work, I expected the story of a man who died at Vancouver International Airport would be a simple one and short-lived, as are most police blotter incidents.

That was only the first of several mistaken assumptions I made about the death of Robert Dziekanski. The second was tacitly accepting the easy story that "bad cops" killed him. It was a simple, smug, and seductive narrative. After all, I thought, what else mattered outside of the twenty-six seconds between a Mountie's cordial "How's it goin', bud?" and the crack of a Taser that brought Dziekanski to the floor? It was caught on video. The camera doesn't lie, or so the aphorism goes. A less comforting reality, however, is that a camera doesn't tell the whole story and sometimes what it doesn't see is worse than a lie.

As those twenty-six seconds stretched into years, I examined a more troubling possibility: the Mounties who confronted Dziekanski did what they'd been trained to do and those who sat in judgment were inevitably influenced by repeatedly watching the video of a man die. Frame by frame. In slow motion. Over and over again. Every single person who has ever watched what has become known as the Pritchard video — so named after the bystander who recorded it — has something the four

Mounties involved never had at the time: knowledge of how it ends. Yet, over the years, the media, politicians, the public, and the criminal courts summarily dismissed that inconvenient fact, just as quickly as they did the notion that Dziekanski had anything to do with his own fate. Not even Thomas Braidwood, the retired judge who conducted a public inquiry and ultimately condemned the Mounties, believed they intended to harm Dziekanski. Yet their split-second actions were viewed, by judges and journalists alike, through a distorting lens, making them all seem guilty.

It is impossible to overestimate the impact of the Pritchard video in an era before everyone had a high-quality video camera built into the cellphone in their pocket or purse. While civil rights experts and police critics occasionally highlighted cases of deaths in police custody, few people had ever seen one. Few people understood how the Taser worked, with many believing it "electrocuted" its target. For many, seeing and *hearing* Dziekanski's reaction, knowing that he died, made it easy to conclude that four brutal police officers killed him.

———

The oxygen feeding that flame is, of course, the fact that police do kill people, sometimes in encounters that seem entirely avoidable. It was a viral video in 2014 showing an unarmed black man being shot and killed by police in Ferguson, Missouri, that was the impetus for the *Washington Post* to create a database — the first of its kind — to get a handle on the problem of people killed by police bullets. Journalists logged 995 deaths in the United States in 2015 — double what police themselves had reported. Similar figures were produced in subsequent years.

Today, video — shot by both bystanders and police themelves — has become commonplace. Fresh examples are served up on social media regularly, often with an attached condemnation that people are being brutalized or killed by the police. Minority groups feel that they are targeted: Indigenous leaders in Canada have argued this point on numerous occasions, and groups such as Black Lives Matter have protested against the violence that they feel the police subject them to for committing the crime of "living while black."

In Canada, the number of people killed by police is lower, drastically so, than it is in the United States. But it is still an issue. It took a lot of hard work by a number of dedicated journalists to put a spotlight on an issue police agencies and governments didn't track, or want to talk about. An investigation by CBC calculated 461 people were killed by police in Canada between 2000 and 2017. That's about twenty-seven people a year — a tiny fraction of the number killed in the United States each year. However, similar trends were discovered in the data: blacks and Indigenous people, the mentally ill, and people with addictions are overrepresented in the deaths.

A year before Michael Brown was killed in Missouri, Sammy Yatim was gunned down on a streetcar in Toronto. The eighteen-year-old was alone in the vehicle while bystanders recorded the incident on cellphones. Constable James Forcillo shot his gun nine times, the first few bullets being the ones that killed Yatim. Forcillo was eventually convicted of attempted murder and sentenced to prison. This incident cast a dark shadow over police in general, and over the Toronto Police Service in particular.

The TPS regained some of its reputation in 2018, however, when another video emerged showing traffic constable Ken Lam coolly confronting Alek Minassian, identified as the driver of a van that deliberately struck two dozen pedestrians on a stretch of city sidewalk. Ten people died. Though Minassian provoked Lam by pretending to point a gun at him, Lam took his time, determined Minassian was unarmed, and arrested him without a shot.

There is a temptation today, just as there was in 2007, when Robert Dziekanski's death was captured on video, to regard all police who use force as suspect, and all cases as equivalent. They are not. Four officers using a weapon they were told was less likely to cause harm than physically tackling someone is not the same as one officer drawing a firearm and knowing one squeeze of the trigger could end someone's life.

Blamed and Broken is more than a story about one of most notorious police encounters ever caught on video. It is a deliberate and detailed dissection of a deadly event that saw not one, but three men die in its wake. It is an examination of how an unrelenting quest to hold someone responsible for Robert Dziekanski's death led to a costly and convoluted result that has little to do with justice. The pages ahead take you behind the stiff, impenetrable curtain that was drawn shut the moment Dziekanski died and into the backstage realm of police and prosecutors. You'll read how public outrage, political interference, and corrosive bias led to a decade of wasted lives. It is a persuasive indictment of the RCMP and an exposé of what some lawyers consider in moments of sly candor to be the best justice system the nineteenth century has to offer us. *Blamed and Broken* illustrates how the RCMP publicly threw four front-line officers under the bus, while it made major changes to its Taser and de-escalation training across the country. That in itself is a tacit acknowledgement that its procedures and blind faith in a dubious weapon contributed to Dziekanski's death.

The events documented in *Blamed and Broken* occurred over a period of more than ten years. To create a narrative that conveys the passage of time and also reveals an interconnected train of facts, I have chosen to write in the present tense to give a better sense of how and why the case against the four Mounties evolved and to put you in someone else's skin as much as possible. That has required some judicious blending of some material without directly attributing sources. In most cases, what you read in direct quotes came from hundreds of hours of interviews I did myself. In some cases, comments come from other on-the-record sources, including news media. I have personally been a witness to many of the events in these pages, thanks to the enlightened wisdom and support of my editorial bosses at CBC, where I worked as a senior journalist. Many of the stories I wrote on the case, and in some cases broke, can still be found online.

At this point, I must emphasize what this book is not. It is not a mere recitation or recap of old news, dusty discoveries, or a facile transcript of courtroom testimony. Official records from the Braidwood Commission of Inquiry and the subsequent criminal cases against the Mounties do form a foundation for exploring what happened. Much like the Pritchard video, however, they do not tell the whole story. Far from it. I conducted literally hundreds of hours of interviews with dozens of people in order to take you, the reader, behind the veil of news releases, prepared statements, and vetted reports, into what noted journalist Carl Bernstein coined as "the best obtainable version of the truth." In the process, I reached out to many people with first-hand knowledge of these events. The fact that a good number declined to speak about these matters, a decade after they occurred, should tell you that there are things that happened in the wake of Dziekanski's death that some people want to keep forever in the past.

Some — many, I imagine — will regard the facts ahead with the same disdain and discomfort they did when first learning of Dziekanski's death, or when first viewing the horrible video of his last moments alive. As someone who has developed immeasurable sympathy for Zofia Cisowski — Robert Dziekanski's mother — I understand why any sympathetic portrayal of the police involved is unsettling. Yet, as a journalist, I owe a duty to asking questions about the unknown. So much about those at the centre of what happened has been blank at best, and at worst, assumed. Until now. I have come to evaluate the evidence against the Mounties in a new light. Not a light that ignores the grief of a mother mourning the loss of her only child, but one that makes it possible to understand how the rush to judgment sharpened her pain.

The perspective I've been afforded by time, persistence, and presence has revealed to me the hard-wired tendency we all have to slot characters into the roles of villain or victim, sinner or saint. Journalists — even the most seemingly objective in the profession — are not immune. Neither are judges, gowns and gavels notwithstanding. It is beyond dispute that four police officers were typecast as one-dimensional villains and provocateurs from the get-go. Dziekanski's posthumous role became that of blameless victim. Indeed, as one of his friends would declaim at the inquiry into his death, "Who among us would not also have smashed furniture against glass walls, threatened people trying to help, and brandished a metal stapler when confronted by four police officers because we didn't know how to get out of an airport?"

This is not to say the Mounties involved in this sad tale were perfect police officers. That they were not doesn't mean they are murderers, as Dziekanski's mother has frequently asserted without question. It doesn't mean they were involved in a conspiracy, as the prosecutors who were desperate for a conviction hypothesized. If anything, it means they are human. If only someone had bothered to ask.

1 | WHY ARE THE POLICE NOT HERE?

AT FIRST, NO ONE notices him. He's dressed in tan pants and a wind-breaker that's nearly white. His clothes are loose-fitting and flap as he walks, as if he were covered with a sheet like a Halloween ghost. He could be a ghost, if not for the luggage cart he's pushing toward the meeting area of Vancouver International Airport. There aren't many people here to notice him, anyway. It's nearly one on a Sunday morning. Flights have all but ceased. The normally crowded greeting hall is now populated by perhaps a dozen tired-looking figures dressed for the city's mid-October chill. Bleary-eyed, most are patiently focused on the swing-ing glass doors that automatically open as each newly arrived passenger emerges from the International Reception Lobby, known as the IRL. The IRL is a semi-secure part of the airport, just outside the cavern-ous high-security hall that houses baggage carousels, Customs, and Immigration. Beyond the one-way glass doors on the public side, there are repeated scenes of welcome: parents hugging children, reunited part-ners kissing, and friends shaking hands. The touching sentiments are brief in these wee hours and most head quickly toward the exit and home, arm-in-arm or holding hands.

No one is waiting for the invisible man as he approaches the auto-matic doors with three suitcases piled neatly on his cart. As he crosses the threshold, the doors close behind him. He follows the long walkway marked by a wood and steel railing, which ends in the public greeting hall. He pauses briefly. His head moves from side to side as if he's scanning for something or someone. Instead of heading for the exit he turns his cart sharply and almost trips as he steers his luggage back toward the glass wall from behind which he had just appeared. A few minutes later, the man hoists his bags from his cart up and over the railing, piling them on the floor by the automatic doors, like a barricade. Once over the railing himself, he begins hitting the glass doors with his hands. He is no longer invisible. People turn and stare.

The banging reverberates to a section of the hall where a young man is stretched out on a row of bench chairs. Paul Pritchard is trying to get some sleep after several seemingly interminable flights from Shenzhen, China. A rootless traveller at twenty-five, Pritchard has been on the road for years, having left his home in Victoria, B.C., at eighteen. Pritchard was teaching English in China when his father called him to say the lung cancer he was battling was terminal, and could Paul come home? Hours earlier he had made it to San Francisco to catch a connecting flight to Vancouver.

Pritchard has never been one to embrace convention or authority — as a teen he had encounters with the police. He used a fake university degree and bogus teaching certificate to land the job in China. Pritchard routinely refuses to stand in line while planes are boarding. As fate would have it, as he sat waiting for the Vancouver flight lineup to shorten, he fell asleep in a chair right beside the gate. He awoke half an hour later. The plane was gone. The only other flight he could get put him in Vancouver long past the deadline to catch the last ferry to Vancouver Island, where his father waited in Victoria.

Pritchard has no money for a hotel room, so he crashes on the benches in the airport terminal with his big blue backpack. In countless ways, Pritchard's long-standing suspicion of authority and penchant for shortcuts has carved the path that has brought him to this moment. Unable to sleep, Pritchard stands up to get a better look at the spectacle unfolding by the glass doors.

In 2007, cellphones are not nearly as ubiquitous as they are today. Those that have built-in cameras can manage to record only notoriously bad, pixilated images. The first iPhone, which has a slightly better resolution, isn't on the market in Canada yet. Pritchard is not using his phone to record the scene, however; he is making use of the digital camera he bought for his travels. He instinctively grabs it, but doesn't turn it on.

As Pritchard looks on, he strikes up a conversation with a traveller from Texas, who is just as curious about why the hell that guy is banging on the glass. They are trading thoughts and speculation, when a man in a suit with his hands in his pockets strides up to the peculiar scene.

Lorne Meltzer wants to get through the doors that are now blocked by suitcases and their increasingly irrational owner. Meltzer is a limo driver here to pick up a client coming in on a flight from New York City. Meltzer has an access card that allows him to open the swinging glass doors so he can wait in the IRL for his fare. He approaches just as the wild-eyed man smashes a chair against the glass.

"Hold on!" Meltzer yells, as he reaches inside his coat for his access card. The man clenches his fist as if anticipating Meltzer's hand will emerge from his jacket gripping a weapon. Meltzer thinks that on a scale of one to ten, with ten being the point at which the man is ready to attack, this guy is at nine. Meltzer swipes his card on the reader. The doors open.

When the man doesn't budge, Meltzer loses it. "Look you fuckin' asshole, I need to get through here," Meltzer yells, just inches from the man's face, which is now glistening with perspiration. The man's black hair is matted with sweat. His eyes are glassy. He slowly backs down and starts hauling his bags through the open doors. He begins to build a makeshift barricade on the threshold using his luggage and some stools from a dark and deserted information counter beside the doorway.

Why am I not filming this? Pritchard suddenly thinks. Years of travel have taught him to point a camera at anything that might be worth a look later on.

Pritchard starts recording the man who has barricaded himself at the entrance of the IRL. The man sounds like he's talking to himself, alternately yelling and muttering under his breath. Whatever language he's speaking, it's not English.

Lorne Meltzer's only priority is his customer on the Cathay Pacific flight from New York City. "Five minutes before Cathay comes down with three hundred people on it," he says loudly, with frustration. Before disappearing to try to find security, Meltzer appeals to the handful of people in the waiting area, and asks if anyone speaks any other languages.

A woman, who's been watching the man's erratic behaviour since it began, approaches. Sima Ashrafinia is here to pick up her husband, who's also on that flight from New York City. She's concerned that there is no sign of security to deal with this man who's running amok and is clearly manic. He's sweating profusely. He seems out of breath and angry as he stands between the absurdly flapping automatic doors. He shouts to the onlookers in a language no one understands, except him. If anyone spoke Polish, they'd know the man is not only lucid, he is dead serious.

"I will trash this office. Fuck off!"

The man's tone alone is enough to make some people fear his next move. Ashrafinia isn't immediately worried. There is a wood and steel railing between her and the man, and, she thinks to herself, *It's not like he has a knife or a gun.*

Ashrafinia knows what that threat is like. Nearly thirty years earlier, in the midst of the Iranian revolution, living in Tehran meant falling asleep to the sound of machine-gun fire. Back then, when she and her friends engaged in protests and shouting matches with Islamist supporters of Ayatollah Khomeini, the worst she feared was being pelted with eggs and tomatoes. She carried a newspaper and matches, believing smoke would reduce the effects of tear gas. Her sense of danger changed suddenly during a massive demonstration prompted by the edict that all women had to start wearing head scarves. That day, gunshots rang out. People started running. They ducked into alleys. They knocked furiously on doors to get off the street. As people scrambled, Ashrafinia thought her friend — pregnant at the time — had tripped. Turning to help her up, Ashrafinia noticed blood on the pavement. The gunmen were approaching. Ashrafinia's decision to run with everyone else has haunted her every day since. Her decision to flee the country came after she spent a couple of weeks in prison. Authorities found her with books by Karl Marx and Jean-Paul Sartre. She was jailed after the banned material was burned in her backyard.

The man behind the makeshift barricade is now wielding a folding wooden table like the kind you might have beside an easy chair to hold your snacks while watching TV. He's holding it at chest height, legs pointed toward Ashrafinia.

"Russia?" she says to him, hoping for recognition. There is none. She tries words in Turkish and Italian. Ashrafinia has two deaf siblings, and tries some sign language she knows. It only seems to anger him. He's thrusting the wooden table legs like a weapon.

"For fuck's sake. I will sue you and everybody else," the man yells in Polish. It's gibberish to everyone else. He's breathing so heavily his chest is heaving. It's not from any physical exertion because he's not really moving, except to step in front of his improvised wall of luggage and chairs to threaten people. "Fine, fine," he utters in Polish. "We are in a different country so ... " he trails off unintelligibly. He understands that what he's doing is probably a bad idea. He is not irrational.

Ashrafinia approaches with an outstretched hand, the same sort of gesture you might use to try to tame the fear of a frightened pet. There's no mistaking her body language and demeanour. Anyone can tell she means to help. Yet it only seems to anger him. He thrusts the wooden table legs again.

"I will smash the entire desk. I will smash the entire desk ... leave me alone, everybody! Go away I said."

Ashrafinia, oblivious to the man's violent intentions, persists. She gestures with her hand, beckoning him to come out from the doorway. The man retreats instead and focuses the pointed table legs directly at Ashrafinia's head, a few feet away.

"For fuck's sake!" he says to the woman trying to help him.

Paul Pritchard has been recording the exchange but stops when he notices he's running out of room on his camera's memory card. He takes a moment to flip through its contents, deleting images he doesn't want to gain some recording time. When he begins recording again, it seems like this standoff could last a while. Pritchard chuckles at the prospect of having a story to entertain friends and family.

Pritchard isn't the only person whose accidental presence here will profoundly affect the lives of many people. Lois Steckley has come to the airport to pick up her son from a flight arriving from Mexico. She doesn't know it yet, but she's mixed up the date of the flight, and her son won't arrive until tomorrow. Steckley is not supposed to be here tonight. Now she's aghast and a little angry that this man has been allowed to run rampant for half an hour with nary a cop in sight. Steckley looks for security guards, and can't find any. She picks up a white airport courtesy phone that connects her to no one. Then she dials 9-1-1.

"Airport Operations, what's your emergency?" a female voice comes down the line.

"There's a guy over here and he's really aggressive … he's really drunk and he's throwing suitcases around," Steckley says breathlessly.

"I'm just going to send the police," the operator tells her. "Could I get a description?"

"You can't miss him," Steckley offers.

"He doesn't seem to have any weapons? He's just throwing suitcases?"

"I have no idea."

Steckley is concerned about her son. She's worried he's somewhere on the other side of the glass. The same side as the "lunatic," she tells the operator.

"He's pissed, he's been drinking. He's not white … I guess he's in his fifties, forties, I don't know."

"Alright, I'll have somebody come down right away." The operator puts Steckley on hold for a minute or two and returns. "I've called the police. They're on their way."

"Oh, now this guy's going to start throwing furniture around, right through the glass," Steckley warns.

The operator hears a smash. "He threw it through the glass?" she asks.

"He's doing it now, yup," Steckley confirms.

As Steckley watches, the man rips a keyboard from a computer on the vacant information desk, raises it above his head, takes aim at the glass between him and Ashrafinia and throws it with both hands. It bounces and hits the floor. It does not break the glass, but the Airport Operations dispatcher believes otherwise.

Ashrafinia has tried for many minutes to get through to the man in the most calm and non-threatening ways possible. But her persistent efforts have been futile. Not even a yellow-jacketed security guard who has shown up is enough to deter the man now. The guard is permitted only to observe and report. He stands safely several metres away and watches the man pick up the wooden table next.

"He's freaking out!" Lorne Meltzer yells.

The man uses all his might to whip the table at the glass wall between him and everyone else. The glass holds but the force of his throw shatters the furniture into pieces.

"Jesus Christ," Pritchard says, as the man next grabs a computer monitor. He winds up to try again. Now those in the waiting area yell back at him. "No, no, no!" It's a word that must be universally understood. The man puts the heavy video screen down on the floor. He casually examines his hands for any harm he may have done to himself during his violent bout of vandalism. "Why are the police not here?" Pritchard wonders aloud.

The police are eating lunch. Just a minute's drive from the terminal, a group of Mounties makes small talk during their meal break on the nightshift. Even though in 2007 seventeen million people will come and go through YVR — the common shorthand for the Vancouver airport using the international airport code — the RCMP's base of operations here is too small to be a full detachment. So it's deemed a subdetachment and its members deal only with such police matters at the airport as lost or stolen passports and the like. They haven't been to many violent calls. It's been a quiet night for these rookies. As they sit in a small office that doubles as a lunchroom, their radios crackle alive in unison. There is an instinctive "holy shit" moment as the adrenaline kicks in.

"Intoxicated male, throwing luggage around, Level Two."

One officer responds immediately with his unique radio call sign to indicate both "message received" and "we're on our way": "Two-three," says Constable Kwesi Millington into his radio.

As the three drop their food, the dispatcher continues.

"Copy two-three. We don't have much information. It came from Ops. Report of a fifty-five-year-old male at the Arrivals Reception Lobby throwing luggage around. He's non-white. Has dark hair and a white coat."

Millington's supervisor at the YVR subdetachment hears the back-and-forth. Corporal Monty Robinson is in another part of the building talking to one of the civilian volunteers who help the police do licence-plate checks. It's rare that Robinson leaves the building to go out on a call. As he listens, he decides to accompany them, and see how they handle themselves.

Like the other Mounties, Millington is wearing his Sam Browne — a heavy, leather belt, supported by a thinner strap slung over one shoulder running diagonally across the chest. It's named after a British Army captain who lost an arm in the Indian Rebellion of 1857. He came up with the modification to his belt so he could continue to use a sword and scabbard. Millington and his contemporaries can carry ten to fifteen pounds of gear on their modern Sam Brownes. Everything from handcuffs and flashlights to their side arms.

Tonight, Millington is also carrying a weapon the inventor of his belt could never have imagined. Millington has one of the subdetachment's two new Tasers. A few months ago, they all had training on the stun gun. They were taught that it is not only safe, but less harmful than a baton or pepper spray. In the little over two years since graduating from the RCMP Academy, known colloquially as Depot, Millington has used none of his weapons, including the Taser, outside of training. Hours ago, at the start of his shift, Millington signed out the new device. To make sure it was working, he did a "spark test": he removed the cartridge at the front of the Taser's barrel containing the steel probes and wires that deliver the current. Once the device was unloaded, Millington pulled the trigger and watched a blue bolt of electricity arc across the gun's electrodes.

Without speaking, Millington, Robinson, and two other constables head to the front door, then out into the parking lot where each climbs into a patrol car.

2 | WELCOME TO CANADA

FOR NEARLY A DECADE, the connection between mother and son has been a telephone. Zofia lives in Kamloops, British Columbia, and works as a janitor. Her only child, Robert, ekes out a hardscrabble life doing odd jobs in Gliwice, a sombre industrial city in the south of Poland. Cheap long-distance phone calls somehow shrink the eight thousand kilometres between them, though it can't lessen the differences between their worlds. Kamloops is surrounded by natural mountain playgrounds: skiing, hiking, and river sports. Gliwice is a blue-collar centre for coal, chemical, and steel production, with architecture dating to the Middle Ages.

The Polish city had been home to them both. Zofia had married young, taking her husband's family name: Dziekanski. Robert was born shortly after, when Zofia was just twenty-one. The marriage, however, eventually disintegrated. Robert was fourteen when his father left them. After that, mother and son shared a dingy flat in a rundown apartment building, managing an existence with little hope of prosperity.

As a teen, Robert was troubled. Reports would eventually detail several arrests for theft and violence, all under the influence of alcohol. His education led him to trade school, where he trained to work as a miner. He had trouble finding a steady job, though. He ended up earning a meagre living by doing house painting and manual labour whenever he could get it. Medical reports would conclude that, by the time he was forty, Robert was an alcoholic with a troubling heart condition.

Long before then, it had become apparent that Zofia's golden years would not be sweet in Gliwice. In 1999, fate stepped in when an acquaintance suggested Zofia reach out to Wladyslaw Cisowski — a man of Polish descent living in Canada. Wladyslaw — who went by the name Peter — was looking for a wife. Zofia was initially hesitant. She was in her fifties. Her suitor was more than twenty years older. Zofia would take her new husband's last name. Within a few years of their marriage he would be in a nursing home.

Zofia Cisowski longed to be reunited with her only son. They discussed the subject during their frequent phone calls, and eventually they agreed that he should emigrate to Canada, too. The plan was cemented when Zofia returned to Poland for a visit in the summer of 2007. Now, in October, Robert Dziekanski is about to join his mother in what he has boastfully told his friends is the place "where there is milk and honey." Dziekanski arrives at Vancouver International Airport on a connecting flight from Frankfurt.

It's a crisp mid-October Saturday afternoon at the bustling terminal. All Dziekanski has to do once he steps off the plane is collect his bags from the luggage carousel, present himself at the Immigration counter to show his newly minted permanent resident papers, and walk out into the greeting hall where his mother is waiting. A new country. A new life. A new start. There is just one problem: the telephone — the thing that kept mother and son together for so many years — is about to become the instrument that will seal their separation for good.

Cisowski has been at the airport since just after lunchtime, having made the four-hour drive from Kamloops to Vancouver. She was so anxious about her son's arrival that she didn't have the confidence to drive herself, and so, days ago, Cisowski asked a neighbour in her apartment building if he would act as a chauffeur. Richard Hutchinson, a drywaller in his fifties, offered to do it for $120. For several hours they take turns watching the stream of passengers coming through automatic glass doors into the meet-and-greet area, scanning for Dziekanski's face. Cisowski and Hutchinson become increasingly impatient when Dziekanski doesn't show.

Cisowski's frustration turns to distress. She realizes she told her son to meet her by the baggage carousel, not realizing it's in a secure part of the airport and there's no way she can go in there. Over the course of the afternoon Cisowski beseeches a man behind an information counter. Her son should have emerged from the secure side of the airport hours ago, she tells him. His flight landed at 3:30 p.m. He doesn't speak English. Can she go inside to look for him?

The man behind the counter is sympathetic, but unable to do much. He doesn't have access to airline passenger lists. He's wearing a shirt with a "Supernatural British Columbia" logo on it. He sells bus tickets, sightseeing tours, and hotel stays.

He tells Cisowski there's no way to get inside the secure area. Be patient, he tells her. Check the giant Arrivals board visible to everyone, and one more thing: check with Immigration. He gives her directions to the Immigration office down a nearby corridor. Over the course of the afternoon, Cisowski approaches him at least three times with the same concern. Each time, he tells her that she might want to check with Immigration. Neither Cisowski nor Hutchinson takes his advice. It is a fateful decision. They opt to keep asking the same impotent people the same questions, hoping for a different result.

They find Janet Sullivan working at another Information counter just up an escalator. Sullivan is a former airline employee. She quickly checks flight arrivals and confidently tells Cisowski that all the flights from Europe have long since landed for the day.

It's now seven o'clock. Hutchinson is frustrated. He wants to know how they can find out if Robert Dziekanski was on a flight from Germany.

"You can't," Sullivan answers. "Not without an RCMP search warrant."

Cisowski asks if Sullivan can page her son. She gives Sullivan instructions on how to say his name: "juh-CAN-ski."

"I can page him," Sullivan says before calling out his name on the public address system, "but it doesn't go into the Customs area. If he's still inside Customs or Immigration, he'll not be able to hear it."

Sullivan calls out Dziekanski's name once, then again ten minutes later. There's no response.

It's only when Sullivan begins making small talk with Cisowski that she learns Dziekanski isn't coming for a visit. He's immigrating to Canada. "Well," Sullivan says, "the best place to go is Immigration." Sullivan is unaware the two have been told that all afternoon.

This time they follow the advice. Cisowski, who's concerned about her shaky English, opts to let Hutchinson make the inquiries. He heads down a hallway tucked between the Burger King and the Tim Hortons restaurants in the international terminal building. He sees a closed office door at the end. There's a telephone and a sign. It reads simply, PICK UP THE PHONE. As Hutchinson puts the phone to his ear, he hears it ring.

Somewhere on the other side of the door, desk phones in empty cubicles awaken and light up line eight. Immigration officer Tina Zadravec is the only one to see the dedicated line spring to life. "Canada Immigration," Zadravec says as she picks up the receiver.

"We're looking for this Polish fellow who's supposed to be here," Hutchinson begins to explain, telling the voice on the phone that Dziekanski's flight was supposed to have landed some six hours ago. "We're not finding him. He's thirty-eight years old," Hutchinson says, making a mistake about the forty-year-old Dziekanski's age. "He can't speak English and his name is Robert. I can't pronounce his last name but I can spell it for you."

Zadravec, alone in the office, stops him, saying that privacy law forbids her from revealing who has arrived on a flight. "I don't see how we can help you," she says. "You've been here too long. It doesn't take that long to get through Immigration." Zadravec suggests that perhaps the man Hutchinson is looking for never made his flight. "Have you tried phoning Poland?" she asks. But Hutchinson is insistent.

While Zadravec listens to him, she glances at the Detention board, which lists the name, sex, and citizenship of any new arrival being held. Dziekanski is not on it. Zadravec puts the phone down, and walks into the area where the public sit and wait to be questioned by an Immigration officer. It's empty except for one man. Zadravec asks who he is and is told he's an Iranian refugee claimant. Zadravec picks up the phone again. While Zadravec has the ability to make a page that can be heard throughout the secure Customs hall, she doesn't. She can make a quick call to someone on the Primary Inspection Line. It's the point all arriving passengers pass through by showing their passport. That would confirm whether Dziekanski has arrived. Zadravec doesn't do that. Her whole search takes less than a minute. She just doesn't think Dziekanski is there. It's just not believable that a grown man would be wandering around the Customs hall six or seven hours after landing. She's never heard of that happening. Refugee claimants, maybe. But a landed immigrant? Never.

Zadravec picks up the phone again. "Without breaking confidentiality," she tells Hutchinson, "I can honestly tell you that there is no one here from Poland in a landed immigrant situation."

Hutchinson listens as Zadravec tells him to check with the airline and call Poland. Had they done that, they might have been told that indeed Dziekanski got on the plane. They might have discovered his two suitcases had arrived in Vancouver. A Lufthansa baggage agent had seen them unclaimed by the carousel and secured them behind the airline's counter in the Arrivals hall. But they don't make those calls. Instead, Hutchinson tells Zadravec that Dziekanski's mother is worried. Hutchinson hears the Immigration officer say Dziekanski is a grown man. "He's big enough to take care of himself ... you might as well go home."

None of this is making sense. How could a grown man who wants to be reunited with his mother disappear in a secure airport without triggering concern? If Dziekanski has landed, why hasn't he called his mother's cellphone number? There are pay phones in the Customs hall. Before leaving Poland he had a cellphone, yet Dziekanski hasn't used it. After another hour or so, Hutchinson is resigned to a wasted day. "He's not here," he tells Cisowski. Hutchinson is now sure of it. There's one more futile trip up the escalator to vent to Janet Sullivan. Immigration was no help, they complain.

It's at this point Sullivan adds to the series of unfortunate choices made by so many people. Sullivan could make a call to another information employee who works near the Primary Inspection Line, just to see if they can try and find Dziekanski. Sullivan decides there's no point, if Immigration has determined Dziekanski isn't there.

Seeing the time, Hutchinson says he's anxious to get going. It's a four-hour drive back to Kamloops and he wants to be up early for church services on Sunday morning. "You don't need to be," Sullivan offers. "There's a chapel on Level Two." Hutchinson and Cisowski wander away. They wait until about ten o'clock before deciding to go home. As they leave the terminal and head to the parking lot, Robert Dziekanski, the invisible man, emerges out of nowhere and shuffles toward the exit.

3 | THE COWBOYS RIDE IN

THE FOUR MOUNTIES speed through the dark along the road that forms a broad loop in front of the airport. The ride from the RCMP subdetachment on the other side of the loop takes all of one minute. None of them feels a need to flip on their flashing lights or sirens, but in police lingo this is still a priority call. Translation: hurry up and get there. The drive is just long enough for their radios to crackle again with an update taken directly from Lois Steckley's breathless description of the lunatic at the airport: "Male is now throwing chairs through glass windows in that area," comes the dispatcher's voice.

The police pull up one behind the other at the curb in front of the terminal doors. They move quickly from their cars to the entrance. Corporal Monty Robinson, expecting to find broken glass, puts on a pair of black gloves as a precaution. Constable Bill Bentley is first across the building's threshold. The red-haired, freckle-faced officer looks even younger than his twenty-seven years. He's the youngest of the bunch and also the greenest. He graduated from the RCMP training program just last year. He's been stationed at the airport subdetachment for only a month. As Bentley enters the airport leading the squad, an airline employee who's been watching the spectacle blurts out, "He's over by the glass!"

Bentley doesn't stop moving. He makes a beeline for a man with a booming voice.

"*Policja!*" the man yells. "*Policja!*"

Instantly Bentley turns his head to his partners behind him and does a quick tool check. "Do you have a Taser?" he asks the group.

Constable Kwesi Millington reveals he's carrying the stun gun, with a one-word answer: "Yes."

Millington is a little older than Bentley — thirty-one — and he's been out of Depot longer. He graduated more than two years ago. Millington is dressed identically to his partners. Each wears a blue Kevlar duty vest that can stop a small-calibre handgun bullet or a knife slash. But Millington is conspicuous. He's easily the biggest of the bunch at six foot one. Millington is also black.

Constable Gerry Rundel is just a step behind him. Rundel is just ten days shy of his second anniversary as a Mountie, though he's come to his policing career late in life. He's forty-six — practically old enough to be Bentley's father. The most senior officer, experience-wise, initially hangs back.

Corporal Monty Robinson wants to observe the rookies handle what seems like a fairly routine call, compared to some in his more than ten years on the job. Robinson's career is peppered with bloody, traumatic, life-and-death encounters. As a member of the Osoyoos First Nation, he's the only one of the four who's worked and lived in parts of the province outside of Metro Vancouver.

The limo driver, Lorne Meltzer, anxiously offers information to the police. "He's right inside there! He speaks Russian!" he advises incorrectly. "He's freaking out."

None of the officers are acting as if they're anxious. They don't seem to be in a hurry to get to the man behind the glass doors who's now standing amid fragments of broken furniture and equipment.

Meltzer isn't the only one in the waiting area happy to see the police arrive. Paul Pritchard has repeatedly stopped his camera to delete old pictures so he can make room on the memory card to keep recording. Pritchard trains his lens on the officers as they slowly walk up to him and pass. "Now the good stuff," Pritchard says out loud, in a tone of gleeful anticipation.

There is no indication, however, that Pritchard will have much "good stuff" to show when it's all over. Bentley, Millington, and Rundel walk calmly, almost casually toward the shouting man's position. As they reach the glass doors, however, they realize they've arrived on the wrong side of the railing that separates the man from the public waiting area. One by one, each officer hops over the waist-high barrier, landing in front of the doorway the man has barricaded.

Based on what he can see, Bentley doesn't think this guy is behaving rationally. As he looks more closely at the wide-eyed, sweaty, and agitated man behind the glass, Bentley's gut kicks in and tells him to be ready in case the guy wants to start a fight.

Bentley has wanted to be a cop since he was a kid. The RCMP motto is *Maintiens le droit*, "Defending the law." Bentley takes that pledge seriously and he's anticipating they will have reasonable and probable grounds to arrest the man — for mischief, at least. Right now, however, he is focused on figuring out what's happened, how to defuse a situation that has caused a number of panicky people to call 9-1-1.

Bentley doesn't know it, but the moment he opens his mouth, a virtual clock starts counting the seconds to a tragedy that will mark all their lives. Three people will die in the ripples from this moment. The lives of many others will be devastated for years to come. Bentley stands outside the doorway, looks across the threshold at the nervous-looking man a couple of metres away, and offers a polite, friendly greeting.

"How are you, sir?"

The man is mute.

One second.

"How's it goin', bud?" Bentley tries again, unsuccessfully.

Two seconds.

Millington closes the gap between them in the doorway and takes control of the encounter.

Three seconds.

Millington motions with a hand palm down toward the floor, conveying a request to calm down.

Four seconds.

"Passport?" Millington asks.

Five seconds.

"Identification?" Millington tries again.

The man stares blankly.

Six seconds.

Rundel is now behind Bentley and Millington and hears the man speaking but it's unintelligible.

Seven seconds.

Robinson decides he needs to get closer to what's going on so he hops over the railing.

Eight seconds.

Rundel thinks the man appears intoxicated.

Nine seconds.

Millington mimes using a pen in the air, hoping the man understands he needs to show ID.

Ten seconds.

The man begins to bend down toward his luggage on the floor.

Eleven seconds.

Robinson steps in.

Twelve seconds.

"NO!" Robinson shouts before the man touches his bags. They don't know much yet, except that the man has been volatile and violent. Allowing him to go to his suitcase is a safety breach Robinson won't allow.

Thirteen seconds.

The man stands back up, and looks impatiently back and forth between the officers and his luggage.

Fourteen seconds.

Robinson motions to the man with his hand to calm down.

Fifteen seconds.

Robinson decides this is going to be by the book. He wants the man to put his hands up on the information desk beside them. Robinson straightens his arm and makes a universally understood gesture. He points toward the counter.

Sixteen seconds.

The man throws up his arms and turns around and walks away from the officers. Bentley thinks the man is telling them "The hell with you guys, I'm out of here."

Seventeen seconds.

The Mounties follow.

Eighteen seconds.

Robinson keeps his finger pointed to the desk as the man looks over his shoulder at him.

Nineteen seconds.

An arrest is imminent. The man puts his hands on the desk, with his back to the officers.

Twenty seconds.

The man swiftly turns to face the police. There's something in his right hand. It's an office stapler he must have grabbed from the counter. He's opened it up, gripping it in the middle as if he's intending to swing it at something. His other hand is a fist.

Twenty-one seconds.

Bentley is just an arm's length from the man when he notices the metal stapler. Bentley jumps back almost two metres. Simultaneously, he pulls out a collapsible baton and snaps it open.

Twenty-two seconds.

Robinson sees the stapler, too. He sees the man squeeze it in his palm. Ejected staples fall feebly onto the carpet in front of him. Robinson thinks he sees the man begin to move toward him. He pulls out his baton.

Twenty-three seconds.

"Leave me alone," the man yells in a language no one understands. He's not standing still. He definitely doesn't have his hands on the counter. "Leave me alone! Did you become stupid? Why?"

Twenty-four seconds.

The officers are spread out in a semicircle around the man, but not so far away that it wouldn't take less than a second for him to reach any of them.

Twenty-five seconds.

"Hit him!" Robinson commands to Millington, pointing at the man.

Millington doesn't hear the order. He's riveted by the man's behaviour. The sweaty man who's caused the disturbance is definitely moving now. Millington thinks he's taking a step forward. Everything he's seeing is textbook: the man now appears both aggressive and combative.

At some point in the last moments of this rapidly escalating encounter, Millington pulls the Taser from its holster, and flicks off the safety switch. Millington's training is clear to him. When confronted by someone threatening to use force, an RCMP officer should use enough force to overcome it, not just match it. It's a strategy known as "force plus one." The Taser is an intermediate weapon, and ranked as less lethal or potentially harmful than pepper spray, a steel baton, or even a physical struggle. Millington's whole analysis is automatic.

Twenty-six seconds.

Millington pulls the trigger.

In an instant, compressed nitrogen explodes two metal probes through the plastic-covered cartridge at the front of the weapon. The probes are tipped with barbs like fish hooks, designed to sink beneath the skin. They fly to their target, each trailing a gossamer wire that carries enough electrical current to disrupt a body's normal electrical signals, the way a tsunami obliterates a coastline by inundation. Just like a tidal wave, the Taser jolt is frightening and extremely painful.

There is a loud electric snap when the probes hit their mark. The man lets out a wild yell, as if he's been set on fire. But something's not right. He's not falling down. He should be falling down. In training Millington was taught most suspects will succumb and drop. This guy is still standing. He's shaking. He's flailing as if he's trying to put out invisible flames on his body. He's grabbing his chest where the Taser probes have hit him. But he's still standing and he's still gripping the stapler in his hand. A few seconds later, he begins to lose his balance and stumble away from the desk. He falls to the floor a couple seconds after that.

Millington pulls the trigger a second time and there's another crackling buzz as the officers move in and circle the man on the floor. He's still not immobile. He's on his side on the carpet, forcefully spinning around as if he were running on a treadmill.

"Put your hands behind your back," Robinson barks. The man may not understand English but Robinson's command is automatic. It's adrenaline. Robinson, Rundel, and Bentley get down on the floor and begin wrestling with the man to get his hands cuffed. Yet all three working together can't do it. The man is on his stomach. Whether his resistance is involuntary — a result of the Taser jolt — or willful, or both, this isn't easy.

"Hit him again! Hit him again!" Robinson orders.

Millington pulls the trigger a third time and it seems to have some effect. Still, the man continues to struggle as three police officers grapple with his arms and legs.

For a full minute they wrestle. Two more times Millington uses the Taser, but not to send an incapacitating shock through the probes. He removes the cartridge and aggressively drives the front of the weapon into the man's back near his shoulders. The weapon's push-stun mode causes pain only as long as the Taser's built-in electrodes are in contact with the skin. The man is struggling so Millington is unsure how effective it is.

Bentley has ahold of the man's left arm and the struggle is so strenuous Bentley's handcuffs go flying. Robinson gets the right arm free and Rundel slaps on a steel cuff. It then takes all three to lock the man's left wrist. There's absolutely no doubt that four well-trained, physically fit police officers are having trouble.

"Jesus," Pritchard says while watching it all. "How is he still fighting them off?"

A man in a black trench coat enters the fray to help. Trevor Enchelmaier is the shift supervisor for the contracted airport security guards, the ones who only observe and report. Enchelmaier kneels down with the police and grabs on to the moaning man's flailing legs. He lets go and stands up only when the man stops moving.

"I put him out," Robinson announces. The officers shift the man onto his side. Robinson sends Rundel out to one of the patrol cars to retrieve some hobbles — a set of straps used to link a suspect's ankles to their handcuffs to prevent the person from getting up again.

Pritchard is pleased with what he just witnessed. "Prime footage for my home videos," he boasts. "At an airport, man!" he adds, incredulously.

It is an understandable reaction. How could anyone not understand that pulling the kind of stuff this guy did at an airport wouldn't end well?

Sima Ashrafinia suggests to another woman observing the scene that it was inevitable. "Yeah, I think they have no other choice because he's out of control," Ashrafinia says before hearing a voice call her name from behind her. She turns away from the scene to meet her husband arriving from New York.

The man on the floor is breathing heavily, deeply, and loudly, as if he's just run a mile. His eyes are closed. Bentley's training kicks in again. He presses the mic button for his radio. He asks the dispatch to contact Emergency Health Services and send medical assistance. It's a routine call. He'd do the same for anyone unconscious and breathing.

In less than a minute, however, Bentley notices the man's face is turning blue. He's still breathing. His chest is rising and falling, but he's decidedly blue. Bentley goes back on the radio and upgrades the call to Code 3, meaning lights and sirens on the emergency vehicles being dispatched to the airport.

It all happens on the other side of the glass from Pritchard but he thinks he can hear the officers talking about what's happening to the guy on the floor.

"Is he dead?" he asks the man standing beside him in the waiting area. "I heard him say Code Red."

Pritchard watches as each of the officers takes a task. Millington busies himself coiling up the Taser wires. He knows he's going to have to account for his use of the weapon. Robinson puts his hand on the man's chest and leans in to listen to his breathing. Enchelmaier places his fingers on the man's carotid artery. He feels a strong, fast pulse like that of someone who's just been running. The man's breathing sounds like snoring.

Robinson sends Bentley out to his car to get a camera and an audio recorder so he can start interviewing witnesses. There is no doubt in Robinson's mind that many people saw what happened. *That's a good thing*, he thinks. Even if they wanted to, the Mounties couldn't suppress details of the event from the investigation. They have an audience. Who knows how many security cameras are looking down on them?

When Rundel returns with the hobbles Robinson tells him they're no longer needed. The man is unconscious.

They do a pat-down and Rundel pulls a wallet and a credit card holder from the man's pocket. Among the items investigators will find inside are paper money — euros and Polish zloty — worth about fifty bucks. There is also an identity card from the Republic of Poland with the man's photo on it. Going by the details on the card, the man is forty years old. His name is Robert Dziekanski. Robinson sends Rundel out to the public side of the Arrivals area to join Bentley in getting witness statements.

The disturbance, which has become a medical emergency, is unfolding right where arriving passengers flood out into the terminal. Ashrafinia brings her husband by the arm to the glass wall to see what's happening. Fariborz Farahani isn't interested. He wants to leave.

"No, no!" Ashrafinia insists. "Come."

There are now airport security people blocking much of the view through the glass, but she can see Dziekanski on his back. He's not moving but he's breathing heavily. His chest is rising and falling.

Ashrafinia was stressed and unhappy before any of this had happened. Her marriage is shaky, at best. Ashrafinia and Farahani knew each other from high school in Iran. They had reconnected after each had been married and divorced. Ashrafinia had sponsored him to come to Canada and they married. However, things had started to go wrong in the marriage; she believed Farahani had an opium addiction. She

Robert Dziekanski's identity is discovered by going through his wallet shortly after he died, early on October 14, 2007.

estimated he was spending upward of a thousand dollars a month on the drug. He'd become depressed and she'd suggested he visit an Iranian friend in New York. It would be a break. Now Farahani is standing beside his wife near the glass. Just beyond lies Dziekanski, still.

"Let's go. We've seen enough of this. Let's go," he commands.

Ashrafinia is teary and upset. She protests, then relents. Outside the terminal building Ashrafinia thinks she sees an RCMP officer. Whoever he is, though, he's not a Mountie. The only RCMP officers at the terminal right now are inside dealing with the scene. Ashrafinia offers to tell the man what she saw. He simply replies, "No, thank you."

Ashrafinia's husband commands her again. "Let's go." His reluctance to be caught up in a police matter is not surprising, given his drug habit. On the drive home, however, the incident at the airport becomes a life-changing catalyst for Ashrafinia. Farahani berates her while she drives. "Why do you get involved? It's none of your business."

They argue. "He's a human being," Ashrafinia counters. "It's everybody's business."

Robert Dziekanski, manic and sweaty, blocks the only public door to the International Reception Lounge at YVR.

Robert Dziekanski wields a wooden table at Sima Ashrafinia as she tries to calm him down before the police arrive.

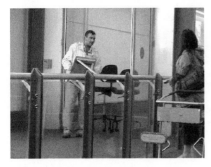

Robert Dziekanksi responds with anger to Sima Ashrafinia's calm voice and offer to help.

Robert Dziekanski points the legs of a wooden table directly at the only person appearing to help.

Robert Dziekanski does not drop his guard when bystander Sima Ashrafinia turns away after failing to calm him.

A glass wall is all that separates Sima Ashrafinia from Robert Dziekanski as he grabs items off of a counter.

Robert Dziekanski raises a desktop computer to launch at the glass. Onlookers shout, "No!" before he puts it down.

Robert Dziekanski, an instant before he actually smashes the computer against the glass wall of the IRL.

When the computer equipment fails to break the glass, Robert Dziekanski tries again with the wooden table.

The four Mounties arrive. They hop the railing to approach Dziekanski. Monty Robinson (foreground) initially hangs back to see how the rookies handle the call.

All four Mounties wrestle with Robert Dziekanski to apply handcuffs even after several Taser deployments. Debate about whether Dziekanski's resistance was caused by the Taser would be used against the police.

Airport employees attempt to block Paul Pritchard's view as he records Mounties struggling with Robert Dziekanski.

Her husband is unmoved. "No," he tells her. "Just leave everything and just live your simple life. You always want to find something, even when you were a teenager; you used to be like that."

Ashrafinia heads away from the airport. A fire truck races toward it.

————————

Six minutes after Bentley's first call for medical help, the truck pulls up at the terminal and three firefighters enter the IRL. They see a man lying flat on his stomach, head turned to the side, hands cuffed behind his back. The man is motionless. His eyes are open and unblinking. No one is doing anything that looks like first aid.

Firefighter Sonia Duranleau starts talking to Dziekanski. She hears one of the Mounties say he won't understand because he's Polish. Duranleau tries to get a reaction from Dziekanski by administering a squeeze of his neck bones. It should be painful. There's no response. Another police voice tells her Dziekanski has been down a few minutes after having been Tasered several times. She feels for a pulse in his wrist. Nothing. Her partner Glen Cameron puts his ear near Dziekanski's mouth. No sound of breathing. No chest movement. Duranleau feels Dziekanski's carotid artery. No pulse. Cameron wants the cuffs off and Dziekanski flipped onto his back because he needs CPR. Robinson refuses to remove the handcuffs. "He's been violent. We're not going to take the cuffs off," he tells them.

Just as they finish their assessment, ambulance paramedics come through the door with a stretcher between them. From the door, some fifteen metres from Dziekanski's body, attendant Mike Egli can tell the man down is cyanotic: blue.

No one seems to be doing any first aid, including the firefighters. It's 1:47 a.m. Dziekanski was Tasered nearly twenty minutes ago.

Paramedic Allan Maciak wants to start CPR immediately. He asks Robinson to remove the handcuffs but again Robinson balks, still concerned Dziekanski might come to and start swinging.

"We need the cuffs off now," Maciak barks and Robinson complies. The two paramedics roll Dziekanski over.

"Oh, look at his colour," Maciak says.

Egli yells at the idle firefighters. "Get the damn oxygen on him now. High flow. Fifteen litres on a non-rebreather mask."

Dziekanski's lips are blue. His tongue is blue and protruding. His pants are soaked in urine. Maciak thinks he's looking at a dead man. They cut away Dziekanski's shirt and pants.

Maciak says, "Let's get on the chest," and tells Duranleau to start chest compressions. They attach a defibrillator to Dziekanski's chest. But the device displays the message, "No shock advised." A shock is useful only if there's a heart rhythm to restore, even an irregular one. Dziekanski has none. The advanced life-support team arrives. The fresh paramedics join the efforts of the other first responders doing chest compressions.

———————

Rundel and Bentley are now on the other side of the glass. Their job is straightforward: get the name of every witness and start taking statements. Rundel can see the urgent efforts to resuscitate Dziekanski, who's lying bare-chested and limp on the floor. Sickness pelts the Mountie in the stomach like a wave with every desperate chest compression he sees. While Bentley goes from person to person, collecting names and details from the numerous eyewitnesses to what just happened, an airport security guard tells Rundel the whole thing was caught on tape. He points out the guy who had the camera. Pritchard has stopped recording and is now just watching what, for him, was entertainment a mere moment ago.

Pritchard had the best view of the event through his digital camera. He saw the Taser have little effect on Dziekanski when it was first fired. He saw how Dziekanski struggled with the police on the ground. It looked to him like Dziekanski was trying to get up. He saw the Mounties flip Dziekanski over once he was under control. Yet even with this vantage point, Pritchard missed key parts of the encounter. He never saw Dziekanski grab a stapler off the desk right in front of him. He couldn't see how Dziekanski held it, or the fist he made with his other hand. Pritchard could see only Dziekanksi's back, because he was facing the police. Not only did he not see things that did happen, Pritchard thinks he saw things that didn't happen: he thinks police shot Dziekanski in the back.

The video could clear up any confusion about what actually happened, but when he sees a security guard pointing him out to Constable Rundel, Pritchard's first instinct isn't to offer up the evidence. He walks in the other direction to the spot where he's left his backpack. He opens it up and stuffs the camera to the bottom to hide it.

Rundel approaches with one thought in his mind: he's gathering information to see if there's enough to charge Dziekanski with mischief. Rundel begins to ask Pritchard what he saw and about some video he might have shot. Pritchard acknowledges he recorded much of what happened with his camera. When Rundel tells him he wants it as evidence, Pritchard balks. He tells Rundel he won't part with it. He's just come back from China and the memory card is loaded with personal photos. He's on his way home to visit his father, who's ill and dying in Victoria. There is some discussion about whether Pritchard could keep the memory card, but give up the camera itself. Rundel knows so little about how a digital camera works that he thinks that might be okay.

It's at this point that a police officer who is worried about incriminating video might simply put his foot down, and demand the whole lot. In Rundel's mind, however, it's just another piece of evidence, and he feels some sympathy and compassion after hearing Pritchard's reasons for refusing to part with the camera. So, rather than flex his power and just confiscate the device, Rundel goes back to Robinson to tell him there's a video of the encounter, but the guy who shot it doesn't want to give it up. Robinson is busy on a phone alerting various supervisors and managers about the ongoing incident.

His direct supervisor is listening to the corporal describe what's happened. Staff Sergeant Doug Wright orders Robinson to hold both Pritchard and his camera until officers with the Integrated Homicide Investigation Team, or IHIT, arrive. Robinson relays that to the rookie: "We don't have a choice. Go back and seize it, Gerry. It's evidence."

Meanwhile Wright gives Robinson some advice: "Make excellent notes," Wright tells him. "Don't allow members at the scene to talk to each other about the incident." Wright tells Robinson they're all essentially witnesses to a homicide.

———

The advanced life-support team is not giving up on Dziekanski. They inject him with epinephrine to artificially boost his blood pressure. They insert a breathing tube into his lungs. They give him atropine to prevent his heart from beating too slowly. An intravenous bag pumps sodium bicarbonate into his veins to counteract the acidification of the blood that happens when breathing and heartbeat stop. They don't stop trying to restart Dziekanski's heart with chest compressions. They have a doctor on the phone who's at Richmond General Hospital a few kilometres away. After about twenty minutes trying to revive Dziekanski, the ER physician makes the call: stop resuscitation.

Robert Dziekanski is pronounced dead. It's 2:10 a.m. It will be some time before the Mounties realize this is no longer a case of investigating someone for mischief and that now they are the ones under investigation.

———

Once again, Rundel is by Pritchard's side, explaining that they have no choice but to seize the camera. Pritchard hands it to him and Rundel places it in a plastic evidence bag. He begins to take a statement from Pritchard.

A few minutes later, another uniformed Mountie approaches and interrupts. Corporal Joe Johal from the Richmond detachment has just arrived at the airport. He tells Rundel to stop what he's doing and hand him the evidence bag with the camera. Johal tells Rundel he's under investigation.

Rundel and Bentley go back to Robinson and discover what's going on. "He's expired," Robinson tells them. "You need to shut down what you're doing and take no more statements. Make sure you've got everyone's names. I've already called IHIT."

IHIT, the Integrated Homicide Investigation Team, is the largest homicide unit in Canada. It's made up mainly of RCMP officers, and includes police from a number of municipal forces in Vancouver's lower mainland.

"People are going to be coming out," Robinson says matter-of-factly.

Bentley looks stunned, as if someone has just sucker-punched him. "Expired?" Bentley asks.

"Yes, he's expired," Robinson repeats. Robinson is trying not to be blunt by making a big announcement. It's not uncommon for police to detach emotionally from something traumatic. This is one of those times. None of them thought Dziekanski was going to die. Robinson's effort at being discreet is failing.

"He's dead?" Bentley asks.

"Yes, you need to shut down what you're doing," Robinson repeats. He doesn't think any of them have done anything wrong. "You need to go back to the subdetachment, take a breather, grab a pop, and make your notes." The three junior officers leave the building and drive away. Robinson stays behind to wait for the homicide investigators and secure the scene.

It's an hour later when the IHIT members show up. Seven investigators fan out and begin the task of trying to determine what happened and why. Constable Pat Mulhall is one of them. Johal hands Mulhall the camera and identifies Pritchard as the owner. Mulhall begins taking a statement from Pritchard, who suggests that at one point people in the airport were concerned Dziekanski could be a terrorist and his suitcases weren't just filled with clothes.

"And then we're thinkin', okay, maybe we should actually get out of here," Pritchard tells him. Dziekanski looked "intoxicated ... on drugs ... crazy," Pritchard says, describing the dead man.

Pritchard is certain the first blast from the Taser didn't seem to hit Dziekanski. "Everybody's going, oh, it didn't even do anything."

Once Dziekanski was on the floor, the cops "had a lot of trouble controlling him ... it seemed like he had some abnormal amount of strength" and Dziekanski was "yelling and screaming and tryin' ta get up."

Even after he was subdued and handcuffed, Pritchard says, Dziekanski lifted his head, and the police seemed to be saying, "He's okay, he's okay." Then, Pritchard remembers, the police flipped Dziekanski onto his back. It was a few minutes more before the first wave of paramedics arrived and Pritchard offers that he didn't see the police administer any emergency medical treatment. "I wasn't in there and I don't know what his state was."

Mulhall wants Pritchard to be clear about what the four Mounties did, and he asks to see Pritchard's video. They sit together on a bench. Pritchard holds the camera, and presses PLAY. They watch everything Pritchard shot. Mulhall is happy and congratulates Pritchard, telling him that the video will be invaluable in clearing up their questions about what happened. He suggests Pritchard accompany him to the IHIT office so they can make a copy, and he can arrange for Pritchard to get a lift to the ferry terminal so he can get over to the island to be with his ailing father. It's a while later when Mulhall returns and says the investigators can't leave the airport anytime soon. There's also a problem with the machine that makes digital copies. If Pritchard will voluntarily give him the camera's memory card, Mulhall promises to FedEx it back to him in a couple of days. Pritchard agrees.

4 | THE PHONE CALL

ZOFIA CISOWSKI HAD ALWAYS imagined the drive home from the air-port would be different. It would be daylight. Her son would be with her. There would be bursts of Polish in the car as she introduced her son to his new homeland. The mountains and valleys marking the miles between Vancouver and Kamloops would have impressed Robert Dziekanski, who has always been enthralled with geography. So much so that he agonized over leaving his collection of worn and dusty geog-raphy books behind. Cisowski had told him to forget about clothes, she would buy whatever he needed in Canada. Just bring the books, she told her son.

Now, as her neighbour Richard Hutchinson speeds along the high-way, the spectacular scenery that would have wowed Dziekanski is hidden by the darkness. There is no jubilant conversation in Polish. There are long stretches of silence on the four-hour journey home.

It's nearing midnight when Cisowski's phone rings in her empty apartment. Her answering machine picks up the call. It's a woman. She doesn't leave her name. She leaves a message: "It's Canada Immigration calling," the woman says. "Vancouver International Airport ... for Sofia." The voice doesn't offer much information, beyond what almost sounds like a scolding. "Well, we're expecting her to be here picking up her relative." The caller tells Cisowski to contact a supervisor, and leaves a phone number. At the airport, Border Services officer Juliette Van

Agteren hangs up the phone and turns back to the sweaty, dishevelled, and distracted man in front of her.

Dziekanski had been brought into the office as he tried to leave the secure Customs hall without any paperwork. Canadians or visitors arriving from international trips must have a stamped declaration card to show to the Border Services officer at the exit. New immigrants need documentation, too, such as a Confirmed Permanent Resident document, or CPR. Dziekanski had neither.

"Where have you been?" one officer had asked him, while pointing to her watch and shrugging her shoulders. Dziekanski uttered a few words in Polish. She tried again, this time putting her hands together at the side of her head to mime sleeping. "Were you sleeping?" the officer asked. Dziekanski nodded.

He had been sleeping. In a secure section of an airport. Invisible for nearly six hours. It is a troubling and potentially dangerous lapse in airport security, yet none of the Border Services officers working tonight realizes it. If they do, they show no interest in investigating the breach or solving the mystery. They just want to send Dziekanski on his way.

Van Agteren has already tried paging Dziekanski's mother twice. When that fails, she goes out into the public area to find her, unaware Cisowski left minutes earlier. The Customs hall is a closed box. Arriving passengers enter at one end, and leave from the other. Had the Border Services officers exercised any integrated system of monitoring passengers who enter the hall but fail to exit, Dziekanski would have been found hours before. Had officer Tina Zadravec bothered to check the computer systems to see if Dziekanski had entered the box after the person on line eight told her he should be there, the logical course of action would have been to initiate a search. Now, hours later, Zadravec walks into the office where Dziekanski is being processed. She sees a man pacing and speaking to himself. *Dziekanski looks like he's been drinking,* she thinks to herself. He drank on the plane, got off drunk and fell asleep, and woke up drunk.

"What?" Zadravec exclaims to the other officers. "Is that man still here? His family have been waiting for him all day and they've just left for

Kamloops." Zadravec doesn't tell anyone that she was the one who sent them home. When it's suggested that Dziekanski is confused and tired and should probably stay at the airport, "Oh, he's a big boy," is the reply.

Border Services officer Adam Chapin steps in to help because he knows a few words in Polish. Enough to ask the basic questions to confirm details on Dziekanski's immigration papers: "Are you married? Do you have children? Have you ever been arrested?"

"No," is Dziekanski's reply to all three.

The whole process to certify Dziekanski as a new permanent resident has taken just under two hours. He's been given four or five cups of water to quench his thirst. Chapin escorts Dziekanski back out to the exit, where he was first intercepted. "Thank you and have a good night," Chapin offers in his best Polish. Dziekanski says the same. His speech is slurred. He's unsteady on his feet, and stumbles as if intoxicated as he heads toward the door leading to the greeting hall, hoping to find his mother.

Less than an hour later, he would be dead.

The last time Dziekanski and his mother spoke, he was frantic. He was gripping the radiator in his neighbour's apartment with both hands. His flight to Germany, where he would catch a plane to Vancouver, was due to depart in just a few hours. Dziekanski did not want to go.

His neighbour, Robert Dylski, was to drive Dziekanski to the airport. As a result of the delays caused by Dziekanski's last-minute panic attacks, Dylski became increasingly worried they'd miss the flight. While he and a couple of friends pleaded, Zofia Cisowski was on the phone begging her son. His hysteria had forced her to cancel this trip once already, and she made it clear it would be very expensive if not impossible to change the ticket again. Dziekanski clearly did not want to fly.

"Don't worry," his mother told him. "Everybody will help you."

Dziekanski seemed unconvinced in the days leading up to the flight, frequently trembling and grabbing on to furniture to steady himself. He hadn't slept in a couple of days. He hadn't eaten. Given

Dziekanski's obvious panic and complete ignorance about air travel, Cisowski could have requested assistance from the airline ahead of time. Once in Vancouver, someone would have been assigned to help Dziekanski through the Primary Inspection Line and on to the Canada Border Services Agency (CBSA) officers for processing. She didn't. He was on his own.

Despite his mania, Dziekanski seemed to want to leave Poland. Days before the flight, he had brought all his belongings — his money, passport, plane tickets, and luggage — to Dylski's apartment for safe-keeping. Dziekanski had been afraid the woman he lived with would take it. Elzbieta Dibon was not happy Dziekanski was leaving. She was also an alcoholic, according to some who knew her, and Dziekanski was looking to avoid any last-minute drama.

Dziekanski knew something of the effects of alcohol abuse himself. While his friends would describe him as merely a social drinker, his liver didn't lie. Just forty years old, he carried a record of chronic alcoholism. His other vice was also substantial. Dziekanski smoked a pack of cigarettes a day. More, just prior to his departure. As a gesture for his mother, he quit cold turkey just before his flight. By the time he got to Vancouver, he'd gone from two packs a day to none, with all the nicotine withdrawal symptoms you'd expect.

Dziekanski's addictions were perhaps, at least in part, a by-product of his circumstances. Dziekanski had no job prospects to speak of and his mother knew it. When they lived together in Poland, she scrimped to afford a brief vacation once a year, but they didn't have enough money for even a used car. Years after she moved to Canada, Cisowski sent him money from her own meagre savings as a cleaner.

Despite his rather depressing life, Dziekanski seemed, by all accounts, an affable man. One neighbour knew him as the person who cheerfully helped store the annual supply of coal for her furnace. He liked to play chess with another. Those digging into his identity, however, would find a man with a troubled past: a thick police file, with a record of several thefts and one act of violence committed under the influence of alcohol. There was a five-year jail term for robbery.

THE PHONE CALL | 55

Cisowski saw only her son's potential, as all good mothers do. She imagined that, in Canada, Dziekanski would find steady employment, learn English, find a wife, and make her a grandmother. A fairy-tale ending to what had been a hard life.

The son she knew was big-hearted and loved his mother. He was obsessed with geography, in an almost naive, childlike fashion: he kept a collection of atlases and picture books dealing with topography, population, and other facts about places he would never even dream of visiting. Sometimes he watched the game show *Jeopardy*, and tried to decipher the meaning of questions dealing with far-off places.

He had tried to learn English years ago. Dziekanski had worked his way through a series of thin *Easy English* magazines. The periodicals were published in Eastern Europe to introduce the vocabulary and grammar of the language. In one issue that featured the English alphabet, Dziekanski had carefully written a pronunciation guide in Polish above each letter. The cover of another issue showed a picture of Mounties in red serge on horseback.

Dziekanski packed those magazines and dozens of atlases into one of his suitcases for the trip to Canada. He put a few clothes in another: a canvas safari vest, which he wore the last time his mother visited; and a pair of low-rise leather cowboy boots she'd bought for him and brought to Poland. It wasn't the only gift from Canada Cisowski had given him that he didn't want to leave behind. Buried in his bags was a plastic resin ornament, the kind you might hang on a Christmas tree or tack on to a fridge door. It's a cartoonish, grinning face — just the head and shoulders — of a Stetson-wearing Mountie.

By the time his friends had convinced Dziekanski to let go of the radiator, he had vomited at least twice. They took a bucket in the car with them just in case, but at the airport Dziekanski seemed resigned to what was happening. He went to the washroom. He had a soft drink. They said goodbye.

More than an hour after Adam Chapin used his best Polish to bid Dziekanski goodnight, the phone in the Customs and Immigration office rings. Chapin answers it. Zofia Cisowski has heard the message left by Juliette Van Agteren. Chapin tells Cisowski that indeed her son had arrived and had cleared Immigration.

"Where was he?" Cisowski asks.

"We're not quite sure. We think he may have been sleeping," Chapin tells her. "I assume he'll get a hotel room for the night, or he'll be sleeping on a bench in the airport." Chapin offers to go into the public area and bring Dziekanski back to have him call his mother.

Cisowski hangs up and begins making plans to go back to Vancouver. She can't impose on her neighbour again. Cisowski decides to fly. She calls a cab and the driver convinces her that it's a waste of money. The next available flight likely won't get her into Vancouver much faster than taking the next bus in a few hours.

As Cisowski tries to grab a little sleep, Chapin searches for Dziekanski. He can't find him. Chapin sees an RCMP officer and asks if he's seen an intoxicated Polish immigrant. The Mountie gives Chapin an odd look.

"Do you have any information?" the officer asks.

After explaining he's trying to relay a message from the man's mother, the police officer walks Chapin around a corner to the spot where paramedics are feverishly trying to revive a man on the floor. Chapin watches as they give up, and declare the man dead. He helps the RCMP find Dziekanski's documents in his luggage, and gives them the phone number of the dead man's mother.

5 | SUSPECTS

THE MOUNTIES KNOW very little about the dead man they left behind at the airport. Their scribbled notes show his name and passport number and his general description. They have no idea Dziekanski has a mother who'd been waiting for him all day. They haven't a clue that she still thinks her son is alive. They're oblivious to the reason why Dziekanski spent hours essentially ignored by Canadian Customs and Immigration officers in a secure part of the terminal, his physical and mental condition deteriorating to the point at which threatening people and smashing property seemed reasonable. They're not even sure about the actions they took just a few hours ago. It all happened so fast. The man turned, he had a stapler in one hand. He made a fist with the other. He appeared to take a step. He's dead.

Bentley is in shock. Nothing like this has happened before in his short career. Yes, there have been a few dust-ups. There was the time he and a partner stopped a man from attacking his wife in their condo. The man had a knife. He believed she had cheated on him. He had slashed her. She was screaming.

Bentley's partner had wrestled with the man and disarmed him, while Bentley doused the suspect's face with pepper spray. Bentley used the tools he had. It was automatic. Muscle memory, learned from training at Depot. If someone has a weapon, you act to stop them.

He'd never seen anyone die before.

Bentley, Millington, and Rundel sit quietly, in an area of the sub-detachment known as "the pit," where there are a number of cubicles. They're making their notes and waiting for what's to come. Those notes, jotted down in the stunned silence as Dziekanski's death sinks in, are meagre and brief. In a few minutes, however, they will begin to give the first of several very detailed descriptions of what happened.

Robinson is still at the airport, securing the scene. He's also fielding calls on his cellphone. There are more than a few people in the RCMP chain of command who want to know what's going on. Is protocol being followed? Are any of the members hurt or do they need anything? He assures his watch commander that everything is under control. "Don't worry, Staff," Robinson says to his boss, Staff Sergeant Ken Ackles. "We got it. It's all covered. There's a video that shows everything."

Despite the tragic outcome, Robinson doesn't believe he or the other members did anything wrong. He thinks the video is a bonus because it will show what happened.

It's nearly 4:00 a.m. when Sergeant Derek Brassington, the primary investigator on the homicide investigation team, gets to the airport, takes control of the scene from Robinson, and gets investigators to work. At the very same time, Staff Sergeant Mike Ingles forces the last remaining cobwebs from his mind and walks into the airport subdetachment. Ingles has been awakened in the middle of the night by news of Dziekanski's death, but his focus is on the three rookies waiting for him.

Ingles is no-nonsense and somewhat intimidating if you don't know him. His immaculately bald head, piercing eyes, and businesslike staccato speech are enough to put any stranger on guard. Even if you do know Ingles, it is impossible to act in a casual fashion with him; he commands attention. That's especially true if you're involved in someone's death and he's all that stands between you and the homicide investigators. There is no RCMP union. The closest thing to one is the Staff Relations Representative program. That's a network of officers like Ingles who advise and advocate on behalf of members. This morning, these three sombre, silent constables need it.

Robert Dziekanski's worldly possessions became evidence for the homicide investigators who secured the scene in the International Reception Lobby (IRL) of Vancouver's international terminal early on the morning of October 14, 2007. Dziekanski, deceased, is shielded from the public by a green screen.

Wide shot of the scene, showing luggage, clothes, and smashed furniture. One of the first photos taken by homicide investigators, it shows the scene inside the IRL in the early morning hours of October 14, 2007. Visible are the smashed table and computer on the floor near the door Dziekanski barricaded. His luggage, still on the cart, is on the left. His clothes, removed by paramedics, sit in a pile beside a green screen that shields his body from public view.

Ingles has no qualms about putting away bad cops. In the past he's been assigned to represent members he knew were guilty of misconduct. What Ingles tries to do in those cases is get them out of the force with what they deserve. On this morning, Ingles walks into the pit and sees Bentley, Millington, and Rundel sitting solemnly, drained of emotion. They tell him what happened. When they're done, it's apparent to Ingles that they've just been through the most traumatic event in their careers as police officers.

Then Ingles does the talking. One of the first things he says to them is not to discuss the details with anyone else. There's going to be a lot of investigation, he tells them. An in-custody death — the term for when police have any involvement with someone who dies — automatically triggers a coroner's inquest in British Columbia. There will be other scrutiny, too. Internal investigations. Perhaps the civilian oversight body for the RCMP — the Commission for Public Complaints — will be compelled to examine what happened. Then there's IHIT, which has already taken over the case.

Police officers have the same rights as any other citizen when it comes to answering questions about their role in a homicide. They are, however, expected to explain their actions. "You have a duty to account," Ingles tells the three Mounties in front of him. Every officer must describe in basic detail what happened.

Ingles adds a caveat in the form of strong advice: speak to a lawyer before submitting to any lengthy interview by homicide investigators. Bentley, Millington, and Rundel reject Ingles's caution outright. They tell their rep they don't need to speak to a lawyer.

Ingles hears them agree: "If we didn't do anything wrong, why wouldn't we just give a statement and tell what happened?"

Ingles doesn't have an argument for that. At least not a successful one.

There is not the slightest suggestion that the Mounties want time to get their stories straight. They don't need to see the video they seized before they describe what happened. Yet they know their actions were caught on camera. They are also aware there are eyewitness accounts from more than a dozen people. The Mounties simply don't think they have anything to hide.

In the weeks, months, and years to come, that fact will be erased from the narrative adopted by some media, the public, prosecutors, and judges, who will insist the police hatched a cover-up from the beginning. They will be wrong, but the Mounties' decision to speak to investigators right away is a fateful one that will saddle them with guilt and suspicion for the rest of their lives.

Just before 5:00 a.m., however, there is no reason to think their actions were anything less than what was expected of them according to their training. Sergeant Brassington and several homicide investigators arrive at the subdetachment and Brassington tells the three pensive police officers they don't need to be worried. "This doesn't look like it's going to be a big deal, guys," Brassington says. Brassington is of the mind that there's no criminal offence or even misconduct to investigate.

In keeping with his assessment, when the tape recorders come out none of the Mounties are cautioned that what they're about to say could be used as evidence against them. Unlike the somewhat lengthy Miranda rights process in the United States, Canadian police use a simple warning based on guarantees in the Canadian Charter of Rights and Freedoms. The so-called Charter warning is given to tell them why they're being arrested or detained, that they have a right to a lawyer, and are allowed to speak to a lawyer. There is no Charter warning given to the three Mounties before they start talking, because the investigators don't believe there's been a crime. Over the next hour the officers are interviewed, separately and simultaneously.

IHIT Sergeant Dave Attew sits down with Gerry Rundel, and it's clear the constable is anything but rehearsed. Just a couple of minutes into the questions his speech is halting, peppered with *ums*, pauses, and stuttering as he retrieves from his memory the chaotic stream of events that was crammed into a few seconds.

"He picked up a stapler, and he started … clenching his fists," Rundel recalls. "And, putting the stapler up above his head, mo-motioning … making motions with it, uh … towards us … and then at that point, Constable Millington had … pulled out his … Taser, and … activated it."

Rundel believes — wrongly — that Millington pulled the trigger on the Taser twice before Dziekanski went down. Then he makes another mistake. "Corporal Robinson, and uh, Bentley and myself, then, made contact with the male and … wrestled him to the ground."

He goes on to tell Sergeant Attew that Dziekanski continued to resist, fiercely fighting the officers' attempt to get his hands in cuffs.

"So, it was just a matter of … wrestling, and putting the pressure on his arms, uh … and shoulders, until we got his arms … out from underneath 'im, and … managed to get 'im handcuffed."

What is clear in Rundel's mind is the same thing that was obvious to bystanders like Paul Pritchard: the officers spent a lot of time wrestling with Dziekanski. They spent more time wrestling with him than anything else.

While that point is clear in Rundel's mind, there are many others that are not. His confusion, and the confusion of his fellow officers, will be a source of great harm for them. In the months and years to come, the public, an inquiry commissioner, indignant prosecutors, two trial judges, and seven justices of the Supreme Court of Canada will adamantly assert that by dint of their training, police officers are imbued with special powers of memory and attention to detail not available to the frail minds of civilian witnesses. It will be a catch-all courtroom explanation for why the errors the Mounties made can't possibly be the product of, well, … error. They can only be the artifacts of a conspiracy to mislead. Lives will be ruined, men will go to jail, and another will die because of the judicial system's self-serving bias.

In the interview, Rundel demonstrates that his recollection is genuinely imperfect, and his answers make clear that this imperfection is entirely predictable given the adrenaline resulting from the sudden escalation of events. Rundel was so focused on what he perceived was a threat that he can't recall any basic or uncontroversial details from an event that happened just a few hours ago.

Attew asks him where the Taser probes hit Dziekanski.

"Ya know, I don't even … I don't know," Rundel says.

Was security dealing with Dziekanski when the Mounties arrived?

"You know, there again, it was, um … I don't recall."

Was Dziekanski's voice loud?

"I really don't recall," Rundel repeats.

Who called for the ambulance?

Rundel doesn't know. Rundel can't even remember if Dziekanski was wearing jeans or dress pants.

———————

In another part of the subdetachment, Constable Bill Bentley isn't doing much better. IHIT Corporal Dave Teboul asks Bentley what Dziekanski looked like. Bentley thinks he was wearing a T-shirt. He wasn't. Bentley can't even remember that he was the one who first tried speaking to Dziekanski, with his "How's it goin', bud?" greeting.

"I forget what member engaged him, I know it wasn't me," Bentley tells Teboul, incorrectly. There is absolutely no conceivable reason why Bentley would lie about this detail, yet he gets it wrong. It's strong evidence Bentley's memory is genuinely faulty. His accusers, who will relentlessly try to prove Bentley's a liar, will conveniently ignore it.

Like Rundel, what sticks in Bentley's mind is the threat he felt as Dziekanski's behaviour escalated.

"He basically grabbed the stapler and he kind of flings it out in front of him," Bentley says. "And he's kind of holding it up … pointing it towards the members … the way he grabbed the stapler, he kind of swung it right out in a fast motion, almost like he was trying to hit, um, myself and Corporal Robinson."

It is a scene not visible in the viewfinder of Pritchard's camera because Dziekanski is facing the officers in the second or two it happens. Then the Taser is fired.

"I see the subject kind of fighting through it, uh, fists are clenched and, uh, subject is eventually taken down. Uh, all happened so fast, I … I can't remember if I was involved in the take-down or not. I don't believe I was."

Bentley thinks Dziekanski is "taken down," but he's not sure. Bentley is pretty sure he wasn't involved either way. What is significant is what Bentley doesn't say. He doesn't use the word *wrestled* to describe how Dziekanski ended up on the floor.

Teboul asks him again whether Dziekanski hit the ground on his own or was "taken" to the ground. Bentley is tentative, as if he's not sure.

"I believe he was, he was taken down to the ground, from what I can recall. Yeah, he was taken down to the ground … uh, I don't think it took much force to get him down. I don't recall."

Bentley's uncertain, almost waffling reply doesn't sound like someone holding up their end of a conspiracy to bullshit a homicide detective. Just as with Rundel, there are things that are a blur to Bentley, for instance during the struggle.

"Is he still being Tasered?" Teboul asks.

"I can't remember. I don't know," Bentley replies.

"Were his legs moving?"

"I can't remember."

Bentley does remember that Dziekanski was breathing when he saw him, because he called for the ambulance and moments later upgraded the call to Code 3.

"It was kinda strange because his skin was turning bluish colour but you could still hear him breathing and, uh, Corporal Robinson said he could still feel a pulse."

It is the team leader of the homicide investigation who sits down with Constable Kwesi Millington at the same time Millington's partners are giving their own versions of events.

———————

"He didn't listen to anything we were saying," Millington tells Sergeant Derek Brassington.

"Okay, so after he was Tasered then you mentioned that he was, and I — I don't remember if you said he was put to the ground or wrestled to the ground or struggled on the ground or whatever," Brassington probes. "What happened after he was Tasered?"

Millington replies, "Uh, well he seemed to feel the effects of the Taser but he didn't fall due to that." Then Millington makes a mistake. "Members had to wrestle him to the ground."

Millington hasn't seen any video of the encounter. He can only draw on what he perceives was the actual experience, and it's immediately clear there is something wrong with Millington's perception of the event when Brassington follows up.

"From the time when he was … you first saw him … to the time when he was handcuffed, how much time do you think went by?"

Millington's reply is telling. "I think it was less than ten minutes."

It was actually less than three. In Millington's mind it all took much longer: the sudden appearance of a stapler, Dziekanski's time on his feet, the wrestling on the ground.

Millington then suggests that he's aware Dziekanski had gone down and was on the floor before he pulled the Taser trigger a second time, when Brassington asks about the second stun.

"The connectors were still attached, but he was already on the ground," Millington explains. "But he wasn't under control."

The next day, after he's had a night's sleep, Millington adds to his statement.

"He seemed more paranoid than angry," Millington says about Dziekanski. "He knocked over some things that were on the desk and, ah, then he reached and grabbed the stapler, had it in the open position and had it raised high and then started advancing towards us."

Millington refers to his training to explain his decision to use the Taser: "To stop the threat."

Robinson gets no sleep before making his initial statement at nearly 6:00 a.m. He's been on the job fourteen hours and he's not done yet. Robinson arrives back at the subdetachment after everyone's already been interviewed and begins answering Corporal Teboul's questions.

"It all went down pretty quick," Robinson sums up.

He tells Teboul that Dziekanski was very agitated from the get-go. "Pissed off, angry," is how he describes it.

"I was trying to give him directions to put his hands on the table," Robinson says. "At that point he grabbed a stapler and tried to hit us with it."

Robinson describes a swift motion that wasn't visible to most witnesses because, he says, it happened while Dziekanski was facing the officers, with his back to most of the onlookers.

What Robinson says next is important, because it will be largely ignored by those seeking to make him out to be a liar.

"The male still wasn't going down, um, and ... and I can hear the Taser cycling ..." Robinson says.

"I wasn't too sure if it, the cycle had ended or not and I was instructing [Millington], to use it again, because the male still, um, was not going down. So I didn't know if the cycle ended or, um, he depressed it again. The male finally started going down at that point ..."

The first time Robinson describes what happened, he thinks Dziekanski went down on his own. Later on in the interview Teboul goes back to the same thing.

"How did he get to the ground?" Teboul asks.

"Um, oh, he had to be wrestled to the ground."

Teboul follows up. "He didn't collapse on his own?"

"No," Robinson says.

"And who, ah, brought him down to the ground?" Teboul presses.

"I don't know which one of us engaged him first, but it was, he was up and we were on him and he was still fighting through all of us."

Like the other officers, Robinson appears to blend Dziekanski's apparent resistance to the first Taser stun with the struggle on the ground a few seconds later. In any event, he doesn't seem to think it's significant how Dziekanski got to the ground. First it was on his own, then it was an imagined take-down. Robinson doesn't remember who was involved because no one was. No officer volunteered the idea that Dziekanski had to be "wrestled" to the ground. Even when they say that's what happened, their memories are incomplete and far from identical. What is uniform is the struggle — the wrestling — on the ground.

The rest of Robinson's interview is disjointed. He repeats himself a number of times. "It happened really quick to where he grabbed the stapler and started swinging at us. And [I] took a step back, trying to think, Can you run? What can you do? Where's he going? And who's he gonna hit, or who's he gonna attack?"

Robinson describes trying to position Dziekanski so he can't flee through the terminal.

"I remember him taking a step forward and then he was swinging the stapler and that's um, ah, like he's swinging the stapler up high ... then he's just, like, he's swinging it, um, to try to push us back or, ah, an attempt to hit us. So we — I didn't know at that point where he's gonna go ... it's aggressively step, swing ..."

Robinson uses the word swing twelve times in his statement. It's a critical mistake, which will end up as evidence that he tried to mislead Teboul about Dziekanski's actions.

Robinson describes a chaotic scene of the officers yelling at each other while they struggled to get Dziekanski under control.

"He was fighting all the way through it. Kicking ... pulling his arms in. I remember he pulled one arm back under. The members would get the arm, lose the arm."

Robinson is certain that Dziekanski was breathing, and had a pulse until the first responders arrived.

He isn't talking like a cop who has something to hide.

Teboul finishes up the interview: "Is there anything else that I haven't asked you, or anything that you feel is important?"

Robinson doesn't hesitate. "Other than there was a lot of witnesses right there," he says. "Watching everything."

These aren't the only statements the officers give. Four days later, when they are back on shift again, each is approached a second time. Rundel still describes Dziekanski as aggressive and combative and maintains it took two Taser blasts to bring him down. Now, however, Rundel disowns the misremembered notion that Dziekanski was wrestled to the ground. He tells Sergeant Brassington, "after the second [Taser stun] he went down, and that's when ... um, Constable Bentley, Robinson, and myself then got on ... uh, on top and ... got 'im into the handcuffs." The Taser, Rundel insists, was the most appropriate weapon in this case. "That's what our training has taught us to do, and that's what we did."

Brassington reinterviews Bentley about his thoughts on the appropriateness of the Taser.

"I feel it was justified," Bentley says. "Had I had my Taser on me, and, ah, had Constable Millington not deployed his Taser, I would have, ah, I would have deployed mine."

Bentley says Dziekanski had become combative when he grabbed the stapler. Pepper spray would have affected the police as well as Dziekanski and could have drifted into the public area.

When Brassington meets Millington again that morning, the investigator wants to know just one thing.

"What can you remember, if anything, about conversations that you ... that, uh, was had between the four Members about ... the use of the Taser?"

Millington is matter-of-fact. "I think someone asked if ... anyone had a Taser."

It wasn't a conversation, Millington insists. He can't even be sure who asked him when he answered, "Yes."

Brassington is also focused on the Taser when he sits down with Robinson again. "I'll ask you this point-blank," Brassington says. "Why was the Taser used that night?"

"The individual was exhibiting combative behaviour," Robinson answers. "The options were baton or Taser. One member had a baton. Millington had a Taser."

Pepper spray was risky.

"I deemed the most appropriate tool to use was the Taser at that time."

Robinson adds that Dziekanski knew who they were, despite any language barrier.

"He was saying 'policia, policia,' so he still was able to identify the members ahead of me as police."

A month later, after Paul Pritchard's video is made public, Bentley will phone IHIT to clarify something that he has recalled. However, Bentley won't be concerned about any of the so-called discrepancies in the police accounts of what happened. News media are focusing on a muddy section of audio at the beginning of the Pritchard video, the part where it sounds like the police are talking about using the Taser. It will prompt Bentley to set the record straight with Corporal Teboul.

"I remember turning around and directing a question to the Members asking them whether one of them had a Taser on them. The reason why I asked this is that I wanted to know that we had a Taser available as an intervention option if we needed to in fact use it. There was no mention whether I 'could' use the Taser, or 'can I use the Taser', contrary to what, um I've seen listed in the newspapers."

Bentley's effort to clarify his initial statement is notable for what he doesn't do. Despite having seen the video, which clearly shows Dziekanski falling to the ground on his own, Bentley makes no attempt to correct that part of his recollection. Someone who knowingly fabricated that detail would be compelled to address the inconsistency. Bentley doesn't see it as significant.

Taken together, there is no question each officer makes errors in describing the same event, either in the timing or their perception of what happened. Prosecutors will argue those errors are like a poker player's tell, revealing a scheme to close ranks and collude. If that was the case, the officers were lousy at conspiracy. Just hours after the incident, with no opportunity to collude, only three of the four believe Dziekanski had to be wrestled to the ground. There's no unanimity about how many times the Taser was used and when precisely it was fired. There are more differences between each man's recollections than there are what some will deceptively refer to as "striking similarities." What is apparent, as the men are interviewed, separately and simultaneously, is that their brains aren't video cameras.

6 | COVER-UP

THE SHRILL WARBLE of Pierre Lemaitre's home phone echoes through his dark house, rousing the family dogs from slumber, waking his wife, Sheila. Pierre, still asleep, doesn't stir when Sheila answers. It's work. They want Pierre. They need Pierre. Now. At 4:30 a.m.

It isn't the first time he's received such a middle-of-the-night call in his long career. As the chief media spokesperson for the RCMP's E Division — the largest in British Columbia — he has learned that calls after hours and before hours aren't unusual. The RCMP has always had a lot of explaining to do, and lately, it seems, there have been more cases to manage.

Sheila unceremoniously wakes her husband. He abandons the dream he's having and takes the phone. Lemaitre recognizes the voice of Corporal Dale Carr, the media spokesperson for IHIT. At this point, Carr has been up for a couple of hours, rising after being told of the in-custody death at the airport.

"Pierre," Carr says, "I think you should come down."

Carr wants Lemaitre's help because this incident has the potential to ring bells well beyond Vancouver. An international traveller is dead after an encounter with police. It involves a Taser.

The media may not be aware of it now, but it won't take long for details of the very obvious ongoing investigation at a public airport to land in Vancouver newsrooms. It's a Sunday — typically a slow news day. Local media outlets are usually desperate for any story to fill their Sunday lineups. This will be national, for sure, if not bigger. Since Lemaitre is bilingual, he can handle media in French, also.

Carr, who has been IHIT's public face on well over a hundred homicide cases, has no idea how critical the next few hours will be to the man he's asked for help. Lemaitre hangs up the phone and searches for his uniform. He has always worn it with pride. Even now, as he dresses in the dark, Lemaitre draws on his sense of duty and feels like it's all worth it because he's doing something important and honourable. Lemaitre doesn't know it will become his last honourable day as a member of the RCMP.

It takes Lemaitre about an hour to drive in to Richmond from his rural home east of the city. He's tired but ready to start work when he meets Carr in the parking lot of the Richmond detachment. They head upstairs to a briefing room.

Homicide investigators are setting up a command centre. There are laptops and wires and plugs and chatter as they begin the task of coordinating the information that's being gathered: interviews, photographs, and names and numbers of witnesses.

At one point, Corporal Robinson enters the room and is talking to investigators. Carr and Lemaitre barely notice him.

Lemaitre understands his role and gets right to it. "Dale, what do you have for me to say? What information can be released?" he asks Carr.

Lemaitre and Carr are both fully trained police officers with years of front-line experience dealing with crimes. Carr has actually worked as a homicide investigator himself. Today, however, they are media spokespeople. Their job is well defined: relay information to the public. They are not involved in the investigation into Dziekanski's death. They do not have access to the growing file of information and evidence being gathered by the investigators. They are messengers, given limited details by other officers, who decide what can be released to the public in the middle of an investigation. It is a fact that will be downplayed and discarded in the crush of criticism that's to come.

This morning, however, Lemaitre is only thinking about what information he needs to do his job. While a dozen or so police go about their business, Carr sits down at a laptop with Lemaitre and plays part of a video. Lemaitre sees what appears to be a man stunned with a Taser, and three officers struggling with him on the ground. It's a short sequence that takes less than a minute and then Lemaitre turns to the matter at hand: "What's our strategy, Dale?"

Carr says his superiors have cleared the information they're allowed to release and it's pretty basic: A man of unknown origin caused a disturbance at YVR. He went past some glass doors. He was banging on the glass. He threw some chairs around. He threw a computer to the ground. The RCMP arrived and attempted to calm him down. At some point the man had something in his hand and was swinging it at the members. Police deployed a Taser. The man continued to fight and struggled with police. His vital signs were monitored. He passed away after emergency medical services arrived.

Carr knows a bit more. He knows Dziekanski's name. His nationality. His date of birth. None of that makes it to Lemaitre before the two men head to the airport terminal, where media are already waiting. Lemaitre runs through the information one more time with Carr before putting on his game face.

Lemaitre sees every interview — as repetitive as they become — as vital and important work. Over and over he does it. In front of cameras, microphones, and on a cellphone for journalists who aren't on the scene. He recounts the same basic information while Carr is preoccupied with his phone, which is going off every thirty seconds. The level of media attention is building and Carr is focused on trying to handle the calls. He barely pays attention to the script Lemaitre is reciting.

At one point this morning, Lemaitre thought he heard that RCMP members involved fired the Taser twice. It's not a critical point right now because the media don't seem to be focusing on that, as much as they are on the fact that a man died after what appeared to be bizarre and inexplicable behaviour at a public airport. In any event, the precise number of times the Taser trigger was pulled is not something anyone could know, with the exception of the officer who fired it. Millington's own notes say he used the weapon four times. Lemaitre hasn't seen those notes. The actual number won't be known for days, when the data from the device is downloaded by a specialist with an outside police force. There's no doubt the true total will be known and it will be part of the coroner's inquest. That's inevitable.

There is also a very big fly on the wall, overlooking this case. Rick Grounds, a civilian representative of the Commission for Public Complaints Against the RCMP — the CPC — has a direct line to homicide investigators. Grounds has access to the complete file police are developing. In real time. The CPC has never shied away from exposing bias and error and misconduct in the force. The CPC will know how many times the Taser was fired when investigators know. There is nothing about this investigation that can be indefinitely withheld from the public. Carr and Lemaitre both know that.

So, when Lemaitre fields questions about whether cameras in the airport captured video of what happened, he tells reporters there is no such video. It's true. There were no working cameras in the area where Dziekanski and the police squared off. It would also be some time before the relatively poor-quality footage shot from a distance by the airport's security cameras would turn up.

Lemaitre knows full well there is video of what happened. He saw a brief scene. That isn't airport video, though. It is evidence. Acknowledging evidence is anathema to police while an investigation is still underway, let alone one that's just begun. Lemaitre doesn't reveal to any journalist that he's seen a snippet of what took place from the same perspective Paul Pritchard had. He hasn't been cleared to do that, and he wouldn't do it on his own, even if asked.

After a number of hours, Lemaitre calls it a day. Back at home, Lemaitre composes and issues a written news release. Other than the fact that Lemaitre writes that there were only three officers who "attempted to speak with the man," there is nothing factually different in his release from what any witness who was there might have seen.

In his written news release, Lemaitre describes Dziekanski as having been violent and agitated. Certainly, based on what he's been told and what little he saw in that snippet of video, it did appear that Dziekanski wasn't complying. Lemaitre is first and foremost a police officer. He's been in countless one-on-one situations that escalated quickly from seemingly small movements by a subject, like grabbing an object or taking a defiant stance. Dziekanski's erratic and destructive behaviour is not in dispute or doubt. He had willfully smashed airport property and seemed intent on causing more damage when police showed up.

Should the officers have taken more time? Was there another way to handle the situation? Would it have made any difference? Those are all questions in Lemaitre's thoughts, but they are not relevant to his job of describing to the public what happened, as best as he can, within the limitations of what he knows and what he's been cleared to say. Lemaitre can't get inside the head of any of the officers involved. He wasn't there. He doesn't know what they saw or how they felt when Dziekanski turned to face them with something in his hand. Anyway, their actions are now the subject of an investigation. *It'll all come out,* Lemaitre thinks.

7 | GRIEF

ZOFIA CISOWSKI CLUTCHES a bouquet of white roses with red-fringed petals, holding the flowers as if she were holding a flickering candle to illuminate a pitch-black passageway in a haunted castle. Cisowski walks zombielike across the carpeted floor of the International Arrivals lounge at Vancouver International Airport in a ritual she repeats twice a year: once on October 14, the anniversary of her son's death, and once on April 15, her son's birthday.

Cisowski approaches the clear glass wall dividing the public side of the Arrivals lounge from the secure side. It's the same barrier through which Paul Pritchard recorded her son's last moments alive, a decade earlier. It's the same structure Robert Dziekanski mysteriously believed prevented him from leaving the airport. With ironic ease the airport chaplain waves his key card against a door in the wall and Cisowski crosses the threshold to stand on the very spot her son's heart stopped beating.

Up until now, Cisowski has been at times joking, at times businesslike in her preparations for this moment. Now, she bursts into tears as a stream of bewildered passengers, arriving from around the world, walk past her toward the same exit Robert Dziekanski never found.

Cisowski lays the flowers — the same colours as both Canada's and Poland's national flags — on an information counter that has long since replaced the one where Dziekanski stood against the Mounties.

Every year, as here in October 2015, Zofia Cisowski marks the anniversary of her son's death by placing a bouquet of red-and-white roses on a commemorative bench installed by the airport outside the international terminal. The flowers are in the colours of both the Canadian and Polish flags. The plaques are in English and Polish and say, controversially, only that Dziekanski's death is remembered "with sadness."

The chaplain tries to console her. "This is a sacred spot," he says before leading Cisowski in a prayer amid the bustling pedestrian traffic moving around them. The chaplain, eyes tightly closed, delivers words urging Cisowski to forgive.

"It's too late for me," Cisowski spits out bitterly. That door closed ten years ago.

———

The sun isn't up when Cisowski boards a bus bound for Vancouver. She's feeling a mixture of frustration, anger, and relief. All she can think of is the previous day spent waiting for Robert, finally being told to go home, and then finding out from a voicemail message she had missed him by just minutes.

Her son had been asleep, the Immigration officer had told her. Asleep? She expected he might be tired because his send-off by friends in Poland had been something of a drinking party.

Once at the airport, Cisowski is unsure where to go. She ascends the escalator to the same information booth she went to the night before. Janet Sullivan, the woman who was behind the counter last night, is here again this morning.

Sullivan recognizes Cisowski. "Oh, you're the lady from last night," she says and inquires about her son. "You didn't find him?"

"No," Cisowski replies. "But when I got home there was a message from Immigration."

Cisowski's accent is thick and sometimes she struggles for the right word in English. Sullivan hears Cisowski say she was told by Immigration her son was "sick." At least that's what it sounded like. Cisowski has a phone number written on a piece of paper, and Sullivan dials it for her. A CBSA officer answers and Sullivan explains why she's calling.

"Send her down," comes the reply over the phone.

Unaware of what's happened, Sullivan once more directs Cisowski to the Immigration office that the night before had turned her away.

Cisowski is worried. A friend of hers had recently told her that her own son from Poland had been held for a day by Immigration officials, only to be put on the next flight back to Poland.

Cisowski identifies herself to the first person she sees, and is wordlessly escorted to a room in which she is the sole occupant. Her questions in halting, broken English about the whereabouts of her son go unanswered by officers who tell her to "wait."

Cisowski's heart is pumping with anxiety, worry, and anticipation.

At one point, two police officers in plain clothes enter the room, exchange a few words, look at her, and leave again.

An hour passes.

It isn't until well after 2:00 p.m. that several Immigration officers, and someone from RCMP Victim Services, in the company of an airport chaplain, open the door and walk in. Cisowski is expecting to hear that her son is sleeping, or that he's free to go. They tell her bluntly that

Robert passed away. They tell her that his body was taken to the morgue at Vancouver General Hospital.

Cisowski falls to the floor, screaming. "My only son, my only son," she repeats over and over. "What did you do? What did he do?" she bawls.

There are no answers, only what seems like a barrage of questions. "Do you have family? Can someone come and get you and take you back to Kamloops?"

Through her tears and confusion, Cisowski explains she has no family. She doesn't count her husband, Peter, who is under constant care in a nursing home. She was waiting for her only son.

What happens next for Cisowski is a painful blur, punctuated by her own random, convulsive, and uncontrollable screams and sobs. Cisowski is driven to the Richmond detachment where a police officer arranges to take her to a women's shelter in nearby Burnaby.

Cisowski is asked whether she works ... does she have a boss or someone who can help? Cisowski gives the Mounties Teresa Collavini's name and number. She's the owner of the janitorial company that employs Cisowski in Kamloops. On the phone, Collavini agrees to make the four-hour drive to pick up Cisowski from the shelter later in the day.

In the meantime, Cisowski is loaded into the front seat of an unmarked police car, and driven by one of the homicide investigators. Along the way the officer stops the car and asks if he can record Cisowski's answers to some questions he has. She agrees.

The Mountie seems focused on Dziekanski's suitcases. Does Cisowski know what would have been in them? Cisowski describes what she expected her son would pack: a few clothes and a pile of books dealing with geography and travel. There would also be a bottle of vodka, intended for Cisowski's aging husband.

At the shelter, Cisowski is offered a couch on which to lie down and rest. There's food, she's told.

"What?" Cisowski exclaims. "Rest? My son died! They killed my son. [If] I have to take rest and stay overnight I will kill myself!"

Cisowski doesn't have to stay at the shelter. Collavini arrives that evening, but, given the lateness of the hour, they stay at the house of one of Collavini's relatives before heading back to Kamloops the next morning.

As they set out, Cisowski hasn't slept. She had always imagined it would be a happy trip with her only child at her side; instead, she is in the back seat of Collavini's car for the heart-wrenching journey. It takes nearly five hours. Cisowski screams most of the way home.

It is only when Cisowski arrives home and turns on the TV that she learns what happened to her son after she left the airport the day before. She had assumed her son died from natural causes, something that would be revealed by an autopsy. On the news, however, the main story deals with a man who died at the airport after an altercation with police. The dead man's name isn't mentioned, but there was only one person who died at the airport. Cisowski watches along with everyone else that night and the next morning, as RCMP Sergeant Pierre Lemaitre solemnly describes the few details he's been given, in sound bites carved up by media who strive to tell stories — even unusual ones like a man Tasered at the airport — as economically as possible.

"He was pounding on the windows behind us," Lemaitre says, looking off-camera at an unseen reporter. "He was throwing chairs. At one point he grabbed some computer equipment off the desk ... it appeared he was not going to calm down."

So far, Lemaitre has described, as best as he can, what eyewitnesses saw.

Lemaitre continues: "Three officers arrived. One had a Taser. It looked like he picked something up and was going to throw it at the officers so they discharged the weapon."

Other than Lemaitre's inaccurate statement concerning how many police officers were involved, he again describes exactly what happened. There is a reason he stated that there were "three officers" involved and not four; Lemaitre had seen just three officers struggling with Dziekanski in the brief clip of the video he was shown. Constable Kwesi Millington, who fired the Taser, was at times out of frame and was not immediately involved in the effort to get Dziekanski into handcuffs.

There is no conceivable reason for Lemaitre to lie about the number of police officers involved in the incident with Dziekanski. None. It is a mistake, and nothing more.

The next day, Lemaitre agrees to an interview before dawn at a Vancouver TV studio in order to accommodate an eastern Canadian audience. "They found the man in the secure area," Lemaitre repeats, "with his luggage cart and chairs set around him. They tried to … communicate with him."

What follows next will haunt Lemaitre for the rest of his life, and damn the Mounties involved in Dziekanski's death and the RCMP. From these few snowflakes an avalanche will form — one that will bury what's left of the RCMP's already tarnished credibility.

"Chairs went flying," Lemaitre continues. "He grabbed a computer off a desk and threw that. They just weren't getting through to this guy and the violence once again, escalating."

Lemaitre is tired and is being pressed repeatedly to describe a series of events that he hasn't personally seen. He knows numerous witnesses saw Dziekanski do the things he described. There is no question Dziekanski threw the furniture and computer equipment, but it happened before police arrived on the scene. Lemaitre is wrong about the order of events and makes it sound as if Dziekanski was in full flight when he was Tasered, instead of having just grabbed something the police could legitimately perceive was a weapon.

Sima Ashrafinia is at home with her husband, Fariborz Farahani, when she sees coverage of the incident on TV news. That's when the couple resurrect the argument from the night before and the tension in their already shaky marriage boils over into another ugly, angry battle.

"You know what?" Farahani barks. "He deserved to die. Why are you shouting in the airport? You should know better."

Ashrafinia is livid. "Nobody deserves to die like that."

Ashrafinia is beyond upset. She's now angry that no one from the RCMP has called her to take her statement. The ninety-second TV piece Ashrafinia sees doesn't have any clips from any of the eyewitnesses, who would have long since left the airport when the media showed up.

The story on TV primarily relies on sound bites from Lemaitre, and he wasn't there when it happened.

It's not uncommon for people to feel unsatisfied when they watch a short, formulaic story on TV about something that's important to them or that they were personally involved in. It's a big reason why journalists are often accused of bias or worse: fake news.

Ashrafinia was face to face with Dziekanski when he was exploding. Despite her best efforts, over a period of time, she was unable to calm him down and get through to him. She watched the result with her own eyes before being dragged away by a husband who couldn't care less. Now, she sees Lemaitre on TV and he seems to mischaracterize what happened. She's angry, she's triggered, and makes a snap judgment. *That police officer is totally lying!* she tells herself.

She grabs the *Yellow Pages* phone book and looks under *Media*. She calls the first outlet she sees and the next day a crew from CTV shows up at her door in North Vancouver.

Ashrafinia reveals that she captured some of what happened on her cellphone camera. It's 2007 and the technology on her flip phone produces only a few unsteady shots so short and of such poor quality it would be impossible to tell what was going on if you hadn't seen what happened for yourself. The audio is unintelligible. Ashrafinia recorded one of the scenes while she stood face to face with Dziekanski. She just stared at him, holding the camera up between them as if she were documenting his bizarre behaviour, or simply to record a weird event, as Paul Pritchard did.

Echoes of her traumatic experience and anger with authorities in Iran nurture Ashrafinia's ardent complaint to the eager news crew: "The RCMP is covering something up. Dziekanski wasn't a threat. He wasn't combative. I was there. I saw it. There were four officers, not three. Lemaitre said the police deployed a single Taser, and said it was used to deliver two pulses to Dziekanski."

Ashrafinia claims to have heard it go off four times, and she insists two officers had Tasers and stunned Dziekanski simultaneously. What Ashrafinia says doesn't add up.

When her version is reported, Lemaitre doubles down and defends what he's relayed to the media. He's certain that at some point in his briefing with Dale Carr he learned the Taser was discharged twice. That's what he tells the media who confront him with Ashrafinia's claim.

It makes no sense that Lemaitre would intentionally lie about it.

Constable Millington's own notes — inaccurate as they are — record that he pulled the trigger four times. Lemaitre hadn't seen those notes. No one from IHIT spoke to him about the number of times the Taser was used. Lemaitre must have thought he heard it from Carr that morning.

Without a doubt, Lemaitre was wrong. It's a mistake. One that will quickly be assumed by the public and many in the media to be a deliberate lie. It would lay the foundation for a theory that the RCMP was actively involved in a conspiracy to cover up what happened to Robert Dziekanski.

8 | THE CAMERA DOESN'T LIE

TWO DAYS AFTER Dziekanski died, the Taser begins to take on a critical role as far as the media is concerned. It's reported that, in the five years before Dziekanski's death, eight people died in British Columbia after they were hit with a Taser.

An RCMP constable emails Lemaitre with a personal complaint. Chris Newel tells Lemaitre that the public misunderstands the value of the stun gun. He asks the media spokesperson to "put out something indicating how many times the Taser has successfully be [*sic*] used.... Our only other option will be FATAL. I don't know how many people understand that. How many would have died if we didn't have the Taser. Of those eight how many had pre-existing conditions that likely contributed if not were the cause of death? Don't forget the 15,000 members that have been Tasered in training. I think we are all okay."

Lemaitre responds with a polite thank you and then adds, "Stand by for the autopsy results! We might be in for a surprise … like … Tasers didn't kill this guy … pre existing medical conditions and or drugs in the system … wait and see."

An hour after Lemaitre sends the email, the forensic pathologist begins his post-mortem examination of Robert Dziekanski. It will be months before the full analysis is complete. Lemaitre doesn't have nearly that long.

He is removed as the RCMP spokesperson for the file and Dale Carr is put in charge of dealing with the media. It's a decision that's made ostensibly because Lemaitre is based in Vancouver and Carr is with IHIT in Surrey. However, the switch will become more evidence that the RCMP is trying to cover up the truth of what happened the night Dziekanski died. The notion of a conspiracy will be cemented when Paul Pritchard goes public with news that the Mounties are refusing to give him his video back.

Pritchard watches the TV news of the incident along with everyone else, and comes away disappointed that neither he, nor his video, is mentioned, let alone shown. *Holy shit,* Pritchard thinks. He was expecting his fifteen minutes of fame for what he'd done. When it doesn't come, he decides that what Lemaitre told the reporters was "completely different" from what he remembers.

Indignation turns to outrage when Constable Pat Mulhall calls to tell him the RCMP will not return the video as promised. Mulhall says it's evidence for their investigation and it will likely be kept until after a coroner's inquest, which will be held sometime in the next two and half years.

What have I done? Pritchard thinks to himself. *Why would I be so stupid to trust the police?* That's a good question for Pritchard. He had dealings with police as a younger man, and they weren't pleasant.

After Mulhall's call, Pritchard feels duped. Through a family connection, he gets the phone number for Victoria lawyer Paul Pearson. "You have two choices," Pearson tells him. "You can do nothing, which I would understand, or I can write a letter demanding the video back."

Pearson offers to write the letter for free. Pritchard takes a day to think about it. He's nervous about confronting the police because of his past run-ins. Pritchard's father offers a warning that the police could bring up his past; they could attack his credibility. Pritchard is unmoved, however. "The cop screwed me over. If there's a way for me to go after them, I'm going to go after them."

Pritchard is adamant with Pearson when they meet: the video he shot shows what happened to Dziekanski with crystal clarity, and it shows something that is inconsistent with what the police say happened. Pearson, a criminal defence lawyer with lots of experience working to get police to return property, is intrigued by what Pritchard is telling him. Almost immediately he suspects the police are spinning a false narrative. *They've got a motivation to do this*, he thinks.

Pearson goes over everything with Pritchard, capturing all the details Pritchard can remember about what happened and his interactions with the police. Pearson drafts the demand letter telling the RCMP to give back Pritchard's property.

By Friday, less than a week after Dziekanski died, Constable Mulhall gets back to Pearson and the Mountie is optimistic. "We're going to get it back to you," Mulhall tells Pearson. Mulhall starts to make arrangements: *Would Pritchard be okay with just a copy of the footage so the RCMP can retain custody of the original memory card?* Pearson doesn't think that's a problem. Mulhall wants to know if Pritchard wants IHIT spokesperson Dale Carr to release the video to the public on his behalf. Pearson says he'll check. The following Monday morning Mulhall calls again to finalize the arrangements about getting a DVD copy returned to Pritchard. The RCMP officer confirms it'll be there by Wednesday and the RCMP will be putting out a news release indicating the video has been returned. It's a done deal.

Until Pearson goes out for lunch.

There's a voicemail waiting for him when he gets back. It's Mulhall. He's retracting the statements he made. "The superintendent has mulled it over and is not happy with releasing it while the investigation is underway." *They're really trying to sit on this*, Pearson thinks.

In order to get a copy of the video returned, Pearson believes that it's necessary to put the RCMP on trial by filing a lawsuit. However, Pearson knows the Mounties can drag a case out and mess around in court for months. That's why he isn't content to only argue the case via the legal system. Pearson, on Pritchard's behalf, will enlist the media in their battle to put pressure on the RCMP. The court may eventually compel the cops to return the video, but it will be the blunt force of media criticism and public embarrassment that will make them cave.

The media won't have the benefit of independently viewing the video before detailing what Pritchard says it allegedly shows. Yet most will unquestioningly report it.

Pearson drafts a writ of summons, suing the RCMP *in detinue*—an old cause of action used to achieve the return of wrongly detained property. Further, Pearson alleges the RCMP has breached Pritchard's rights under the Canadian Charter of Rights and Freedoms, which protects against unreasonable search and seizure.

The suit is ready-made for media tempted to make David and Goliath comparisons, even subliminally. The term *cover-up* now springs immediately to mind in public discussion and media coverage of the unfolding investigation.

The team commander for the IHIT investigation doesn't see it coming.

Superintendent Wayne Rideout had gone on a popular radio program in Vancouver just two days after Dziekanski died. On air he acknowledged that the RCMP had a video and that it had been passed to the coroner, the prosecutors, and senior managers within the RCMP. All of this, he claimed, showed that there was no cover-up.

Rideout wants the video kept away from the public because investigators haven't tracked down all the witnesses. The airlines that carried Dziekanski to Vancouver have so far been unwilling to provide passenger manifests to enable police to speak with people who might have been sitting near the Polish traveller. Also, Rideout doesn't think it's up to him to release a video that B.C. prosecutors might want preserved if they ultimately determine charges are warranted. It's the way investigations work.

Then two major investigations divert the RCMP's attention from the Dziekanski matter almost entirely. A light plane crashes into a building not far from the airport on the same day that the bodies of six people are found executed in a Surrey apartment building. The Mounties who had custody of Pritchard's video have bigger things to manage than growing public sentiment about a week-old in-custody death.

Pearson is worried the police narrative is starting to sink in and be accepted. He doesn't buy the RCMP claim that releasing the video could alter witness statements. *They just don't like what's on the video. That's why they're sitting on it*, he tells himself before filing the lawsuit. However, a lawsuit will take time, he knows. It will be weeks before the RCMP is even obliged to respond in the courts. Discovery and arguments will take months. Pearson decides to wield another weapon: the media.

There is already the start of suspicion in news coverage.

The coroner has shared details of Dziekanski's autopsy with Zofia Cisowski, before giving them to the RCMP. Very quickly the toxicology results are in the hands of Cisowski's lawyer, Walter Kosteckyj. When Sergeant Brassington, who's leading the IHIT investigation, learns of it, he calls Kosteckyj and pleads with him not to release it to the media. Kosteckyj tells Brassington it's too late. He already has.

A hungry media hears that no drugs or alcohol were found in Dziekanski's blood. While true, this news creates the false impression that alcohol was not a factor in Dziekanski's death. It's the embarrassment of finding out from the media, however, that prompts RCMP chief superintendent Dick Bent to pick up the phone and complain to the coroner about how it makes the force look. Bent is told the coroner tried several times to convey the results to the police first, but Superintendent Rideout didn't return his phone calls.

It isn't just the toxicology report that Kosteckyj has. The coroner, Owen Court, actually meets with him and Cisowski and shows them the Pritchard video. Court has already told the RCMP that it appears to him the four officers quickly resorted to a Taser without much effort to try to calm Dziekanski, and he wants to exercise his statutory powers to interview all four of them. Court's actions are an alarming surprise to some senior Mounties because Court is ex-RCMP. Now Kosteckyj is saying he's going to hold a news conference about it all.

The RCMP hastily organize a video conference with B.C.'s solicitor general, John Les, to soften what could be a public relations disaster. Les is concerned the RCMP's use of the weapon has become more casual than intended in provincial policies. When he learns Kosteckyj is slated to speak to the media, Les wants to get out in front of it by immediately issuing new, more restrictive rules to police for stun guns.

The RCMP spends a good deal of time walking Les through the video, making the case that what it actually shows is four Mounties properly assessing the situation, judiciously using the Taser out of necessity. "They followed our training and policy exactly," is how Chief Superintendent Dick Bent sums it up. Les, however, is still uneasy about how it will play out in the media.

When Kosteckyj goes public, he describes the video as "something that will be shown to police academies around North America as not the way to intervene in this kind of situation." Polish Canadians are described in the news as outraged. One woman calls the Mounties "dogs" for the way they dealt with Dziekanski. The case against the police hits the tipping point when Pearson calls a news conference with Paul Pritchard as the focus. Pritchard plants a number of ideas in the public consciousness that will turn out to be just as false as Lemaitre's mistakes about what happened.

"They definitely decided they were going to Taser him before they got to Mr. Dziekanski, before they even cross the glass doors to get in there," Pritchard says into the microphones. Pritchard tells reporters that he bases that on having overheard the officer who fired the weapon ask if he could or should use it. Pritchard's hearing and memory will ultimately be shown to be flawed on this point, but the wheels that will crush the cops are now in motion. Pritchard describes the Mounties as having "ran in" to the airport. He goes on to say the RCMP cornered Dziekanski behind a desk. Pritchard offers his own use-of-force guidelines for police: "Three big police officers. Take the guy down. I mean he's forty or fifty years old. He doesn't have weapons. Take the guy down."

The RCMP manages a timid response, which, in light of their reluctance to part with the video or discuss details of exactly what happened, comes across as evasion. The force's national Taser expert is trotted out to challenge the notion that open-hand combat is better than using a Taser — a weapon that is ranked by the RCMP as a device less harmful than a baton. Corporal Gregg Gillis tries to explain why tackling someone isn't always the best option. "If we end up, for example, down on the ground and officers get injured, we potentially increase the risk to the public ... if we're not able to get quick and effective control."

The media, however, flush out other law enforcement and legal sources who openly question why the Mounties didn't just step back and take a minute before using force. Much is made of the RCMP's training documents that stipulate force can only be used when a subject has the ability, the intent, and the means to injure or kill someone. Jokes about the lethality of a stapler aside, it is nonetheless something that could be used as a weapon to resist arrest or injure a police officer. The Mounties had been trained to disarm someone who picks up an item that could be used as a weapon. They used the device they had believed was the quickest and safest means to do that. In one particularly tense back-and-forth with reporters, Dale Carr says it's not in their job description to be injured in a fight with someone they're trying to control.

To drive the point home that the RCMP screwed up and are trying to cover up, Pritchard alludes to his stint as an ESL teacher in China, declaring that he "took great pride in telling his adult students about the rights and freedoms Canadians enjoy. It's too bad that so soon after coming back to Canada I've been made to feel like I may have been overstating those rights."

In the media relations battle, Pritchard's comparison of human rights in Canada with those in China is devastating. It is, however, another false ingredient that the media blithely fold into the cover-up recipe. There is no comparison with China that can be made, of course. Had Pritchard dared to record a police encounter while abroad, he likely would have been arrested and beaten before being "asked" for the video. He wouldn't have been able to speak out about it. He certainly wouldn't have been able to sue for it back.

So, before the public has even seen the video, heard any evidence, or been offered any real explanation for the Mounties' actions, the officers are condemned. They are tried, convicted, and hanged. Prevailing public sentiment is that it's all but certain the RCMP has deliberately tried to conceal the Pritchard video. The media, in turn, primes the public. Not just on what the video shows and what it means, but also what should not be questioned or second-guessed. This is the narrative that will stick.

It is becoming rapidly apparent the RCMP cannot hold on to Pritchard's video. The investigation is not a criminal investigation. IHIT has been essentially gathering evidence on behalf of the B.C. Coroner's Office, and the coroner, in a surprising reversal, tells the RCMP he takes no issue with the release of the video, thereby eliminating any reason to hold it under the Coroner's Act. It's an embarrassing development for investigators who've argued against releasing the recording.

Superintendant Wayne Rideout tells his superiors, "We are essentially being forced into making a preliminary determination of criminal activity before we have completed the very investigation that is meant to arrive at that decision. We are in a difficult situation. In my opinion, we should not call our investigation criminal to satisfy issues pertaining to the video. However, if we do not, we must release the video."

Federal Department of Justice lawyers tell the RCMP that they don't have a legal right to hold on to the video any longer. It's not a criminal investigation.

At the first court hearing in early November, there is nothing to discuss. The lawyers representing the RCMP tell Pearson and Pritchard the video will be returned. In his Victoria office on Vancouver Island, Pearson's phone rings. It's the RCMP in Vancouver. They don't want to use a courier. They will hand deliver a DVD of Pritchard's video.

Two plainclothes RCMP officers make the ninety-minute ferry journey to Victoria and solemnly hand Pearson the disc and offer cryptic advice: "You've got what you want. Be careful with it."

Pearson assumes that on top of concern about how the video may impact a live investigation, the RCMP is worried the video will be shot out to the media. Pearson doesn't think much of the comments before scrambling to a conference room and feeding the disc into a DVD player with an audience of office staff.

Dear God, this is unbelievable, Pearson thinks, and probably says out loud as people in the room are transfixed by what they're watching. In Pearson's mind, the video clearly shows Dziekanski wasn't aggressively charging the officers or attacking them. No one publicly had ever said he was, but in the battle over the recording, that was the impression generated by those who couldn't understand why the RCMP would Taser a man just because he'd been violent and then picked up a stapler in a standoff.

Pearson's analysis of the video is apt. "This is going to be atomic." Indeed, as a weapon to hold the RCMP accountable for Dziekanski's death, the blast will unleash an unstoppable shock wave, destroying the lives of many in its path.

With the video in hand, Pritchard has to make a decision about what to do with it.

His father, John, has terminal cancer. A former hairdresser, John Pritchard had tried to lead a healthy life. He didn't drink. He didn't smoke. He'd been a triathlete. Now he has late-stage lung cancer and he is refusing to do chemotherapy because he is against putting "toxic chemicals" into his dying body. Paul, the dutiful son, goes along with his father's wishes, which involve getting mistletoe injections from a clinic. The alternative treatments are costing hundreds of dollars. Reality hits home when Pritchard's credit card is declined at the clinic. There is also the need for a reclining bed and other expenses to keep giving his father palliative care at home. The video is a means to pay for some of that.

Pritchard senior is dead set against it, concerned that his son is going to lose his integrity. He thinks the media will turn on his boy.

"It's not about that," Pritchard tells his dad. "We absolutely need money."

That's when Pritchard turns to the CBC. A producer at the public broadcaster has been talking to Pritchard for a documentary the news organization is working on: What if CBC and the other two major networks, CTV and Global, each kick in some money and agree to share the use of the recording?

The way Pritchard sees it, he's owed something for all the hours he's spent doing interviews and dealing with the media.

"I don't need a lot of money but we need enough to get us through the next couple of months," Pritchard pitches.

The producer sees the video. It doesn't take long to agree on a sum of two thousand dollars from each of the networks; a bargain, considering how much is usually paid to freelance video journalists for routine events like house fires and car crashes.

With the deal done, Pearson works with Kosteckyj to make sure Dziekanski's mother has a copy before it's offered to the clamouring media. Pritchard commits to abandoning the media's money if the sale of the video is vetoed by Zofia Cisowski. There is a chance she will see the last moments of her son's life, and refuse to allow its use.

The imminent release of the Pritchard video sends the RCMP chain of command into near panic.

In British Columbia, emails fly as senior officers scramble for a road map on how to manage the inevitable new wave of public outrage.

Deputy Commissioner Craig Callens, the RCMP's top officer in the province, sparks a flurry of activity when he asks what the strategy is. Chief Superintendent Dick Bent asks for a synopsis of the accounts as told by the Mounties involved in Dziekanski's death. He wants to know why the Taser was used as quickly as it was. "The explanation is important in this case," he writes, saying the RCMP needs to "get our powder dry."

It's an apt metaphor, given the RCMP is headed into a battle, but perhaps a little too on the nose, because the Mounties are essentially being accused of killing a man by shooting first.

It is Staff Sergeant John Ward who injects some common sense into the debate. Ward is Lemaitre's superior and Lemaitre has been agonizing over the mistaken information he relayed that is eroding not just the RCMP's reputation, but his own. Ward is candid. "We believe it is appropriate for us to be as open as possible in describing/explaining our actions at the scene. We should have the same story to tell now and at the [coroner's] inquest. If we do not present as much information as we have, the various groups that continue to pillory us will use our silence against us."

Ward is running counter to the will of the homicide investigators, however, and it is their strategy that carries the day. IHIT's team leader has decreed there will be no correcting of the record and no explanation of the Mounties' actions that night. Superintendent Wayne Rideout warns against "any justification of actions on the video or specific response to the video." Rideout cautions those efforts could be viewed as part of a cover-up. "We are between a rock and a hard place on this," he tells his superiors.

In an email to virtually everyone in the chain of command above him, Dale Carr complains that "throughout this investigation we have been called on to explain or release information that we would not otherwise release or explain in any other investigation."

Carr makes a tactical error in believing that the Dziekanski homicide is like any other investigation.

"It is our thought that by me standing up and offering an explanation as to the members actions, a 'play by play' per say [sic] could come across as though we are defending the members actions. The media is not the forum in which we do that, the coroner's inquest clearly is."

The paralysis throughout E Division in British Columbia is so profound, not even the RCMP commissioner and his advisors can relax the corporate rigor mortis.

At National HQ in Ottawa, the general feeling has been that the Mounties who dealt with Dziekanski followed policy and training. Dziekanski's death was unfortunate. Tragic. It was, however, something the public doesn't necessarily understand can be a consequence of police use of force.

It takes the better part of a day for Assistant Commissioner Bernie Corrigan to download the Pritchard video to his laptop in Ottawa from a source at E Division in Vancouver. There really was no digital cloud at the time, to speak of. As head of the RCMP's public affairs and communications department, Corrigan thinks he should see what is going to be released so the force isn't blindsided. Deputy Commissioner Bill Sweeney is at his side when he clicks the play button.

The silence between them is broken as each utters "holy shit," and then a stream of F-bombs. "This is going to be a problem." Corrigan wasn't expecting what he saw and he knows the media is going to go full tilt with it.

This is going to be bad, Corrigan thinks.

It had already been a bad few years for the RCMP. There had been revelations of the RCMP's involvement in the extraordinary rendition and torture of Maher Arar and others who were falsely linked to terrorism. The commissioner of the day, Giuliano Zaccardelli, resigned in disgrace over false testimony he gave to Parliament. In Houston, British Columbia, twenty-two-year-old Ian Bush died after being shot in the back of the head at the RCMP detachment by an officer who claimed self-defence. Now this.

It is Corrigan's job to show the video to Commissioner Bill Elliott, who has a reputation for struggling with anger management issues. After Elliott watches the video there is only one question in the room: "Now what do we do?"

Privately, there is another thought running through Corrigan's mind, one concerning the four Mounties in Pritchard's video. *Their world has changed as of right now.*

Broadcast and print media share a common approach to publicizing the video: they draw conclusions even when the recording doesn't capture a critical moment in the event. The camera doesn't lie, but some moments in the Pritchard video are obscured and there are others that can't be honestly understood without verifiable explanation. There is another problem with the video: it doesn't show what the four officers saw from their vantage point because Dziekanski had his back to the camera, and he was partially blocked by a desk. Many media reports are embellished with interpretations that either come from speculation or are spun from the firmly accepted narrative that the police murdered a man.

A story by Canadian Press on the eve of the video's release tries to jump the gun, offering matter-of-fact assertions that Dziekanski's hands were raised "as if in surrender" before he was stunned with a Taser. The story then insists an RCMP officer used his full weight on Dziekanski's "head and neck." CP attributes the details to descriptions by Pritchard. Both descriptions are false.

CP isn't the only outlet to mistakenly claim a Mountie placed his knee on Dziekanski's neck. Television and radio reports on CBC say the same thing. So does the story on CTV, which also suggests Dziekanski had his hands raised when he was Tasered. Global TV highlights an officer's knee on Dziekanski's neck, as well, and then takes the video to Mike Farnworth, the public safety critic for the opposition New Democratic Party in British Columbia.

Farnworth breaks down in tears on camera after seeing the video. "That's not a nice thing to see," he says before announcing his call for a special prosecutor to investigate.

As the video goes viral on the web, online comment sections and media phone lines fill up with swift and certain condemnation of the Mounties. Many viewers describe feeling disgust, shame, and embarrassment. The RCMP is swamped with emails and comments on its website. "What a sham. It looks like the man was shot in the back in cold blood," reads one. "Nothing more than murderers, and they should be treated as such," says another. "You tasered the shit out of this poor guy.... You murdered him."

The Polish government calls for decisive punishment of the officers involved, based just on what they believe the video shows. Initially, Dziekanski's death prompted what had been a straightforward government-to-government inquiry by Poland. The video amplifies that concern into a full-scale diplomatic incident. The Polish foreign ministry calls for charges against the Mounties for their "excessively brutal and unjustified" treatment of Dziekanski. "We want the matter clarified and we want those guilty named and prosecuted," a spokesperson told the Associated Press, seemingly unconcerned that Poland would find the officers guilty before actually prosecuting them. Polish prosecutors initially deny IHIT investigators access to Dziekanski's medical or criminal records on the grounds that "Dziekanski was the victim of wrongdoing at the hands of the RCMP" and such a request is contrary to Polish law.

Assistant Commissioner Bernie Corrigan saw the condemnation coming. He had brought it up at senior executive meetings. He had wanted to have B.C.'s top police officer, Deputy Commissioner Gary Bass, out in the public to meet criticism head-on. Corrigan ran up against the strategy at E Division, which was to use media relations officers instead of the bosses who the public were desperate to hear from. By the time Corrigan got Bass on the phone to make the case for going out in public on the YVR incident, it was too late. A tide of outrage and resentment was washing over what was left of the RCMP's reputation. Corrigan takes some of the responsibility for not doing what it took to get Bass or anyone else in front of the story.

The RCMP is left to deliver a feeble and impotent response that only infuriates those who believe the video is proof of an attempt to cover up what happened to Dziekanski. Sticking to his script, Dale Carr recites his lines for a dissatisfied media scrum. "It's just one piece of evidence, one person's view," Carr says. "What I urge is that those watching the video take note of that. Put what they've seen aside for the time being. And wait to hear the totality of the evidence at the time of the inquest," Carr pleads, with all the bravado of the little Dutch boy with his finger in the dyke.

9 | IN THE EYE OF THE STORM

THE PRITCHARD VIDEO flies around the world like the stone from David's sling. Every time it's played, the RCMP takes a hit right between the eyes. The police force Goliath is knocked down, but like the proverbial David at this point in the battle, Pritchard hasn't quite finished either. There's still the matter of the giant's head, which must be removed.

Pritchard is awakened by his father, who eagerly relays an urgent message from his lawyer: CBS News in New York wants him in their studio tomorrow morning. "Bottom line: free flight and hotel in New York for a couple of days," Pearson writes.

With every iteration of Pritchard's story, there is a compacting and smoothing of details. The version that is served directly to American audiences on the CBS morning program is no different. Dziekanski is characterized as "calm" when police showed up. While Pritchard himself can be heard on the video exclaiming shock at Dziekanski's behaviour and wondering aloud why the police weren't dealing with him, his opinion now is that Dziekanski was merely acting "a little bit strange."

CBS also makes a serious mistake in describing the events leading up to the use of the Taser: "The video shows him backing up, raising his hands and turning away before the police stun him." The impression, once again, is that Dziekanski was surrendering and was shot in the back, neither of which is true. There is no mention of the stapler

Dziekanski had grabbed in one hand and raised, which prompted the Taser fire.

A week later, Pritchard is feted as a hero at a memorial rally for Dziekanski in Vancouver. He is draped in a flag bearing Poland's national symbol: a white eagle. A thousand people chant, "Thank you, Paul."

———————

"Murderers," says the voice on the phone.

RCMP Sergeant Cheryl Gravelle recoils as message after message left on her voicemail repeats the same sentiment about the officers involved in Dziekanski's death. The frequency of the messages and ire of the callers becomes so overwhelming for the switchboard at the Richmond detachment that the people making them are told to phone the Commission for Public Complaints Against the RCMP.

The CPC has opened a file on the case. Paul Kennedy, the chair of the commission, has launched his own examinations of how the Mounties handled Dziekanski, and the kind of job homicide investigators are doing. As well, the federal public safety minister has asked Kennedy to scrutinize the RCMP's rules and training for Taser use, and whether those protocols are being followed.

In the meantime, the question of whether the four officers involved screwed up and should be disciplined falls on Gravelle's shoulders. She is the RCMP's internal affairs officer for the Richmond detachment, the third-largest in the country, with 275 staff.

The incident at the airport was tragic. The video is not pleasant. *Could they have taken different actions at the time?* Gravelle asks herself. *Should they have slowed down a bit before jumping to the Taser?* Gravelle thinks so. *Did they do anything that was against policy, or how they were trained?* Gravelle's answer is decidedly *No.*

Ultimately, it's up to the officer in charge of the airport subdetachment, Inspector Renny Nesset, to order a conduct review. Nesset had wanted the RCMP to release the video with a frame-by-frame explanation of what people were seeing, from the point of view of how and why police use force. His advice to senior managers was either never heeded, or never heard. Then, as now, he sees no reason to launch a code of conduct complaint against the officers, based on all the facts.

Gravelle can overrule him. She wouldn't shrink from it. She is the real-life version of the TV-show cop every officer loathes because of the power they wield to ruin careers. She can't find anything the Mounties did wrong, either. Gravelle says as much when a representative from the complaint commission phones to ask why nothing is being done to discipline the four. Gravelle senses the person on the other end of the line isn't happy. The public wants blood. They want the Mounties' heads on a platter.

The mounting condemnation sends their commanding officer into a fit. Superintendent Ward Clapham is now faced with a public seething with contempt for anyone wearing a police uniform. "We have people booing and hissing at our officers while they're on patrol," Clapham says, in a rare outburst to a reporter.

Complaint letters are the least of it. "There are even death threats," Clapham says.

It's obvious to senior officers in British Columbia that it's bad. "We are being crucified," Assistant Commissioner Dale McGowan writes to two others in the chain of command.

Back in Ottawa, however, they don't seem to realize the front of the ship has struck an iceberg. The commissioner of the RCMP seems oblivious to the level of public outrage. Not a single mention of the impact of the YVR incident on RCMP employees has been made in any communication by national headquarters staff. Bill Elliott breaks his silence a few days after the Pritchard video is released by sending a brief internal message of support to all members. A separate one that's made public is more verbose. "I would like to make clear that this incident is being treated very seriously by the RCMP," Elliott says in a woefully impotent written statement. Elliott offers an assurance that the RCMP is doing its own review of Tasers, but in the meantime "our experience and that of other police services over the course of many years and thousands of incidents, as well as existing research, have shown deploying the

Taser is often the fastest and safest way to gain control of an individual. We and other police services teach our officers that it is less likely to cause serious injury than other tactics."

What Elliott could have said, but didn't, is that the four officers at the centre of the maelstrom were taught exactly that.

"The four RCMP officers directly involved in the events," Elliott says, in a verbal equivalent of holding a dirty diaper at arm's length, "have been assigned to other duties."

While Elliott gives the public his "concerned face," his true allegiance is to the Mounties. At least, for now. In a rare gesture, Elliott gets on the phone and speaks directly with Robinson, Millington, Bentley, and Rundel. He tells them it was a job well done. Elliott then writes to Gary Bass. "I know this is tough on you and all our folks in E Division. Please be assured of my ongoing support."

Bass is thrilled. "Your calls to the members is a big hit and it is the buzz around [the] Richmond [detachment]." People inside the RCMP often refer to the organization as a family. It's a product of the intense camaraderie that develops under adversity. There is an inevitable us-against-them attitude, despite the understanding that everyone in uniform is a public servant who wields special powers to use lethal force.

Instead of talking to the public, however, the RCMP lurks in the background, secretly ramping up its media monitoring to record the criticism without responding. There is a feeling by many that this will all blow over if the wagons can be circled tight enough.

Superintendent Tim Cogan is a practitioner of the failing "less is more" media strategy. As a spokesperson for the force, he filters media requests and weighs them based on the benefit to the RCMP. When *The Current* — a high-profile, popular radio program on CBC — comes calling for someone to participate in an on-air discussion, Cogan vetoes it. Although it could be an opportunity for the RCMP to make its case to a national audience, Cogan deems it "entertainment journalism." "It's a no win situation for us. There are better ways to get our message out, I think." He is wrong.

On the same day Elliott addresses the nation via just a written statement, because Cogan decides putting Elliott on camera isn't going to help the RCMP, the top officers in British Columbia quietly visit the members in the eye of the storm. The "other duties" to which Elliott said the Mounties had been assigned was, in fact, only one other duty: a week-long course on how to drive all-terrain vehicles. It's at the Pacific Region Training Centre in Chilliwack, an hour and a half east of Vancouver. Deputy Commissioner Gary Bass, Assistant Commissioner Al McIntyre, Superintendent Clapham, and Inspector Nesset all trek out to the sprawling facility near a wooded provincial park to essentially tell the members they are helpless. The incident has gotten away from them. They don't know what to do about it.

The video's wide circulation is now giving people a clear view of exactly who these murderous cops are, and so to protect them (and the force), Clapham puts all four on leave for a week, in a bid to gain some time to figure out how much worse it's going to get. Someone has to figure out what to do with four notorious officers. They certainly can't keep working at the airport. Not now. Even having them continue to work out of the Richmond detachment is a problem. It isn't uncommon for TV cameras to camp out front. The shooters are after shots of the YVR officers, but in the process are potentially compromising the identities of a horde of plainclothes police who come and go from the building. The TV reporters' main target is Kwesi Millington. They may not know his name, but they know the cop who fired the Taser is black. There are very few black officers working in the region.

If Robinson is worried, he's not showing it. Long ago he'd booked a Disney cruise with his kids. He isn't about to cancel it. It may sound like Robinson is lacking compassion. He's going on a vacation while Robert Dziekanski's anguished screams blare from TV screens from Vancouver to Krakow. Robinson isn't heartless. On the one hand, neither he nor the others think they've done anything wrong. They acted according to their training. The outcome was tragic, of course. Yet Robinson has seen a lot as a cop, including death. A part of him is numb. People calling for heads on a platter have no idea how the incident is affecting the officers involved. Even now, it's working its way deeper into each man's consciousness. Substantial psychotherapy is in the offing.

At the moment, they tell themselves they are police officers with a job to do. Indeed, the day after Dziekanski died Robinson was on duty in Surrey. He worked undercover two days straight, busting people for selling street-level crack. At one point a fellow officer asked Robinson point-blank if he was one of the guys involved in the airport death. "Yeah, that was me. I was there," Robinson replied, before he stopped the conversation. *Just don't talk about it,* Robinson thought to himself. Then came the plane crash into the building in Richmond and another adrenaline-filled night while investigators ruled out a terrorist attack.

For several weeks Robinson's superiors all the way up to Commissioner Elliott have seen the YVR incident as a bomb they can defuse. The federal government has ignored the ticking and is rejecting calls for an inquiry. While media strategists and senior managers at the RCMP debate whether to snip the red or the blue wire they run out of time.

The B.C. government pushes the detonator and orders a full-blown public inquiry. While there are already a number of investigations and reviews underway, including a coroner's inquest tentatively set for early in 2008, those are not enough. The global reaction to the Pritchard video has reached a tipping point. The Government of Poland announces it's doing its own investigation into Dziekanski's death. Seven billion dollars are being invested in hosting the 2010 Olympic Games in Vancouver, less than two years away. Right now, in the public's mind, the brochure shows a picture of a Polish man on the airport floor, screaming in agony. The RCMP has so far justified their miserly treatment of the facts with claims about tainting a police investigation. Officials at the Vancouver Airport Authority and Canada Border Services Agency have no such excuse, yet they've been silent for weeks about their roles in what happened.

B.C.'s solicitor general, John Les, says he has little choice: "This incident has British Columbians, Canadians, and people all over the world seeking answers with regard to not only this human tragedy, but how the province welcomes the world to our airport."

B.C.'s attorney general reinforces the idea that the other players forced the government's hand. "Nothing was forthcoming," Wally Oppal complains.

There is a caveat, however. While the inquiry can begin to look into the use of Tasers right away, the examination of what happened to Dziekanski must wait until any criminal charges are dealt with. Calling the inquiry is a calculated gamble for the province. It could be on the hook in any civil suit filed by Dziekanski's mother, because the RCMP in British Columbia is under contract to the provincial government.

Premier Gordon Campbell makes sure his message is included in the announcement. "I'm glad to apologize on behalf of people in British Columbia for what took place," Campbell says publicly, before personally phoning Zofia Cisowski.

The spectre of a public inquiry, fuelled by rabid outrage and the power of subpoena, has the immediate effect of making some of those involved suddenly eager to inoculate themselves. Alain Jolicoeur, president of the Canada Border Services Agency, breaks six weeks of silence to appear at a tightly structured news conference. After an obligatory "sincere and deepest sympathies" to Cisowski, he reveals that after a review — surprise — CBSA did nothing wrong and no one is being disciplined or reprimanded. The review recommends more cameras in the Customs hall — an area the size of four football fields — and more patrols to discover missing passengers. "I'm very, very sorry," Jolicoeur says, "and I really wish we would have found out about Mr. Dziekanski before, but it's a difficult thing to do."

The focus on the main cause of Dziekanski's ordeal lasts about ten seconds before media like the *Toronto Star* retrain their sights. "Whatever the [CBSA] agency's lapses the night Dziekanski died," the newspaper's editorial board declares, "the real issue remains the conduct of the RCMP officers who used a Taser on a man who, while agitated, appeared to pose no immediate threat."

One of the strongest and most rational responses comes from an RCMP officer, though not from the RCMP per se. Superintendent Gord Tomlinson is the officer in charge of the North Vancouver detachment.

He's also president of the B.C. Association of Chiefs of Police when he steps up to the microphone, condemning the outrage surrounding the four Mounties involved in Dziekanski's death. "Critics screaming foul and police rushing to defend their colleagues are not helpful in reaching an understanding of what happened," Tomlinson says. "It is understandable that the family might want quick answers and resolution, but I would ask you to remember that the officers involved have families as well.... I can assure you that no one was more horrified than these four officers when this incident ended in the death of Mr. Dziekanski."

It would seem that even the premier understands that, his apology notwithstanding. Gordon Campbell is in the airport when he bumps into Deputy Commissioner Gary Bass. The two speak for twenty minutes. The meeting is so extraordinary Bass relays it directly to Commissioner Elliott. Campbell is highly complementary of the force, disappointed over the degree of public criticism, and wants to support the four members somehow. Campbell asks Bass for suggestions and pledges that the inquiry "will not be a negative attack on the Force." It is an indication of just how desperate the RCMP is to make this go away that Bass believes Campbell's ridiculous assurance.

In keeping with the theme of making the problem disappear, it's decided Gerry Rundel will be permanently transferred to Nanaimo, near his home, but, more importantly, far away from the airport. The other three Mounties are also moved away from the public and ordered to report to the RCMP's newly formed group handling security for the 2010 Olympics in Vancouver.

Despite being told he did nothing wrong, no one comes to Bill Bentley to explain that it's not safe to work at the airport or even at the nearby Richmond detachment. No one asks Bentley what he wants to do. Bentley has wanted to be a police officer since he was a kid. He thrives on street policing. He understands why he can't work at the airport anymore, but Superintendent Ward Clapham had offered to put him in a plainclothes section, investigating serious crime; even if he was tied to a desk, it would have been meaningful police work. Somewhere up the chain, though, that is overruled.

Coming from Ontario, Bentley has no ties to British Columbia. The other members at Richmond detachment had become like a surrogate family. Things were bad enough. Getting yanked out of what had been a supportive environment just makes it worse. There is literally nothing to do. The Olympics assignment is a complete boondoggle because the games are more than two years away. Bentley sits at a desk in a virtually empty office with no actual work. He checks his emails. He's done nothing wrong but this is clearly punishment. The other bodies who come and go are older officers. Some are retired. Bentley is used to adrenaline. He's prepared to respond to emergencies at a moment's notice. Go, go, go. This is like hitting a brick wall at full speed. On the one hand, Bentley understands the rationale of burying the YVR four well beyond the public eye, but it's taking its toll. Bentley's mental health is tanking and he is seeing a therapist.

Millington is doing no better. The morning of the incident, he called his mother in Toronto. "Hi mom," he said in a subdued voice that put Cynthia Hewitt on edge. "Something happened," Millington told her. "We were arresting a guy and he died." Millington didn't go into detail despite his mother's immediate need to understand. It sounded to her like Millington was on the verge of tears. When she learned more about the incident, Hewitt's heart sank. For her son and for the other mother who lost hers. In the weeks since, Millington has relayed what he is being told by everyone around him: *It'll be over soon and we should be going back to work.* As one week runs into the next and the public anger toward her son grows, Hewitt hears a noticeable change in how her son sounds on the phone.

It is only marginally better for Robinson, a senior officer. At Vancouver 2010 he's given the title of Paralympics Planner. He reads through policies and background material. Then he starts to lose it. It's clear to Robinson that while they've been sent below deck on the S.S. *RCMP*, the wave of public resentment against them is threatening to scuttle the ship and send them to the seabed. There are no less than eleven separate investigations, including the threat of criminal prosecution by Poland.

Robinson tells Mike Ingles that they should probably have legal advice because, despite everyone's assurances that they did nothing wrong, it's looking like it's going to take a turn for the worse. Robinson begins the internal process of applying for funding to speak with a lawyer at public expense. When a bureaucrat in the RCMP civil litigation section stops his application because he hasn't clearly identified what legal process the advice is for, Robinson flips. "How am I supposed to tell you what I want the lawyer to advise me on when I don't know what all the processes are?" he asks her on the phone.

"Well, if you don't apply for it under policy, you may not be covered," is the terse reply.

"This fucking conversation is over," Robinson says, before hanging up.

Robinson calls up Mike Ingles and asks him for help. He angrily tosses the stuff on his desk against the cubicle and tells Bentley and Millington, "I'm fucking out of here," and leaves.

He doesn't come back for a week.

When he returns the inspector asks him for a chat. "You know, usually when people take leave, they put in for a leave pass," he explains.

Robinson is livid. "Who the fuck is going to make up for the time I'm putting in, evenings and weekends dealing with this? I think it works out about fucking even."

His superior isn't looking for a fight. "Okay, Monty, but in future put in a leave pass."

Robinson and the others are starting to feel like pariahs. It was bad enough when they were removed from their jobs, had to go into the office, and clean out their desks on their own time.

Working at the airport was a choice Robinson had made. That's where he wanted to be. Robinson is divorced. The shift schedules allowed him to see his kids on a regular basis. His son, Colby, is six. His daughter, Casey, is nearly twelve. Now there are cameras out front of the 2010 security building as local TV outlets gather visuals for stories about the Olympics. Inside, talk eventually turns to why these three officers have been transferred here. There is a consensus that they acted according to how they were trained.

"Then why don't you fucking go outside and tell them that?" Robinson spits at the superintendent, gesturing to the media outside. "To support me like this and not do it in front of the cameras is fucking meaningless."

No one's spirits are lifted when Solicitor General John Les makes a trip out to the 2010 Olympics building in what is presumed to be a visit of support.

After a few weeks of the mind-numbing charade Bentley and Millington just decide not to show up. No one notices they're AWOL. No one phones either one to check up.

10 | ALL IN

IF ANYONE IN THE RCMP thought the call for a public inquiry would take the pressure off, even temporarily, they were once again misreading the mood of a nation. It wasn't like lancing a boil. The YVR incident is an embedded infection and it's not responding to the treatment prescribed by the Mountie spin doctors in charge.

IHIT investigators are aware that Cisowski's lawyer, Walter Kosteckyj, has made a freedom of information request for the report by the Richmond Fire Department crew. Superintendent Wayne Rideout knows it will show that the Mounties initially refused to remove Dziekanski's handcuffs and that the first responders found no breath and no pulse when they arrived. Rideout alerts senior officers in British Columbia that it's inevitable Kosteckyj will release the report to the media. Rideout decides to reverse his edict that IHIT doesn't talk about evidence. He calls for a pre-emptive news release.

The plan is to push Corporal Carr in front of the mics and cameras to reveal the evidence they do have: the Mounties on scene recognized Dziekanski was in distress and called for medical assistance; they monitored Dziekanski and he was breathing and had a pulse; they didn't remove his handcuffs at first because they thought he was breathing; the ambulance crew thought they had an indication of breath. Rideout acknowledges there is a risk of reigniting public criticism but the alternative is to say nothing and face a media onslaught. "It will at least provide some information that clarifies that RCMP members did not stand by without providing first aid to Dziekanski," Rideout writes.

When news of the plan reaches Commissioner Bill Elliott, he goes ballistic. "Are we sure this is the right strategy?" Elliott writes to his second-in-command and officers in charge of moulding the Mounties' image. "Is E Division consulting HQ? I am concerned we still are not as coordinated as we need to be. I hope my concerns are unfounded ... please get back to me asap to tell me how worried I should be."

Rideout has finally recognized the need to satisfy the public interest in this case outweighs the strict principles of police investigation and case management. Elliott's view is that journalists asking for accountability, as in "Why did the RCMP lie?" are slinging "dirty questions." Elliott is curating a siege mentality and a hostility toward the media and, by extension, the public. His advisors still believe they can control what the public thinks. The top brass in British Columbia fall in line.

RCMP Assistant Commissioner Al McIntyre makes sure everyone else gets it. "In dealing with this matter in its entirely [*sic*] ... specific and global, before any planned release, communiqué or statement is made, please ensure consultation occurs with Tim Cogan and his shop ... before the release is made."

The common theme in virtually every email about the YVR incident revolves around protecting the RCMP. The lives, reputation, and futures of the four officers involved are never mentioned.

While the RCMP continues to take punch after punch, the Vancouver Airport Authority issues its first real response to the event. After self-examination, it declares, its employees are saddened, but blameless.

———

Among the millions of people who form an opinion after watching the Pritchard video, none is more important than Thomas Braidwood. The retired B.C. appeal court judge is a self-described "news freak." He first sees the video as almost everyone else does, by watching it on TV.

Why? Braidwood thinks to himself. He's absolutely appalled by what he sees. His reaction is visceral. *I mean … stapler in his hand? Give me a break. Four cops?*

Braidwood is dismayed by the use of the Taser. His first thought is to wonder why the Mounties didn't try to de-escalate the situation. *It's so obvious.*

Braidwood decides for himself. In his eyes, the video is everything. If the officers gave statements that falsely described how the incident happened, "it's all over then." In Braidwood's mind, there's nothing any one of them can say to explain the errors, believing that "he'd have to backtrack on everything." The speed of Braidwood's condemnation of the police is matched by his instant admiration for Pritchard for having the sense to record the images in the first place.

Braidwood finds most of it disturbing. One sequence jumps out at him. Immediately following the struggle with Dziekanski, after the officers have finally got him in handcuffs, Bill Bentley can be seen collapsing his steel baton, called an ASP, which Bentley had deployed when he saw Dziekanski grab the stapler off the desk.

The ASP is extended with a flick of the wrist, and the sections lock into place with friction. It takes a fair amount of sharp force to push the metal sections of the baton back together. As soon as the crisis was past, that's exactly what Bentley did, by striking it on the floor several times. It bothers Braidwood because it appears Bentley is whacking the weapon on the ground near Dziekanski's head. Braidwood thinks the rookie cop has no emotion or regard for the man on the floor. Braidwood thinks Bentley is detached from what just happened.

Braidwood doesn't like weapons. He never has, during his long career as a defence lawyer and later as a prosecutor.

Thirty years ago, he was hired to defend Santa Singh Tatlay. The East Indian man was so outraged when his daughter married a man of a lower caste that he hatched a plan to kill her and her husband. Tatlay enlisted the help of James Lewis to send the newlyweds a present: an electric kettle packed with dynamite. It exploded when it was plugged in.

Braidwood had lost what became known as the "kettle bomb" case. Both accused were found guilty. The B.C. Court of Appeal upheld the convictions. Lewis took his case to the Supreme Court of Canada on the basis that he had been duped and didn't know what had been in the package he'd mailed. He argued that the trial judge failed to instruct the jury on the issue of the relevance of motive. The prosecutor in the case, a lawyer by the name of Wally Oppal, had failed to prove Lewis had a motive.

The Supreme Court rejected the appeal, and in his reasons Justice Brian Dickson, speaking on behalf of the court, enunciated some legal principles behind the decision. "While motive is always relevant," Dickson wrote, "and the absence of motive is an important fact in favour of the accused, the prosecution doesn't have to prove motive in order to establish criminal responsibility, even when the evidence against the accused is entirely circumstantial."

They are principles that will play a central role in the lives of the four police officers toward whom Braidwood feels an instant dislike.

––––––––

The thing about lawyers that many people find hard to accept is their ability to abandon even the most bitter criticisms of their courtroom opponents after the judge's gavel falls. When court's in session, the black-robed orator on your left may be working overtime to make you look like a fool in front of the judge. His obligatory reference to you as his "friend" notwithstanding, he wants to see you fail. Fail hard. It's not personal, or so they tell each other. Outside the chamber, there are many friendships, even between rivals. Every profession has its club. Lawyers are no different. It just seems odd to some, given the stakes they play with.

For Braidwood, the decades-old murder case was the start of an abiding friendship with Oppal. When the trial ended, the two went to dinner. Braidwood came to the table bearing a gift. Oppal opened the box. Inside was a kettle.

Years later, Oppal and Braidwood sat together on the B.C. Court of Appeal. Oppal went into politics and after he was elected became the attorney general. Braidwood retired. Then, one day, after he had been disgusted by what he saw in the Pritchard video, his phone rings. It's his old friend Wally. Oppal has an offer. "Would you like to run the inquiry you've read about in the papers?" Oppal asks.

Braidwood says yes, without hesitation. In spite of his strong feelings about what he's seen so far, Braidwood is certain his years on the bench have given him the power to overcome any bias and keep an open mind. No sooner does he accept the job than he is stunned at the task he's just taken on. Braidwood's never conducted an inquiry before. He has no idea how to do it. So he goes to see another former judge for advice.

Just a few months prior to Braidwood's agreeing to preside over an inquiry, William Davies had taken on the task of examining what happened in another case of apparent police neglect, indifference, and cruelty. Frank Paul was an Indigenous man who froze to death after he was arrested for public intoxication and then was dumped on the street. "What the hell do I do?" Braidwood asked his old colleague from the bench.

Oppal had already given Braidwood a head start by suggesting a choice for commission counsel — the lawyer who does all of the heavy lifting of deciding which facts to put on the record, who should be interviewed, and, ultimately, who gets put in the witness chair to be questioned and cross-examined. Oppal's recommendation was Art Vertlieb. What Braidwood doesn't know is that Oppal has already got Vertlieb to sign on.

Vertlieb is at his office when Oppal calls. "I've got some thoughts about a commissioner," Oppal explains. "I've been thinking about counsel and I think you'd be ideal for it."

Vertlieb thinks so, too. His experience is in personal injury cases. He's not a criminal lawyer who's big on use-of-force defences. Right out of the gate, Vertlieb is not inclined to examine what happened from the point of view of the police and their rationale. He's drawn to finding the evidence behind the risks of the Taser. *It's clearly an instrument that can cause death,* Vertlieb thinks after seeing the video. As a bencher, a director of the Law Society of B.C., Vertlieb also has a deep understanding of process and the rules of natural justice that will form the foundation of a well- and fairly run public inquiry.

"Absolutely, absolutely," Vertlieb tells Oppal. "If it's something you think I should do, I'd absolutely do it."

Initially Vertlieb didn't pay much attention to the story. Some guy went a bit crazy at the airport, the police intervened, and he died. That was sort of it. Until the video. *Wait a second,* he thought. *That doesn't look like this guy was attacking anybody.*

Oppal had said he wasn't getting answers from anybody, including the RCMP. Vertlieb thinks if the cops had just come out right away and said the officers were mistaken, they thought he was coming at them, they just misapprehended the situation, Oppal wouldn't be calling him. Vertlieb sees himself as the ideal choice for such a controversial case. He thinks of himself as independent. He isn't part of a big firm that has clients implicated in what happened. He's never carried a brief for the government. The RCMP is certainly not his bread and butter.

Braidwood reaches Vertlieb about a week later and makes the formal request. Vertlieb says he'll be happy to do it. "You'll do what you're told, will you?" Braidwood asks, in jest.

"Nearly," Vertlieb replies.

"Close enough," Braidwood tells him.

Braidwood insists that even though the government is expecting him to conduct the first phase of the inquiry as a "study commission," that is, primarily an academic examination of the Taser, he intends to make it a fully public process, with witnesses and cross-examination.

Braidwood is setting the stage for what will be the main event: the exposure of the four men who used the weapon that resulted in a death caught on tape. What Oppal, Braidwood, and Vertlieb don't know is that there is a debate going on inside the RCMP about whether to co-operate.

There is a concern that if the homicide investigation into what happened results in charges, there is no way the Mounties can be put into a witness chair at an inquiry. It would jeopardize their right to a fair trial. There is also a belief that, as a federal police force, the RCMP is not subject to the jurisdiction of a provincial inquiry. RCMP chief superintendent Dick Bent, the deputy head of criminal operations in British Columbia, says as much in an email to the force's second-in-command, Deputy Commissioner Bill Sweeney. "Part of me feels that we need to be as transparent and co-operative as possible and hate to be seen as saying, 'Sorry, province, but you don't have jurisdiction.'

"There is another argument," Bent writes, "larger issues here which potentially affect other federal government agencies."

The debate would be another damning indictment of the force if it were to be made public. That's why Deputy Commissioner Gary Bass puts his foot down on the dallying. "I think we should avoid any legalistic jargon which leaves any room for suggestion that we may opt out at some point or under some circumstances," he tells the chain of command.

No one, however, seems concerned about the jeopardy waiting for the four officers involved in Dziekanski's death. There is an understanding that nothing said in testimony at an inquiry can be used as evidence in a subsequent criminal trial. Such evidence would be tainted. The only exception is for the crime of perjury, but none of the officers intends to lie at the Braidwood Inquiry. Why would they? There's a video of what they did.

11 | A MOTHER'S HOPE

THE WORLD, IT SEEMS, is squarely in Zofia Cisowski's corner. The media, anxious for a clip of the grieving mother, beat a path to her apartment door. Many others reach out to her by phone, shattering what little rest she's able to get. The shock of her son's death, the Pritchard video, the public nature of the tragedy, and the belief that there were many missed opportunities when it could have been prevented have resulted in Cisowski suffering profound post-traumatic stress and depression. She is on medication and seeing a psychologist.

The overwhelming moral support she receives convinces her that her son's death wasn't just the unfortunate result of police doing what they were trained to do. Many people are calling it murder. It certainly feels that way to Cisowski as she looks down into a casket to see her only child — albeit a grown man — lifeless, posed in a burial suit with hands folded neatly as if merely waiting. This is Cisowski's painful duty. It is a moment of grief unmitigated by the mocking cheeriness of the brightly coloured flowers placed near Dziekanski's head and feet. Cisowski takes no solace from the ornate cross on a chain that's conspicuously draped over his unmoving chest. Yet it is a fitting decoration for what many believe Dziekanski has become: a martyr.

The memorial service in his name draws more than six hundred people to the funeral home in Kamloops, with cars and even buses full of pilgrims filled with both sympathy for Cisowski, and anger at the

RCMP. The Pritchard video — or at least the media's interpretation of it — beatified Dziekanski and damned the Mounties. Cisowski is overwhelmed by it all. Grief and loss are handicaps that will never fully recede.

Apart from her grief, Cisowski has almost nothing in her life. She is a woman of very little means. She began the year in a government-subsidized apartment, after having separated from her aging and ailing spouse. She slept on a mattress on the floor until a Polish expat on a mission from the local immigrant services society came knocking to see if she needed anything.

Jurek Baltakis had been president of the Polish Canadian Society in Kamloops. He also knows what it's like to try to make a new life in Canada. Baltakis arrived in 1981 after spending four months in a Polish prison. He was caught under martial law for working with Solidarity. His role with the historic and revolutionary labour union was media coordinator. The skills he learned battling an intransigent government and aiding an irate public would come in handy.

Baltakis has made sure Cisowski has a bed and some other furniture. Those are the basics; now, he knows, her needs are greater. Cisowski spent most of her meagre savings to bring her son to Canada. The cost of his funeral alone is a financial burden. She is not able to work. Although these are the days before online crowd funding, people from all over are so moved by her story that they begin to offer donations. Baltakis and others steer the money to a bank account. Others have already secured Walter Kosteckyj as her lawyer. He has taken on the challenge for no fee upfront, and 40 percent of any settlement if there is one.

In many ways, Kosteckyj is the perfect choice to represent Cisowski. He is not one of Vancouver's legal elite whose suits cost more than many people's monthly mortgage payments. He isn't one of the high-profile procurators frequently quoted in the media. His bread and butter is preparing wills, handling estate planning, and managing personal injury cases. His receding hairline, husky build, and plain speaking lend a common-person authenticity and reasonableness to his persona. Nevertheless, he is a skilled solicitor. Kosteckyj aced his studies in law at the University of Saskatchewan and became law clerk to the chief justice of the province. In the case at hand, with so many taking sides with the Polish community, it doesn't hurt that Kosteckyj's background is Polish.

His real advantage, however, is that before he went to law school, Kosteckyj was a Mountie. He was a good one, too, earning the highest marks in his troop on graduation from Depot. While that was more than twenty years ago, who better to prove the RCMP killed Dziekanski? Kosteckyj is at Cisowski's side in her Kamloops apartment when RCMP deputy commissioner Gary Bass makes an unpublicized personal visit to offer his condolences and to attempt to explain the Mounties' actions. Their meeting carries on at a local church with religious leaders and members of the Polish community. "There was clearly what I would call a trusting atmosphere and a stated desire to ensure this situation does not deteriorate but improves," Bass tells Commissioner Elliott. Bass clearly failed to read the room.

Kosteckyj has already rattled the RCMP's cage by feeding the media details he gleaned from the coroner and freedom of information requests. Now he decides that it's time to strike out at the other players. He and Cisowski trek to Ottawa to testify before Parliament's Standing Committee on Public Safety and National Security. The committee is pursuing its own investigation into the use of Tasers in Canada. Kosteckyj acknowledges that "there are a lot of people who own a piece of what happened to Mr. Dziekanski," but then he leads an assault of rhetoric against the RCMP for an approving group of MPs seated around the room.

"There were four trained police officers there," Kosteckyj says. "Not a single one asked a single question that day. Although they were told that he spoke no English, people thought he spoke Russian. Not a single attempt was made to try to communicate with him." Kosteckyj continues to lay down his version of what happened. "This nonsense about gesturing that the police put out at the beginning is just totally unproven by the tape itself."

Kosteckyj implores the committee members to accept that the statement put out by Sergeant Pierre Lemaitre is hurtful to Cisowski because it misrepresented what actually happened. There is, perhaps, plenty to quarrel with in the statements and news release written by Sergeant Pierre Lemaitre. Kosteckyj, however, is now guilty of misrepresentation. Lemaitre said the officers tried to communicate by using gestures. The Pritchard video clearly shows that. Moreover, Kosteckyj's version of Lemaitre's release leaves out one detail that is critical to understanding why the Taser was used: Dziekanski made a grab for something, which the officers interpreted as something that could be used as a weapon. Yet Kosteckyj goes unchallenged as he urges the committee to take the strongest possible position against the RCMP. "They cannot misrepresent circumstances and expect that they are going to have the public's support." He hammers home, again, that this is a straightforward story of villain and victim. "This guy was a lost soul," he declares.

Kosteckyj delivers a compelling and persuasive case of neglect and abuse, but never touches on the question of why the police were called in the first place; why a forty-year-old, intelligent man would think barricading an airport exit with his luggage was a good idea; why he thought smashing furniture and equipment would be understood universally to mean "where is my mother?" Kosteckyj made a point of insisting there are a lot of people "who own a piece of what happened" to Dziekanski.

One person who is exempt is Dziekanski himself. Not because he didn't do anything that contributed to the crisis, but because he died. Had Dziekanski lived, what happened would have been a news blip. Pritchard's heroic efforts to record what happened would have remained just "prime footage" for his "home videos."

That's not to say the incident doesn't raise critical questions about how the RCMP has trained Mounties for situations like this. Clearly, it does. Even the issue of Taser safety, which this very committee is studying, is rapidly taking a back seat to the main question driven by the furor over the Pritchard video: *Why aren't these cops in jail?* The measured questions about training and whether the Mounties followed it are now conflated with a popular belief that the Mounties either intended

Dziekanski's death or, at the very least, didn't care one way or the other. It's a theory that comes from emotion, not fact.

The RCMP itself has stoked suspicion by behaving much like the child who smashes a window playing baseball and refuses to admit it to their parents, all the while holding a bat in one hand. Yet there's never been any legitimate evidence the Mounties expected Dziekanski to die. Rather, they acted as if they thought he was breathing and had a pulse when first responders arrived. Why would you refuse to remove handcuffs from a man you know is dead? You wouldn't, of course. That answer makes perfect sense if you accept the question is based on what the police believed at that moment. The trouble is, if you're one of the four officers involved, the questions being asked now flow from the knowledge of how this story ends. The refusal, then, when held up simultaneously with the outcome, makes the Mounties malevolent. Dziekanski's death is deliberate. However, the police officers didn't have the luxury of foresight as the incident occurred and now they're being judged as if they did. The four officers will be fettered to the false logic of hindsight in the months and years ahead.

Right now, however, Cisowski believes they are the instruments of her son's death. "These RCMP officers who are expected to help people stood back and chatted as they waited for others to arrive," Cisowski says to the committee, reading from a statement she clearly didn't write. It is enormously difficult for her to speak. The day before would have been Dziekanski's forty-first birthday. "They appeared detached," Cisowski says of the officers, "as if they had played no part in this fatal incident. This is what is truly repulsive to me."

At the very moment Cisowski is expressing her disdain for the Mounties to MPs in Ottawa, a small contingent of RCMP investigators is in Gliwice, asking their own questions about Dziekanski. This trip has taken months to negotiate with Polish authorities. Superintendent Wayne Rideout sees it as critical to a thorough homicide investigation.

Dziekanski's behaviour was unquestionably bizarre. In Rideout's mind it is important to figure out why Dziekanski acted the way he did and whether any clues exist as to why he died after being Tasered.

While the trip will come to be viewed by many, including Cisowski, as a fishing expedition intended to dig up "dirt" on Dziekanski, it is far from the frame-up that will be assumed. All of IHIT's questions were provided in advance to Polish prosecutors and it is they who conduct the interviews in their offices. Rideout, two investigators, and an officer who can speak Polish are able to ask follow-up questions, all in front of senior Polish lawyers. Knowing that the trip would generate controversy, the RCMP made sure the team includes an inspector from the Ontario Provincial Police as an independent observer. His job is to make sure the trip isn't a mission to smear a dead man.

Under oath, Polish authorities interview Dziekanski's doctor and several friends. All of them have seen the Pritchard video. The people the RCMP wants to hear from are well aware the questions being asked are coming from the same police force implicated in Dziekanski's death. Nonetheless, they are co-operative and the results of the interviews are not insignificant.

Dr. Janina Jablonska reveals that she prescribed a beta blocker, a drug commonly used to treat an abnormal heart rhythm. In the interview, Jablonska explains it was just to "tune him up a wee bit," because he had a slightly quickened heartbeat.

Wojciech Dibon, the son of the woman Dziekanski lived with, says that at times Dziekanski "could drink an entire half-litre bottle of liquor" with the woman. Robert Dylski and Aneta Czernel say they occasionally saw Dziekanski under the influence of alcohol. Investigators also discover a letter written by Cisowski to her son indicating she was worried about his drinking.

While it's a fact Dziekanski had no alcohol — or drugs for that matter — in his system when he died, it's possible he was suffering from withdrawal, which could explain his irrational behaviour. Furthermore, chronic alcoholism would have damaged his heart, making him more susceptible to a fatal arrhythmia.

While Rideout and the investigators keep their findings private and share them only with medical experts working on the case, when Cisowski gets wind of the police visit to Poland she is livid. "They are looking for something, I think, dirty, a record of medication," she says, insisting her son "never had any disease like a heart attack or any other diseases. He was a healthy boy."

It is on the basis that Dziekanski was a "healthy boy" that Cisowski pleads for a moratorium on Tasers when she appears at the first phase of the Braidwood Inquiry. Others, such as the B.C. Civil Liberties Association, have long since made the demand. The appeal has more weight coming from Cisowski herself. "I know my son would not die if he would not be Tasered," Cisowski testifies, wiping tears away with a tissue.

Kosteckyj does most of the talking for her, suggesting the lack of uniform standards among police forces for using a Taser is a "cluster-fuck." Braidwood doesn't rule out that he will call for an outright ban, depending on the evidence, which includes technical and scientific reports from international experts.

When the RCMP shows up at the inquiry, it is with a disturbing video of an American female police officer being beaten unconscious by someone she's trying to arrest. The video is offered to show that it's dangerous for police to wait until they're being attacked to use a weapon like a Taser. Under current RCMP policy, the stun guns can be used when someone is just actively resisting arrest by holding on to something or running away.

In contrast to the RCMP's claims, Braidwood hears time and time again from critics who argue the Taser has become a tool of convenience, not necessity.

The weapon's reputation isn't helped with an appearance by Tom Smith, the man who founded Arizona-based Taser International. Smith testifies the gun's origins were influenced in part by the fantasy stun weapons of *Star Trek* and *Star Wars*. *Taser* is actually an acronym for Thomas A. Swift's Electric Rifle. It's a reference to a gun that fires bolts of electricity, invented by the hero of a series of science-fiction novels published in the early twentieth century. The fictional Tom Swift never had a middle name. The weapon's real inventor, Jack Cover, added the initial to make the word pronounceable. Now Smith has to fill in a few other gaps about the device, as he defends it to the inquiry. Smith maintains it is safer than airbags but not risk-free.

"Is one of the possible outcomes, death?" Smith asks the inquiry rhetorically. "I would never say never. It's certainly a possibility of any interaction that includes confrontation."

Smith is one of the thousands of people backing the devices who have volunteered to be stunned to demonstrate its efficacy. RCMP Commissioner Bill Elliott decides that offering up his sizeable frame for Taser target practice is also a shrewd public relations move. Braidwood himself declines an offer to experience the business end of a Taser probe first-hand, before deciding he's heard enough.

12 | FROM BAD TO WORSE

A YEAR AFTER THE YVR incident, many, including the dead man's mother, believe the four Mounties involved have moved on with ease and apathy. It's a popular, but false, assumption that the officers are all unconcerned about consequences. They remain haunted by Dziekanski's death and Cisowski's loss. Each officer is well aware that a decision by B.C.'s Criminal Justice Branch on whether to charge them is imminent. That could ultimately mean going to prison. Even putting any potential prosecution aside, there is the inevitable public inquiry, which will shine a searing searchlight into their lives, lasting well beyond the day or two they can expect to spend in a witness chair. No, there is no casual walking away from the twenty-six seconds that changed their lives. Each moment is a separate car in a freight train bearing down on them.

It's becoming harder to continue to work, for Bentley. Both he and Millington transferred to Ontario in the months after being warehoused at the Vancouver 2010 Integrated Security outfit. At least back east they have families to support them, even if their careers are tanking. Bentley is initially assigned to work in consular operations in Toronto, which involves driving from one downtown consulate to another, keeping the peace. Occasionally, he is seconded to do VIP work, and he becomes a glorified doorman at a hotel or an event. Bentley copes with the anxiety and stress of being a pariah by running.

After the airport incident, the RCMP made Robinson undergo a routine psych evaluation and deemed him fit for duty. He is not well, though. Robinson copes by drinking.

The first anniversary of that horrible night has come and gone, and now with a week to go before Halloween, Robinson has a beer in his hand. It's a party at a friend's house not far from his own home in Delta, south of Vancouver. Robinson's twelve-year-old daughter and seven-year-old son are with him. It's Saturday night. Robinson knocks back five beers in four hours before collecting his kids and heading home around 10:00 p.m. Robinson doesn't know it, but when he gets into his blue Jeep Wrangler for the short drive home, Bentley, Millington, and Rundel are behind the wheel with him.

At about the same time, twenty-one-year-old Orion Hutchinson leaves his mother's house, drunk and in a huff. He straddles his cherished Yamaha FZ6, a motorcycle capable of over 220 kilometres an hour.

Hutchinson's parents would describe their son in much the same way any loving parents of a child would: he loved the outdoors; he was intelligent, caring, and passionate about everything he did.

His mother would also admit her son likely coped with ADHD, which led to a number of poor choices. A close friend described Hutchinson as fearless to the point of being reckless: "Accidents happened to him," the friend confessed for a national magazine story, adding Hutchinson recently appeared "out of control" on his motorcycle. Hutchinson's mother worried about the bike, too, long before the evening he sped away, apparently to visit the grave of a high school sweetheart.

If either Hutchinson or Robinson had gotten on the road just a few seconds earlier or later than they did, things would be different.

Robinson is driving less than thirty kilometres an hour along a residential road when he begins to turn left onto his street.

Bang!

There is a sudden, startling crunch of metal on metal as the front passenger side of the jeep, where Casey is strapped in, collapses. Bits of plastic, glass, and metal rain down over the asphalt. The impact has immediately brought Robinson's vehicle to a stop. As Robinson tries to process what just happened, he asks his kids if they're okay. When he gets out of the car and sees the scene, he is in shock. The twisted remains of a motorcycle are melded into the jeep. Orion Hutchinson is six or seven metres away. He was killed instantly from the impact of slamming nearly broadside into Robinson's jeep at what might be as much as ninety-six kilometres an hour. Robinson never saw him. Even as he sees Hutchinson now, lifeless on the road, it doesn't register.

Robinson wants to get his children away from the scene. He wants to run. He yells, "Someone call 9-1-1," thrusts his driver's licence at a passerby, and takes off on foot with his kids to his house a couple of blocks away. After calmly getting his kids to brush their teeth and into bed, he tells his daughter to keep her phone on while he goes out again.

Robinson grabs a bottle of vodka and pounds back two double shots before leaving the house to return to the crash scene. As he does, Robinson knows from his own experience and training as an accident investigator he's rendering any Breathalyzer test unreliable at best. He knows it is a bad decision, but drinking is what Robinson habitually does in the wake of on-the-job traumatic events.

There is a reminder of his addiction hanging on the wall not far from the bar. It's a certificate of appreciation from the RCMP, given to him nearly a decade earlier when he was a constable in the small B.C. interior town of Chase. David John, a man from the Little Shuswap First Nation, came at Robinson and two other officers with an axe in one hand and a bat in the other. When he wouldn't drop the weapons, Robinson pulled his firearm and for the first time as a police officer shot at someone. Robinson knew John and rather than aim for his centre of mass as he'd been trained, Robinson fired at his legs. The bullets went through his pants. Robinson's sergeant fired, hitting John in the shoulder. The weapons fell to the ground and Robinson helped tackle the man.

Afterward, another member sent Robinson home, in shock, with a case of beer. He drank. He cried. He went to work the next day. The night sweats began.

It wasn't any less stressful the day Kenneth White walked in to the Chase detachment with a sawed-off shotgun. The weapon went off. White ended up wounding himself and spraying the office with shot. As Robinson moved in to arrest him, the injured man hurled a racist slur. "Get away from me, you fucking Paiute." Being a First Nations cop didn't always make it easier to police Indigenous communities. Sometimes it just added to the disdain he endured.

When Robinson walks back to the crash, the Delta Police Department is already on scene, talking to bystanders. Constable Sarah Swallow sees Robinson standing near the jeep in the middle of the debris and she waves at him to get away.

"I believe that you are probably looking for me," Robinson tells her. "I'm the driver."

Under questioning, Robinson admits to drinking before the accident, but says it was only a "couple of beers at 5:30." He adds that at his house he had "two shots" of vodka "to calm his nerves."

In both cases, Robinson misrepresents how much he has had to drink. Swallow believes she can smell the alcohol, and Robinson's speech is slurred.

After being arrested for impaired driving, Robinson is given two Breathalyzer tests at the Delta Police headquarters where, not surprisingly, he blows over the .08 legal limit. Robinson clocks in at .10. When a forensic toxicology specialist with the RCMP does some calculations based on variable amounts of vodka in Robinson's post-crash shots, it's possible he was actually under the limit before he panicked.

It is a cold reality that news stories of car crashes, even fatal ones involving alcohol, are seldom remembered minutes after they are reported. This one is different. When the story breaks, and for months afterward, nothing is revealed about the precise mechanics of the accident, Hutchinson's speed, or his intoxication, which turns out to be .17 — more than twice the legal limit. The bullet points in the narrative are straightforward: Orion Hutchinson is dead and Delta Police are recommending an impaired driving charge against an off-duty RCMP officer.

Almost immediately, the RCMP confirms the driver under investigation is one of the four Mounties who were involved in Dziekanski's death. His name is Monty Robinson.

If there had been a chance of getting the public to believe Dziekanski's death was the tragic outcome of four police officers doing what they were trained to do, it all but vanished when Hutchinson was killed. The public may not know much about the crash, but they know Hutchinson is dead. If not for Robinson, he might be alive. Without the details to judge what actually happened under the street lights that night, many fill in the gaps with a convenient conclusion: Dziekanski and Hutchinson are part of a pattern. Anyone can see it.

Delta Police begin work on what will be a six-thousand-page report to Crown counsel on why Robinson should be charged with Hutchinson's death. Robinson's driver's licence is suspended, and when police are done with his wrecked Jeep, he keeps it, and leaves it permanently parked in front of his house. He doesn't want anyone to accuse him of tampering with evidence and any potential trial is going to be years away. A part of him also wants lookie-loos to see the damage, specifically that it's on the side of the vehicle. Robinson believes the evidence proves he did not hit Hutchinson — it was the other way around.

The coroner will tend to support him, ruling the death accidental and noting that Hutchinson died when "he collided with a passenger car while riding his motorcycle. Speed and alcohol intoxication on the part of Mr. Hutchinson were contributing factors." The coroner will also find that Robinson's alcohol intoxication was "believed to be a contributing factor," though the public report does not explain how.

While some people in Robinson's predicament might prostrate themselves before the public and confess a profound remorse and regret for the loss of Hutchinson's life, notwithstanding who was at fault, the embattled police officer does not. That is not surprising. What offender, let alone one who's a police officer, would utter anything that might be taken as an admission of guilt before a trial?

Robinson is also still coming to grips with Dziekanski's death and the impending public inquiry. Even one of Robinson's harshest critics suggests the stress on the Mountie is extraordinary. Mike Webster, a psychologist with decades of experience working with the RCMP, FBI, and other international police forces, is of the opinion that the officers at YVR abandoned their basic training when dealing with Dziekanski, supplanting it with "their more recent and questionable Taser training, provided for them by their misguided employer."

They "panicked," Webster believes, resorting to "a level-nine response to a level-two threat."

Still, Webster can appreciate the stress Robinson is under. "Not only is he worrying about the Dziekanski incident. Now he is worried about the outcome of this incident. It is the last thing he needed to have happen," Webster says.

That's exactly what Bill Bentley, Kwesi Millington, and Gerry Rundel think.

13 | LAWYER UP

BEFORE A SINGLE WORD has been uttered at the inquiry into what happened to Robert Dziekanski, the rabid anger with the Mounties involved has made other police Taser-shy. Use of the weapon in 2008 is down by 30 percent from the year before. Although thousands of RCMP officers across the country have been stunned without incident as part of their training, the publicity surrounding the YVR debacle sows seeds of doubt in the ranks. The head of the RCMP's civilian oversight agency examines real-world use and chastises the force for relying on the device before trying other means of control, though Paul Kennedy admits the Taser is a valuable tool. "Anybody given the choice between being shot or Tasered, would prefer to be Tasered," Kennedy says. However, no officer wants to star in the next iteration of the Pritchard video. It doesn't help when it's discovered that some of the stun guns made before 2006 can generate shocks higher, and sometimes lower, than their design specifications. The questionable devices are taken out of service around the country.

While the public continues to seethe about Dziekanski's death, prosecutors and bureaucrats in B.C.'s Attorney General's Office are working in silence. Since the summer, in a process shrouded in Masonic-like secrecy, Assistant Deputy Attorney General Robert Gillen has overseen the work of weighing the results of the homicide investigation. The IHIT report to the Crown does not come with a recommendation. The prosecutor assigned to the case will have to make the decision on the basis of his own analysis. He is, however, bound by a strict standard.

The Criminal Justice Branch (CJB) in British Columbia holds to an unyielding two-pronged test when deciding whether to prosecute. The case must be in the public interest and there's little doubt that box has been ticked. The other half of the equation is less certain: there must also be a substantial likelihood of conviction.

In British Columbia, the use of the word *substantial* in this analysis is not casual. While other jurisdictions may approve charges when there is a perceived "reasonable" chance of conviction, B.C.'s bar is qualitatively higher.

This no doubt makes the CJB disinclined to proceed with prosecution. Furthermore, the prosecutors also know that if they elect to charge the officers, it's unlikely they could be compelled to appear at the public inquiry. Already the pace of their deliberations, cloaked in mystery, has postponed the start of the inquiry indefinitely.

The Christmas lights adorning the B.C. legislature building in Victoria have been burning for nearly two weeks when the decision is finally made. Prosecutors give Dziekanski's mother and her lawyer a private preview of their call a day before it's made public. Both are bound by an undertaking not to reveal what they've been told. That doesn't stop Cisowski from describing how she feels. "I'm so disappointed and angry and I don't think it's so good for me." Walter Kosteckyj will only say he's struggling with why it took so long to render the decision he was given.

The Criminal Justice Branch doesn't always proactively acknowledge a decision not to charge someone. When deliberations go the other way and a prosecution is green-lit, the Crown is equally shy about commenting. The public animus and outrage surrounding the YVR case shatters that template, and forces prosecutors to be uncharacteristically chatty, comparatively speaking. Along with the straightforward decision that no charges will be laid against the officers, or anyone else for that matter, the department produces an extraordinarily detailed, seven-page "clear statement" to explain their thinking. Contained in the document is an acknowledgement that the officers' efforts to subdue Dziekanski had something to do with his death, but didn't cause it.

Stan Lowe, the department's spokesperson, tells disbelieving journalists that "factually and legally at law as far as causation, these officers' conduct would be viewed as contributing to the death."

It is a headline for some but not surprising in the least.

"The Officers in question were lawfully engaged in their duties when they encountered Mr. Dziekanski, and the force they used to subdue and restrain him was reasonable and necessary in all the circumstances" the report declares.

Charging the officers with assault or manslaughter would fail hard. An outside police use-of-force expert concludes the officers did what they were trained to do. You can't put a police officer on trial for following his training, just because the outcome is tragic. Three levels of executive managers in the branch unanimously agree "the available evidence falls markedly short" of what would be required to convict the police. This is the determination, even though the Crown knows what many people didn't until now: the Taser wasn't fired two or three times, or even, as Millington believed, four times. It was triggered five times. Yet the three pathologists who were consulted on the case don't think the Taser directly caused Dziekanski's heart to fail.

First, it's questionable whether Dziekanski received the full force of each stun, they say. They also point to other factors, such as the physical restraint, Dziekanski's decreased ability to breathe, his agitated state, and something else: Dziekanski's autopsy and the interviews of people who knew him suggest chronic alcohol abuse. It may have weakened his heart, and the stress of travelling for more than thirty hours without a drink could have induced withdrawal that might explain his bizarre behaviour.

It's long been established in law that, when judging a police officer's conduct, a trier of fact must look at it from the perspective of the officer, and not determine whether it was reasonable based on the outcome.

Almost immediately come the cries of "But the video!" from the media, pundits, and armchair experts. The Crown's decision is seen by many as flawed, a whitewash, and blaming the victim.

"We can not just drop the charges," the Polish government says through its embassy in Ottawa. It lashes out at "factually baseless insinuations of alcohol abuse." Poland believes Dziekanski's mother is owed both "moral redress" and financial compensation.

Zofia Cisowski is angered by the expert results and gives contradictory responses to questions about her son's drinking habits. "In Poland, it's not unusual to drink a lot," she says, before insisting her son "used to drink a lot at one time," but when she last saw him in the spring before he left Poland, "he didn't drink excessively."

It is a shame that a mother should be put in the position of defending her dead son's reputation. It is understandable why she does it. Any parent would. It is also predictable that Cisowski segues from her son to Orion Hutchinson and how Monty Robinson is implicated in both deaths. The second of which occurred after the Mountie had been drinking.

Al McIntyre, the assistant commissioner in British Columbia, tries to disarm the critics by reminding people the RCMP met privately with Cisowski more than a year ago to "express our condolences." Since then, the force has formally restricted Taser use to situations involving threats to officers or public safety. McIntyre makes a case for giving the four officers a break because the incident has been difficult on them, too.

Those who subscribe to the cover-up narrative aren't moved. They see the Crown's decision as further evidence of a conspiracy. The absolution of the officers, however, clears the way for their appearance at the public inquiry. While it is true that inquiries are not criminal trials and, as such, are prohibited from fixing blame, it is also understood the standard for drawing conclusions is lower. Braidwood will not need proof beyond a reasonable doubt to make any findings against the officers. He just has to be satisfied that his opinions about them are probably true. As it stands, before having heard their evidence first-hand, Braidwood's opinions of the officers are not sympathetic.

The officers themselves are being led to believe something quite different. Six months after Dziekanski died, the four Mounties and other representatives of the force finally sit down with Helen Roberts, a lawyer working for the Department of Justice. The message Roberts has for them is clear: they didn't do anything wrong; we've seen this story before; if there's a finding against us, the RCMP will take care of it; just co-operate, do your part, tell the truth, and it'll be fine. There is no jeopardy in testifying, the officers are told.

In the meeting, Robinson is skeptical about the reassurances. "We're not trying to be difficult but no one's talked to us," he says, making the case that each officer needs his own lawyer.

It's Staff Sergeant Mike Ingles's position, as well, that separate counsel are called for. Each officer's role in the incident was different. The members can't be expected to explain or defend what each of the others did. There is also a concern in the room that having the same lawyer representing both them and the RCMP could be a conflict, especially if, ultimately, they testify it was the force that trained them to do what they did.

On the Mountie side of the table there is a feeling that Roberts isn't listening.

Roberts touts her experience, reminding them she is representing the RCMP in the last incident to strike a blow to its image: the death of Ian Bush, a twenty-two-year-old mill worker who was shot in the back of the head by an RCMP constable during a struggle.

They don't need separate lawyers, Roberts tells them. She won't support it. "You're going to be represented by the Department of Justice." Roberts doesn't seem to care if they like it or not.

The Mounties feel Roberts is arrogant and dismissive. What they're told in the meeting is that if they want their own lawyers, it'll be on their own dime.

"We're in some serious fucking trouble," Robinson concludes.

Inside the RCMP, Ingles spends months making the case that nothing less than individual representation is acceptable. It is a challenge. The RCMP is only good for legal fees up to fifty thousand dollars. Any more than that and it has to be approved by the public safety minister. There are four officers facing serious allegations. They can't be represented by articling students. The bill will be staggering, even if the lawyers they hire can be persuaded to bill their time at a basic rate of $250 an hour. That would be a discount from what some of the best litigators command. There is an internal debate in the RCMP about how to make the case for legal representation at public expense. Certainly the officers were on the job and acting in the scope of their duties. One RCMP litigation analyst suggests there is another benchmark that needs to be met: namely, that they acted "honestly, without malice," and met "reasonable departmental expectations."

Lesli Hildebrand writes to an in-house RCMP lawyer that on that basis funding should be approved. "Clearly we do not want the membership second-guessing themselves, given the high risk and litigious environment that they work in. When an allegation is in the 'grey' area, the members need to be supported."

That position is also endorsed by senior RCMP brass in British Columbia, but they don't control the money. Commissioner Elliott has expressed support, but Roberts remains unmoved. Just before Christmas, she fires off an email to those arguing for separate lawyers, saying that she isn't aware of any conflict that would trigger an approval from the Department of Justice for what the officers want. "If you believe there is a conflict," Roberts writes, "please provide the particulars at your earliest opportunity, so that your comments can be considered."

The process she refers to will take months, and the inquiry is expected to start in days. The officers will need an alternative source of cash. The Mounted Police Members Legal Fund is that backstop. The non-profit organization takes payroll deductions and makes them available for legal fees. True to its nature, the RCMP waits until the eleventh hour to make its position clear.

Deputy Commissioner Darrell Madill is in charge of contract policing, which includes the Mounties working in British Columbia. On January 14, he advises senior officers in British Columbia, "Independent council approved by the commissioner. Sorry for the delay."

It's Wednesday. An inquiry that could end the careers and destroy the reputations of four police officers begins in less than a week.

Their lawyers are hired. Robinson is paired with Reg Harris. Harris has been a lawyer for only a decade, but he was a police officer for sixteen years before that. Rundel goes with Ted Beaubier, who practises locally in Nanaimo. Bentley's counsel is David Butcher, who has made a career out of representing police officers. Millington's lawyer is Ravi Hira. Hira has handled just about every kind of case and for years worked on the other side of the courtroom as Crown counsel.

Each receives a memory stick containing all the disclosures they need to represent their clients. There are sixteen and a half gigabytes of files, or the equivalent of more than a million pages of data. It's the kind of case that might take eighteen months to two years to properly prepare. The lawyers don't have that much time. It's Thursday. The inquiry starts Monday.

14 | THAT'S HOW IT IS — GERRY RUNDEL

THE LAWYERS REPRESENTING the four Mounties could ask to adjourn the start of the inquiry. They have been given only a few days to prepare for the first witness. They have the critical task of understanding what their clients did, what they're alleged to have done, and what role anyone else played. They don't. Instead they meet the evidence head-on, as it comes.

To the uninitiated, the inquiry has the feeling of a concrete battleship. How can it possibly move, let alone float, under the weight of its own structure? More than eighty witnesses are scheduled to appear. The battery of lawyers is so dense, Braidwood issues a seating map of the federal courtroom they've taken over. There are no fewer than ten tables, with two dozen lawyers and staff all vying for Braidwood's certitude.

As the inquiry gets underway, there is little made of the fact that two key witnesses to what happened will not be asked to give evidence. Paul Pritchard doesn't want to appear, and, remarkably, no effort is made to subpoena him. It's unclear why that is, given Pritchard saw events unfold from a unique vantage point through a viewfinder trained on the action.

His legal dispute with the RCMP over the return of the video will figure prominently in the inquiry's investigations. The video itself will be played countless times at the inquiry in ways that create a false reality compared to how the police saw it: forward, backward, slow motion, and frame by frame — each fraction of a second frozen, debated, and dealt with before the next slice of time is held up for Braidwood to judge.

Pritchard's own metamorphosis is also captured on the video. He can be heard urging police to intervene and remarking that, even after several stuns, Dziekanski was still resisting arrest. Yet he altered his interpretation of what he saw once he knew the outcome.

He isn't the only witness to do that, but others will be called. Their memories tested. Details of their backgrounds will be invoked in an effort to establish credibility and intention. Lawyers for the police are unaware of Pritchard's background beyond what they read in the news.

Commission counsel Art Vertlieb also determines there is no need to call Dziekanski's mother. On one level, it's understandable. She continues to grieve. Her English is not the best. Yet, if the purpose of the inquiry is to figure out what happened to Dziekanski and why, it's not unreasonable to question why an educated forty-year-old man, regardless of his travel experience, would not have used the cellphone he was given, or make a phone call to his mother from a pay phone, after nearly ten hours on the ground.

Dziekanski's cellphone battery had ample power. He carried a recently purchased GSM card — a piece of plastic the size of a credit card that contains a removable SIM chip that's inserted into the phone, enabling it to make and receive calls. The SIM chip was punched out of the GSM card, as you'd expect. Yet it wasn't in Dziekanski's Nokia cellphone. Police found no trace of it in any of his belongings, which meant his phone was capable of making only emergency calls. It is a mystery Cisowski might have been able to solve. Yet without her testifying, those questions and others about his background, medical conditions, and any behavioural problems are among those that can't be asked of the person who knew him best. If the inquiry wants answers, they will have to be extracted from second- and third-hand sources.

Braidwood leaves little doubt that the Pritchard video, and the public's interpretation of it, forms the inquiry's impetus. "I expect that all of you and many people indeed around the world have seen the video recording of the incident at the International Vancouver Airport in

October of 2007," Braidwood says in his opening remarks on Day 1. "Public reaction to the events at the airport was immediate and intense." The trouble is, that's not entirely true. The reaction to which Braidwood refers was generated through a series of events, not the least of which were the RCMP's misguided attempts to control public reaction, which took some time to unfold. Initially, a number of witnesses, including the man who recorded the video, believed the police response to Dziekanski was understandable.

As he continues his opening remarks, Braidwood leaves little doubt about how the inquiry has already framed Dziekanski's own role in what happened. "As a parent I can imagine nothing more terrible than losing a son or a daughter," Braidwood says directly to Cisowski sitting in the gallery. "As we embark upon these solemn hearings, may I express my profound condolences for your loss. Please be assured that I and the members of our Commission team will make every effort to provide you with a complete record of what happened that night in the hope that it will assist you in finding some closure and peace."

In the first few weeks of hearings, it is patently obvious from testimony that the first people who came into contact with Dziekanski made choices that put him on a collision course with the last people to see him. Among them is immigration officer Tina Zadravec. She could have launched a search for Dziekanski when Richard Hutchinson asked why he hadn't materialized after a number of hours. Instead, Zadravec insisted Dziekanski wasn't in the airport and told Hutchinson and Dziekanski's mother to go home.

She weeps in the witness chair. "It was really shocking," Zadravec testifies. "I think about it a lot but I wouldn't do anything differently. If I knew he was going to die, I would do everything differently. But in doing my job, I did my job."

The inquiry hears also how airport employees essentially stood by and watched Dziekanski's meltdown. Bob Ginter, YVR's response coordinator, admits that when he saw Dziekanski get Tasered he deliberately held back the airport's own first responders because he was worried that calling them in would leave the airport vulnerable in case of another emergency like a plane crash. While Dziekanski was dying on the floor, Ginter spent the time assessing the damage he had caused to the computer and wooden table.

The airport authority takes responsibility for Ginter's decision, arguing that even if he had acted in Dziekanski's interest, the difference in response time would only have been a matter of seconds.

There were some witnesses who tended to support the police actions. Limo driver Lorne Meltzer acknowledged he played a role in ramping up Dziekanski's mania by getting into a shouting match with him, and he testified that police acted calmly until Dziekanski suddenly produced the open stapler in his fist and appeared to move toward them.

Trevor Enchelmaier, the head of security for YVR and a former lifeguard and ambulance attendant, had told police at the time that Dziekanski had continued to struggle with the Mounties on the ground. At the inquiry he backs away from that observation and agrees with commission counsel that maybe Dziekanski was just choking. Yet Enchelmaier holds fast to his claim that he personally checked Dziekanski's pulse and breathing three times before the firefighters arrived.

It is Sima Ashrafinia, however, who presents the biggest challenge to the police ahead of their appearance at the inquiry. In the witness chair, Ashrafinia disowns much of the statement she gave investigators more than a year ago, in which she had said the police Tasered Dziekanski because they "have no other choice because he's out of control."

When asked about that, Ashrafinia offers an explanation for why she now thinks that she was wrong. "That moment, yeah, he was out of control," she agrees, before unintentionally testifying that the outcome of the incident, and her belief in a conspiracy to cover it up, altered her perception of it.

"I believed the airport rule, RCMP rule, and I was 100 percent obedient. But after that day, when I put the puzzle, I realized I shouldn't be that way. That statement that I said three days after incident had fear of authority in it. But now, I don't have any fear of authority. I believe he was just upset guy, angry and lost."

Now, however, she says most of what she told police was her husband's idea and she just somehow went along with it. Sensing that Ashrafinia is changing her story to fit the narrative, Millington's lawyer, Ravi Hira, steers her back to what she told police just days after the incident. "You believed that he deserved to be Tasered. You just felt that the result was a very tragic result. Is that a fair statement by me?"

Ashrafinia's answer suggests exactly that, though she has trouble admitting it. "I am still going through therapy for what I saw," she says. "Yeah. That day, yes, I said that."

Braidwood will ultimately accept what Ashrafinia thinks now as the reality. He will conclude much the same himself.

So far, the push and pull of lawyers at the inquiry has revealed a tale of multiple failings of airport staff and Border Services employees. That evidence and the publicity of it begin to redistribute some of the weight of Dziekanski's death that until now has been carried almost exclusively by the Mounties. Just before the four officers appear to testify, however, RCMP Commissioner Bill Elliott throws a grenade in their path to the witness chair.

A little more than a week before Gerry Rundel is slated to give evidence, Elliott goes before media cameras and microphones to discuss the RCMP's shifting policy on Tasers. No more will officers be permitted to use the weapons on people who are merely resisting. They must pose an active threat. Never mind that the Taser used by the Mounties at YVR was for precisely that: a man suddenly brandishing a weapon.

Worse, in the eyes of many, is the fact that Elliott suggests Tasers pose a risk of death, especially when used on people who are agitated. Elliott acknowledges there have been deaths in cases involving police use of Tasers, and then he digs the hole even deeper, adding, "Well, I think certainly there have been some instances where Tasers have been used in inappropriate circumstances."

Elliott will not talk about the case against the four Mounties, even to clarify whether his comments reflect the RCMP's thinking about what they did.

The CTV news network reaches out to the rank and file for a reaction and snags Sergeant Scott Warren, the chair of the RCMP's Officer Safety Committee. Warren appears on camera and rebuts Elliott's analysis. "Sometimes I think the commissioner is — again, not trying to be disrespectful — but I think he's in over his head." Warren appears calm but beneath the surface he is seething at what he sees was a monumental public relations blunder by the commissioner. "He is not the best person to speak to this new policy." Warren's speech is code for *Elliott doesn't know what he's talking about.*

It doesn't take long for Warren's phone to ring. It's Gary Bass. "The commissioner wants to see you," Bass tells him, meaning Warren needs to get on a plane and fly to Ottawa from Victoria.

Warren refuses. "Yeah, I'm not going. It's my kid's birthday ... I got better things to do. I don't have to go."

Warren hangs up. His phone rings again. It's Bass again.

"You just hung up on me? I am the CO, right?"

Warren is unrepentant. "I understand. I thought we were done talking."

Bass becomes serious. "Scott, I really need you to go there."

Warren won't budge. "Are you ordering me to go?"

Bass says he isn't. Warren hangs up again.

When the phone rings again, Bass won't take no for answer. "It was funny the first time and the second time, but not so funny now. I need a favour. Will you go to Ottawa and meet the commissioner for me?"

Realizing it's inevitable, Warren agrees: "Well, if you'd said that in the first place, I probably would have said 'Yes, sir.'"

There is a caveat, however. Warren wants to take two other Staff Relations representatives with him — Steve Walker and Mike Ingles.

Bass is puzzled. "What do you need them both for?" he asks.

"Steve's there to talk when I take a breath because he's a great speaker," Warren explains. "Mike's there to stop me from going across the table and choking that guy out."

A few days later, Warren, Walker, and Ingles have flown across the country and are in a boardroom at a hotel in Gatineau, Quebec, just across the river from Ottawa. For the first half-hour of the meeting

Elliott reads Warren the riot act. Flanked by his deputies, the commissioner dresses him down for disrespectful comments and undermining
morale. While Elliott rails about how disappointed he is, Warren stews,
frustrated that the commissioner doesn't see how his own comments
threw the four Mounties under the bus.

Warren politely puts his hand up, as if in school. It's a mocking gesture that Warren thinks is going to send Elliott into a fit.

"Yes?" Elliott asks.

"Nobody says they're disappointed in me twice. I let you get away
with it once. You're not getting away with it a second time. My turn."

Elliott is taken aback.

"I need you to tell me right now, truthfully, that I can be honest."

Elliott says he can. "You're a pompous prick and you're in over your
head and you don't know anything about use of force and you should
have shut your mouth and you didn't."

Before Elliott can respond in anger, Warren and his wingmen continue to press. "Listen. I'll stop calling names because we're even now,"
Warren says. "Let's talk about the guys you sewered."

Elliott is having none of it. "Why did you do what you did?" he
demands.

Warren has an instant answer. "I did what I did for the people that
had to go to work that night because you confuse the shit out of everybody. You said the Taser kills people. How do you think those people
are going to respond?"

The feeling on Warren's side of the table is that if the Taser is dangerous, pull it from use. Giving cops a vague reason to doubt their training
or second-guess their ability to make a split-second decision puts people
in danger.

After a couple hours of each side trying not to let it spiral out of
control, they agree to disagree, shake hands, and go home.

I can be a total dick, Warren thinks to himself, while still believing he
made the right call to back the Mounties who are about to face their own
dressing-down at the inquiry. Before they do, they are called to individual,
private interviews with Vertlieb, so he can prepare both them and himself

for the questions that will be asked under oath. The Mounties come away from the experience with a belief that they are being steered to address and accept a set of assumptions about what they did wrong. Bentley can't quite put his finger on it, but it seems to him from the questions Vertlieb asks that Robinson is on the hook for what happened.

Robinson's sit-down with Vertlieb at his lawyer's office takes a decidedly adversarial tone. Robinson is combative. He challenges a host of questions he's asked about his background. "What do you need to know that for?" he says, in reply to queries about his upbringing and education.

When it's over and Vertlieb leaves, it appears he was frustrated by the encounter, as well. Robinson's lawyer, Reg Harris, tells his client that on the way out, Vertlieb told him he wanted to punch Robinson in the head.

Before Rundel even arrives at the interview his lawyer tells him that Vertlieb wants to know if Rundel is willing to testify against the other three. He isn't. In their meeting, Vertlieb asks Rundel repeatedly if he ever discussed details of what happened at YVR with the others. Each time Rundel says no. After the third time, Rundel hears Vertlieb say, "Really?" with a tone of incredulity.

Rundel is the first of the four to be called to the witness chair at the inquiry. He's also the oldest among his former partners. Despite his brief tenure as an RCMP officer before the incident, he's pushing fifty as he walks cautiously into the inquiry hearing room.

Back when Rundel was about twenty, he met with an officer at the detachment in Port Alberni, the small fishing and lumber town on Vancouver Island where he grew up. Rundel wanted to be a Mountie. The officer told him he didn't have a chance. Rundel's father had been a chronic alcoholic. The police had been called to the family home a number of times for alcohol, domestic violence, and firearms complaints. The message Rundel got was that he wasn't Mountie material.

He put the idea out of his head and pursued a life in the fish-farming industry. Rundel married young and divorced before he was thirty. He married again, and had a daughter and son shortly after. Living in Nanaimo with a young family, Rundel went back to university, with the idea of becoming a Fisheries or Natural Resources officer. He hit the honour role, and was voted valedictorian.

Just before he graduated, however, the RCMP was showing up in universities looking for recruits. Rundel attended a presentation and the dream he had a quarter century earlier was reawakened. Within a year he was on his way to Depot. At graduation he was voted by his troop to be the cadet who best exemplified the core values of the RCMP. Rundel was stationed in Richmond and commuted back and forth to Nanaimo.

Since the incident, he's been largely on desk duty doing research and criminal background checks. The stress of what happened and the public notoriety sends him into a dark hole of depression. His marriage buckles and he and his wife, Kelly, don't speak for a year. They pass notes to each other to deal with things that can't be avoided.

At the inquiry, Rundel will not be able to do anything less than speak at length and in detail about what he and his fellow officers did. Rundel did not use any force that night, yet he is asked repeatedly to explain the rationale for using the Taser. The way Rundel sees it, the moment Dziekanski flipped his hands in the air and turned his back on the officers and grabbed a stapler, he went from being non-compliant to resistant.

"My … interpretation of that is saying, 'The hell with you guys. I'm out of here.'"

Walter Kosteckyj tries to coax a confession from Rundel, suggesting that he should have known then what many people believe now. "Do you think now, in retrospect," Kosteckyj presses, "this was a frightened man?"

Rundel admits the obvious. "Well now that I've had the opportunity to look back at the video prior to us arriving … it's possible he was frightened, yes."

Rundel, however, insists the officers were working by the book, and Dziekanski precipitated the use of force when he inexplicably swung around with a stapler in his hand held at chest height. "It could have gone bad," Rundel testifies after two days of grilling. "There's no doubt

Gerry Rundel graduating from the RCMP Academy known as Depot, just shy of his forty-fifth birthday, October 2005.

in my mind he took up the combative stance and had every attempt to injure, harm us officers and anybody else in the public."

What Rundel and the others may have thought at the time becomes the focus of inquiry lawyers, particularly when the statements to homicide investigators appear to read differently from what the video shows. Rundel's notes, written in the aftermath of a lightning-fast sequence of events that he wasn't expecting, portray events accurately but out of order. "Yelling, arms up. Not English. Stepped towards us in front of counter. Cst. Millington deployed tazer," Rundel wrote.

Inquiry lawyer Patrick McGowan is disbelieving. "So today you still say he held the stapler up?"

Rundel clarifies what he meant. "I think in my notes I'm referring to his arms being up in the combative, up towards his chest."

While Dziekanski's back is to the camera in the Pritchard video when he's holding the stapler, his arm does appear to be bent in such a way that his hand, and the stapler he gripped, would be at chest height.

McGowan is unsatisfied with Rundel's explanation and his description of what happened given to a homicide investigator. "He picked up a stapler ..." McGowan reads into the record. "Putting the stapler above his head, mo-motioning ... making motions with it, uh, towards us," he continues. "Is that the truth? Let me start with this: Was that accurate?"

Rundel offers an explanation McGowan didn't ask for. "That was five o'clock in the morning, after a stressful incident and the way I remembered at the time."

McGowan wants Rundel to admit it was false. "Was it accurate?" he repeats.

Rundel tries to explain again. "It can be taken out of context in perhaps the order of the events and the way that they happened. That was how I remembered it that particular moment."

Kosteckyj goes at Rundel again. "Why is it that you felt you had to react so quickly?"

Rundel barely contains his frustration as he turns to face Braidwood. "Commissioner, I feel I've answered this question several times. Would you like me to answer it again?"

Braidwood clearly hasn't tired of hearing the same explanation over and over again. "Oh, I think you should," Braidwood commands.

Although Rundel has his own lawyer at the inquiry, it is the counsel for a fellow officer who gives him an opportunity to explain how he feels about what happened. "I mean, it's obviously a very terrible outcome to the call we had to answer that morning," Rundel testifies. As much as Rundel regrets Dziekanski's death, he insists the police did what they are trained to do in the circumstances they were faced with, and not one of them believed that using a Taser would lead to Dziekanski's death. "I can't say I could have done anything any different. That's unfortunate but that's how it is."

In the order of cross-examination, the lawyer for the Government of Poland gets his crack at the witness after most are done. Yet it is the questions posed by Don Rosenbloom that most closely align with the public's hostility toward the police. Rosenbloom has a reputation for speaking truth to power, with clients such as the David Suzuki Foundation, the Nisga'a in their Supreme Court battle over Indigenous rights, and the National Association of Japanese Canadians who sought settlement for internments during the Second World War. He's come out of retirement to represent Poland at the inquiry. Rosenbloom asks questions that many are thinking, in ways that would make some lawyers in the room cringe, but which set journalists looking for that pithy clip at attention. It's what Rosenbloom is good at. It's what the Government of Poland is paying him to do.

"Faced with the video footage," Rosenbloom asks Rundel, "will you now acknowledge you and your fellow officers fell far short of prudent conduct in how you handled this incident?"

It is acknowledged that it was Rundel himself who seized the Pritchard video. If anyone understood why it would be futile to deliberately mislead investigators or the inquiry for that matter, it would be him.

"We gave statements on the morning of the incident … after a very stressful, traumatic event," Rundel replies. "We gave those statements prior to the release or any viewing of the video. Now, after looking at the video, I see the video fully supports my version of the events and the details I gave in that statement. So my answer to your question is absolutely not."

The experience in the witness chair leaves Rundel so fractured he is unable to return to work.

15 | COPS AND ROBBERS – BILL BENTLEY

BILL BENTLEY WAS the kind of kid who never gave his parents much to worry about. "When he was little," his father, Alan, says, "people would ask him what he wanted to be when he grew up." The answer was always the same: policeman. Bentley was so focused on that career choice as he entered his teens, he eschewed friends who got into trouble or experimented with drugs lest somehow, through guilt-by-association, they would sully his own record and hamper his chances of following his dream.

"Follow your heart," Alan Bentley told his son.

It was clear that he had done just that. Bentley didn't disguise the awe and pride he felt after his first week at Depot in Regina in 2005. The letter he wrote to his family back home in Toronto oozed admiration for the RCMP as an institution. "I absolutely love it here. It is everything I imagined and more. I definitely know now why it is considered the best police training facility in the world. The facilities and people here are top notch. I'm very impressed by the high moral [sic] and professionalism here."

Over the next six months, Bentley sent regular updates about the gruelling and challenging training. He wrote about all of his experience with the same wonder as a kid who got a job in a candy store: "Just wanted everyone to know that I got my posting today. Looks like I'm going to Richmond B.C. Pretty happy with my detachment."

Bill Bentley poses for his graduation photo at the Depot in Regina, Saskatchewan, May 2006, and realizes his childhood dream of becoming a police officer.

Bentley's personal reports also go into detail about the rigorous days of physical and mental training that start before sunrise and end at midnight. The physical tests were significant, even for Bentley, who had been a long-distance runner since he was a child. Although he had earned a university degree in criminology before signing up for the RCMP, the mental side of police work was also a challenge.

> This past week has been really stressful. We had our final detachment scenarios, where we respond to calls and deal with calls as we have been trained. The one thing about policing that you learn early on is that although our laws are written in black and white, policing for the most part is grey and requires a lot of common sense. Without getting too much into my scenario, I was basically dispatched to this address where a lady complained that a friend had outworn her welcome and wanted her to leave. It turned out that the friend had a warrant out for her arrest. When I responded to the call, I got both the complainant and suspect confused because they looked so similar and ended up arresting them both, so I could take prints and figure out who was who. Sounded logical, but they didn't like that here and made me redo another scenario, which I passed with flying colours.

Depot did not prepare Bentley for what happened barely a year after his graduation. While cadets are given some play-acting scenarios on what to expect when called to testify in court, they are nothing like the reality Bentley walks into when it's his turn in Braidwood's witness chair. One thing is certain: there will be no do-overs.

The first things commission counsel Patrick McGowan zeroes in on are Bentley's handwritten notes he made after the chaotic encounter with Dziekanski. "Subject grabbed stapler and came at members screaming," McGowan reads from the officer's notebook.

Bentley testifies he thought it was accurate at the time. He admits it was wrong. "Everything happened so fast. I was tired when I made my notes. After getting adequate amount of sleep, adequate time to reflect on the incident, as well as watching the video to refresh my memory, I realized it was incorrect."

Bentley goes on to say that as he tried to piece together the order of events that played out, he was confused. There is no question Bentley's description of Dziekanski's movements — arm in the air, screaming — is accurate. The problem is they happened the split second after he was Tasered, not before.

"I think it was just out of sequence," Bentley testifies.

Bentley made another error about what happened. He told IHIT Dziekanski ended up on the ground after Rundel and Robinson took Dziekanski down. "After watching the video," Bentley testifies, "he fell to the ground from the energy of the Taser."

Bentley has no explanation for why he made that mistake.

Walter Kosteckyj, not the only lawyer at the inquiry to suggest a theory, asks, "You've heard the CYA principle back at Depot? That's Cover Your Butt … make sure you've got everything covered, right? Well is that what this was about? You were making sure you were justified in using force when you were telling this story?"

Kosteckyj's suggestion ignores the fact that Bentley himself didn't use any force, beyond trying to get Dziekanski in handcuffs. It overlooks the fact that even as Bentley wrote his notes he knew there was a video of what happened.

"There was no cover-up, if that's what you're getting at," Bentley replies.

When it's Don Rosenbloom's turn to pick away at the police officer's testimony, he presses Bentley to justify the use of the Taser, with the hindsight of knowing Dziekanski died.

"I don't know whether he had any voluntary control over his body," Bentley says, "but it was the expression on his face, as well as the screaming and the way he did it that made me believe he was trying to fight through it."

Rosenbloom doesn't like the answer and says so. "I have such trouble with this, I'm sorry."

Bentley's lawyer rises to object at the remark. "With respect, my friend is editorializing," Butcher says.

Braidwood takes Rosenbloom's side and quashes Butcher's complaint. "Oh, I'm against you, I'm afraid."

It will happen again.

Rosenbloom does notice something even the commission counsel haven't picked up on. On the Pritchard video, before Dziekanski throws up his hands and turns away from the police to "flee," as Rundel put it in his testimony, there is a moment when Robinson's black-gloved hand appears to point toward the counter, which Dziekanski then moves toward. The officers are all behind a glass wall, and nothing can be heard of what's said by anyone. The interpretation, however, is that Dziekanski was actually following an instruction given to him.

Bentley has no trouble agreeing that it appears as if Robinson is giving Dziekanski an order, which he appears to follow in that instant.

The discovery is seen by some at the inquiry, including some journalists, as a major contradiction to the Mounties' sense that Dziekanski wasn't being co-operative. However, the officers have been consistent insofar as not really having a coherent understanding of what each of them did and said over the course of those few seconds.

There's a bigger problem with ascribing Robinson's gloved hand as some sort of clue to a cover-up. It doesn't explain why Dziekanski then picked up a stapler when he got to the counter, turned around, and held the metal object at chest height, facing the police. That is when the Taser came out. That is when Millington made the decision to pull the trigger.

There is no doubt people in the benches of the courtroom gallery don't buy a word Bentley is saying. Their jeers, snorts, derisive laughter, and other audible signs of disbelief become so obvious during Bentley's testimony that Vertlieb is forced to address it.

"Mr. Commissioner," Vertlieb says, rising after a break in Bentley's testimony, "we understand that this is a subject that has a great deal of

COPS AND ROBBERS — BILL BENTLEY | 155

emotion around it, but I just want to mention that out of the respect for all of the participants and, as well, the witness, if the people in the courtroom, the spectators, could just try to respect the process and not become too involved in a verbal way. I just want to mention that to you."

With the help of his lawyer, Bentley tries to break out of his training, which has taught him to just answer the question. "Now, you've learned from the media who Mrs. Cisowski is?" David Butcher asks his client.

"Yes," Bentley replies.

"You've seen her today; you know she's in the courtroom today?" Butcher continues.

"I saw her earlier," Bentley agrees.

"Is there anything that you would like to say to her at this point in time?"

The exchange between lawyer and client is obviously planned.

"I'm sorry for her loss," Bentley offers. "My heart goes out to her and her family."

Bentley's sentiment is genuine but it is rejected as self-serving by Cisowski's lawyer as soon as the hearing is adjourned for the day. "I was angered by it, to be perfectly frank," Walter Kosteckyj tells the media. "I thought it was totally inappropriate and so disingenuous, to lead Mrs. Cisowski to literally cry her way out of the courtroom. It was a cheap attempt to get some sympathy."

Few people know it at the time, but as Bentley testifies he is spiralling down into a deep depression that would come to be diagnosed as PTSD. The glare of the spotlight during a few days of testimony is nothing compared to the daily paralysis of doubt, guilt, and anger he has endured most days since Dziekanski died.

Bentley's father follows the inquiry and the fallout as his son leaves the witness chair portrayed as self-serving and soulless, while Robert Dziekanski is "morphed into Paddington Bear."

Father and son speak almost every day by phone. Alan Bentley is haunted by one call that came shortly after Bill started working in Richmond. He was being transferred to the airport subdetachment. "He'd been talking to the other guys," Bentley says of how his son seemed disappointed by the move because he thought it would take him away from real street policing, which he loved. "The airport," Bentley recalls his son telling him, "nothing ever happens there."

16 | TRIAL BY FIRE – KWESI MILLINGTON

CYNTHIA HEWITT wanted to give her baby boy an African name. She was from Trinidad and was living in Montreal in the 1970s when her son was born. Her island nation had once been largely populated by slaves from countries like Ghana in West Africa. She believed that a strong name linking the boy to his roots would serve him well. He was born on a Wednesday, but the Ghanaian word for *Wednesday* is *Kwakou. It just didn't sound right,* she thought. *It's too bad he wasn't born on a Sunday. That name is* Kwesi. *To heck with it,* Hewitt decided. *Kwesi it is.* Sekou, *which means "wise," will also go on the birth certificate as his middle name.*

Kwesi Millington was barely school age when his mother moved the family to Toronto for work. She settled in Rexdale, a mixed community with a significant black community. Whether deserved or not, the area has a reputation as a bed of crime and violence. Eventually, an amateur video would catapult Rexdale to global notoriety. Rob Ford, the stoned and stupefied mayor of Toronto, would be caught on camera smoking crack in Rexdale. When Kwesi was born, Hewitt couldn't possibly have known that the media and a different kind of video would be just as thorough at ruining her son's life.

All kids can be trying and difficult at times. Hewitt was prepared for the rebellious phase as her son became a teenager. It never happened. About the worst trouble Millington ever got into involved going into a local pool hall after his mom had told him not to. If he was not difficult, neither was he dependent. Mother and son were very close, but Millington never really opened up to her. They didn't have the kind of relationship in which it was easy to sit down and talk about feelings. He could count on one hand the number of times he'd seen his mother cry. Showing emotion does not come easy for Millington, either. If anything, he works hard at keeping it in.

And so it was with his thoughts about what to do for a living. His mother encouraged him to go to university after high school so he went, and earned a Bachelor of Commerce degree at Ryerson in Toronto. There was a bank job for a while. Work at a government office. A Jenny Craig weight-loss store. Millington found desk jobs boring and unrewarding.

Being a police officer was never a life-long dream, as it was for Bill Bentley. Yet, when he considered the idea, applied, and was accepted to Depot in 2005, Millington became focused on being the best policeman he could. He was encouraged by the possibility of promotion and advancement. Secretly, he thought of what it would be like to be the first black commissioner of the RCMP. Until October 14, 2007. Now he is notorious. He walks into the Braidwood Inquiry, having spent the past year and a half reading about himself in the news and the blogs, and catching what some people say under their breath. Liar. Murderer. Nigger cop.

Millington has been prepared by his lawyer as well as any of the officers have for the days he will spend in the witness chair. He is not prepared for the audible jeers from people in the gallery or the woman who attends each day conspicuously drawing in a *Pinocchio* colouring book. It's not surprising that he appears uncomfortable. He drains glass after glass of water — five in the first hour — as he is led through the evidence that he pulled the Taser trigger five times before Dziekanski died.

Millington likely doesn't know that the lawyer asking the questions thinks a lot of his evidence is bullshit. Art Vertlieb had heard it already when he interviewed Millington ahead of time. Vertlieb has a fine line to walk. He has to be fair and be seen to be fair so that when he asks the tough, challenging questions it doesn't look like he's already come to his

Kwesi Millington confidently poses for his grad photo on the steps of the chapel – a building dating back to the 1880s – at the RCMP Depot in Regina, May 2005.

own conclusions. Some of that finesse comes from preparation. Some of it is just intuition.

Millington testifies that he fired the Taser because "Mr. Dziekanski was exhibiting combative behaviour and I felt he was a threat to the other officers, and I acted to stop the threat."

That's when Vertlieb gets an idea. He instructs the commission's registrar to unseal a key piece of evidence. Len Giles cuts open a plastic evidence bag and removes a black office stapler.

"Would you be good enough to give that to the officer?" Vertlieb asks. "Given all of the four officers and the tools and the distance, that's what scared you?"

There is spontaneous chortling and guffaws from the gallery.

"That's what made me fear for the officers' safety, yes," Millington replies.

Vertlieb asks him to demonstrate exactly how Dziekanski held the stapler and describe why it was threatening. As Millington obligingly rises and grips the stapler in his hand as Dziekanski did, Vertlieb is secretly thrilled that Millington looks the opposite of menacing.

After a few questions, Vertlieb lets Millington sit down. Not for long. "Would you stand, sir, with the open stapler, please?" Vertlieb asks again. "And keep in mind, of course, that Mr. Dziekanski's perhaps four inches shorter than you and less weight, correct?"

Millington, at six feet tall, agrees.

"Okay," Vertlieb continues, "show us the combative behaviour that made you feel for your officers and your own safety that resulted in the Taser. Show us the combative behaviour, please?"

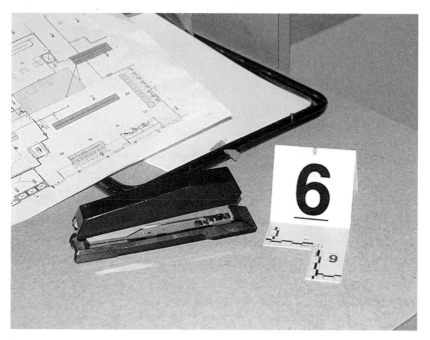

The stapler. Homicide investigators took only one clear photo of what was both the trigger for the Mounties' use of force, and their ridicule by the public. Yet when Robert Dziekanski picked up this stapler and brandished it at police, it became a weapon.

Millington doesn't appear to realize he's being set up.

"Like I said, he had his fist raised, he had the stapler up and he was advancing towards us."

Vertlieb isn't done. "When you think about this event and the questions that we posed to you here and reflect on the fact that there were four of you with handguns and other assorted tools and body armour, is it your evidence that because of this stapler that all of that ended up in Mr. Dziekánski's unfortunate demise that morning?"

Before Millington's own lawyer can rise to object, Braidwood steps in. "I don't think so. Don't go there," the commissioner tells his counsel. "There's certainly no suggestion in the world that any of these officers knew that their conduct would result in the —"

Vertlieb cuts him off. "I agree."

Millington will not get assistance like that again from the commissioner as he is taken back and forth over the Pritchard video and his statements to investigators in an effort to mine all of the discrepancies in his initial account of what happened.

Despite the mild admonishment, Vertlieb is proud of the moment. Millington's credibility has been skewered. The picture news agencies use from his first day of testimony is the image of him standing with the stapler in his hand.

One of the big questions is why Millington thought Dziekanski was still standing when he fired the Taser for the second time.

Braidwood leaves little room for doubt about his view. "Are you telling me," Braidwood asks Millington directly, "that at the moment all this happened and we see he's on his back with his legs up in the air and that's when the second Tasering took place, that you're saying that despite that you thought he was standing?"

It's a question with a built-in assumption that in the hours after the incident, Millington was able to parse his adrenaline-fuelled use of the Taser in the same way Braidwood can, by leisurely looking at split-second frames of a video. Millington knows his original statement is wrong, but that's how he remembered it. "It was a fast-moving situation and I thought he was standing at the time."

Millington's own handwritten notes on the Taser training material he was given by the RCMP indicate multiple stuns are to be avoided because they're hazardous. Walter Kosteckyj pushes him to explain. "You guys don't leave your brains at home. Why did you think that they didn't want you to use multiple charges?" Millington also never gave Dziekanski the warning he was taught to deliver. "You never challenged him. Challenge. As in, 'Stop, or I'll shoot fifty thousand volts into you.'"

Millington testifies it all boils down to time. There wasn't any. It happened so quickly.

Kosteckyj insists Millington panicked, and then made matters worse by failing his basic duty to record how many times he'd fired the Taser in his notebook, and to make sure first responders knew, as well. "Sir, you just abdicated all responsibility for your use of the Taser that night to others, didn't you?"

Millington pauses for a moment before answering. "What does abdicated mean?"

Millington's middle name was intended to instill him with wisdom, but the wisdom and knowledge that he possesses is of little use when he is confronted by a group of unfriendly lawyers trying to hold him responsible for Dziekanski's death.

Millington is questioned about why he told investigators that Dziekanski grabbed the stapler and "had it raised high."

Millington testifies that what he meant by "high," was "above his waist."

When Don Rosenbloom rises to take his shot at Millington's memory, he is relentless. "In the course of your duty as a police officer, if you turned to somebody and said, 'Hands up high,' would you feel there's compliance if a person simply brought their hands to this location as I'm demonstrating to you where the hands are below the shoulder? Would that be compliance?"

"Yes," Millington insisted.

Rosenbloom has heard enough. "You and your fellow officers collaborated to fabricate your story in the expectation it would justify your conduct to your superiors. Do you deny that?"

Millington is unfazed. "Yes. We never did that."

Millington, like Bentley and Robinson but not Rundel, had thought Dziekanski had to be taken to the ground by force.

"I'm going to further suggest to you," Rosenbloom continues, "you were fast at work at the scene, cooking up your story and you continued your collaboration back at the detachment office. Do you deny that?"

Millington is prepped to only answer what he's asked. "Yes," comes his one-word reply.

Unsatisfied, Rosenbloom tries again. "I am suggesting you and your fellow officers intentionally misled IHIT investigators and you continue to lie under oath at this commission. Do you deny that?"

If Rosenbloom was hoping to arouse some ire or spark an emotional reaction, he is disappointed. "Yes, I deny that," Millington says calmly.

Outside the inquiry, Rosenbloom leaves no question about his feelings. "I've been disgusted by the whole event from the day it happened and I think I speak for most Canadians," he tells sympathetic-sounding reporters. "This has obviously been a very sad day in the history of our country. It's a sad day in terms of the reputation of the RCMP."

"You wanna know why Canada feels supposedly a particular way?" Millington's lawyer, Ravi Hira, says to the same reporters, who now take on the adversarial tone of commission counsel. "When you take a little sliver, a little second, and characterize it as the whole movie, of course they're gonna think that way."

In preparation for the case, Hira drove out to the RCMP's Pacific Region Training Centre in Chilliwack to learn more about the Taser, and to receive a stun himself so he'd know what it felt like.

Millington was mistaken about whether Dziekanski was on his feet or on the floor when he was stunned a second time. Hira says everyone makes mistakes. Whether Dziekanski was wrestled to the ground is irrelevant. "What is material is this: we know he was acting up in the secure area of the International Arrivals lounge of an international airport. The second-largest facility in western Canada. When the officers arrive, he was acting in a bizarre fashion. He did not follow their commands. Instead, he picked up a stapler and advanced to them. I'm sorry. They acted in accordance with their training. Nobody wanted this outcome. It's a tragic outcome but that doesn't mean these officers are somehow lying or cooking up a story."

Some question why Millington didn't show more emotion if he believes it was a tragic outcome. "He regrets what happened. We all do," Hira says.

"What's wrong with saying I'm sorry? Why can't he say that?" one reporter asks indignantly.

"I don't recall that question being asked," Hira snaps. "I don't recall what relevance it is with respect to the commissioner's findings, but let me say this. I am sorry. It's a tragic event. We all are."

In fact, Millington is haunted by the event and Dziekanski's death every day. Not long after he steps down from the witness chair and returns to Toronto, depression and PTSD overtake him, and he goes off work.

17 | OUT OF CONTROL — MONTY ROBINSON

"WOULD YOU PLACE your right hand on the Bible, please? Would you state your full name, please?"

"Benjamin Montgomery Robinson."

Monty Robinson is trying to be calm as he's sworn in at the Braidwood Inquiry. Underneath his deliberately cool exterior he is one part angry, one part nervous, and ninety-eight parts certain his time in the witness chair is not going to end well.

Robinson battles a growing anxiety that RCMP management is letting the four members involved in Dziekanski's death take the fall for it. Sure, Assistant Commissioner Al McIntyre had asked the public to consider the strain on the police officers when the Pritchard video was released months ago. But that wasn't a clear defence. McIntyre didn't say the Mounties acted according to the training the RCMP gave them.

Not only is management not coming to the officers' defence, Robinson knows how the constables who have testified before him were attacked with the assumption that they had all conspired to cover up what they knew to be excessive use of force and negligence. Robinson's insistence on having his own lawyer instead of being represented by the woman who assured them they had nothing to worry about now seems like a prescient act of self-preservation.

It is a difficult time for Robinson's parents to watch what has happened to their son. Ben Robinson went to a residential school for six years. That was horrible. He thinks this is worse. It's particularly hard as Robinson thinks back on his boy the way no one else can. On his son's first day of school he had gotten all dressed up. He proudly carried a lunch box just like his older sister. As he stood by the door, Ben Robinson backed up and raised a camera to his eye to take a picture. Through the viewfinder Robinson saw a tear on his son's cheek. He knelt down. "What is it son? What's the matter?"

The boy answered. "It's my first day of school but I don't even know how to read or write."

Robinson's heart broke. "You know Robbie who comes over here and plays with you every day? He doesn't know how to read or write either, that's why you're going to school."

A smile spread across his son's face. The one thing Robinson always hoped was that his son wouldn't follow in his footsteps and take up a life as a commercial fisherman. It is a difficult way to make a living. It was also unlikely his son would emulate his grandfather and become a United Church minister. His graduation from Depot in 1996 was a proud day for the Robinson clan, with many members of the family venturing for the first time out of British Columbia to be at the ceremony in Regina. Ben Robinson believed his son would never be a foot soldier in the force. He was too smart for that.

———————

Before sitting in the witness chair, Robinson has been schooled by his lawyer. *Just answer the questions. Don't say any more. This is what you're supposed to do.* Yet, as one day turns to two and then three, Robinson is certain the inquiry's agenda isn't to dispassionately examine what happened. It's to assign blame.

Robinson's first brush with commission counsel, in the private interview in his lawyer's office, had been testy. It had ended with Robinson hearing that Art Vertlieb wanted to punch him. Now Vertlieb is asking the questions.

Benjamin Montgomery Robinson at his graduation from Depot in July 1996, at the start of a career in the RCMP that would end in disgrace.

"Wouldn't you be [in] charge at the airport that night? Wouldn't you be directing the constables? Would you give them guidance?"

It's a game of cat and mouse, the point being to establish that Robinson, as the senior officer, bears responsibility for what happened to Dziekanski.

A few days earlier he was given a chance to review the statement he gave to homicide investigators more than a year ago. It was a revelation. *Oh my God … my statement's shit*, Robinson thinks, when he sees it again.

The way it's written, Robinson is all over the place. He jumps from one moment to another without regard to timing. He was on adrenaline when he gave it, still reeling from what had happened. The officer who interviewed him never really got him on track to give a step-by-step account and just let him ramble. Now, every word, every misspoken phrase, is laid out in front of him. He must answer for all of it.

Then there is the video. Having to watch it in his lawyer's office was bad enough. Now it is carved up in tenths of a second and served to him like thin slices of fugu, each piece more toxic than the last. Robinson feels each frame kickstart a kind of PTSD from the incident. He's convinced they all did what they were trained to do, but the video is making them appear like goons. If Dziekanski hadn't died, Robinson thinks, Pritchard's video could have been used as a training tool.

The same cannot be said for Robinson's statements, which he must now reconcile with what can be seen in the Pritchard video. As with Millington before him, Robinson admits he was wrong in saying Dziekanski was "wrestled to the ground." Even though that image of wrestling Dziekanski to the floor is one that evolved almost accidentally in his statement, the lawyers treat it like dogs gnaw on a bone.

"Now, I understand you may wish to change that statement in some way about wrestling to the ground," Vertlieb says.

"I was mistaken but I was telling the truth," Robinson replies. "At certain points we did wrestle with him, but like I have on page three [of my statement] he did — he did drop to the ground. So the Taser did take him down, and I sort of blended the whole interaction with him and I was mistaken. But at the time I did the best job I could in articulating it."

Robinson also elects to correct his description of Dziekanski's use of the stapler. Robinson told investigators Dziekanski had been "swinging" the stapler before he was Tasered. What he meant was that Dziekanski had "brandished" the metal object. "At the time I used the articulation of swinging and I didn't clearly articulate it well."

Vertlieb doesn't let Robinson off the hook. "What do you mean you didn't clearly articulate it well?" he asks.

"I didn't articulate it well. At the time I gave my statement, I didn't break everything down to each interaction and I didn't go through to the point in fine details, and those questions weren't posed to me at the time."

Robinson is admitting a mistake. He's admitting the statement he gave is poorly constructed and almost certainly not up to a standard you might expect from a seasoned police officer. "He swung but then he brandished it, and it wasn't swinging initially. But I sort of blended the whole interaction and I was just trying to clarify it. But just because I was mistaken doesn't mean I was lying. I did the best job I could at the time."

Vertlieb turns that admission of error into something more akin to an admission of guilt. "Do you realize that in your statement you used the word 'swinging' twelve times?"

Robinson agrees.

Robinson's training instructs that when faced with someone who suddenly brandishes what could be a weapon, an officer can, depending on circumstances, use force to neutralize that threat. No one gives a plausible explanation for why Dziekanski picked up a stapler, if not to use it defensively or offensively in some fashion. Dziekanski gripped the open stapler like a baton, and squeezed repeatedly, making staples fall to the floor.

Vertlieb runs with the image to make a point. "Tell us about the staples. How far did they come out?" he probes.

Robinson can't recall.

"Would the staples have come out perhaps a foot or so?" Vertlieb presses.

Robinson doesn't know.

"Well, you must have some idea, sir, you were there. They certainly were no threat to you, the staples?"

Robinson realizes he's been led down a path he never intended to take. Vertlieb appears to be riffing on the image of four fit police officers threatened by a delirious man with a stapler.

When Dziekanski is down on the ground and finally in handcuffs, he begins to snore. It's at this point in his statement to investigators that Robinson uses the phrase "I put him out" to describe what he said to the other officers at the time.

"Did you think because you were on top of him, you were the one responsible for his loss of consciousness?" Walter Kosteckyj presses.

"I was trying to draw attention to the members that he's no longer pushing up and he's snoring, so the fact that he went out."

Robinson will not accept that his use of the pronoun *I* in the statement means he felt he was solely responsible.

As lawyers dig deeper for a tighter connection between Dziekanski's death and Robinson's role, they hover over the handful of frames from the Pritchard video that show Robinson positioned near Dziekanski's head during the struggle. The autopsy is quite clear: there are no signs of trauma or injury to Dziekanski's neck that would be consistent with choking or suffocating force placed on it. It doesn't stop more than one run at the theory that what can't quite be seen in the video is Robinson's knee on Dziekanski's neck.

"I thought we — or I — went over this yesterday," Robinson says in frustration when Poland's lawyer, Don Rosenbloom, brings it up again. "I know where my knee was. It was not on there."

Rosenbloom persists. "What about your shin?"

Robinson rejects the idea. "I know where my knee was and it was nowhere near his neck."

Robinson is the last officer to testify and there is a palpable sense that if the four of them are to be found at fault for what happened, the case will have to be made now.

As Dziekanski sunk into medical distress, Robinson insists, he monitored the man's vital signs, along with the airport's head of security, Trevor Enchelmaier. Yet, at times, Robinson can be seen on snippets of the Pritchard video wearing his black gloves. It would be difficult to monitor Dziekanski's pulse wearing tactical gloves. Robinson testifies he removed them and put them on again occasionally, in case Dziekanski suddenly roused and became aggressive.

In a rehearsed exchange between Robinson and his lawyer, the Mountie is given one opportunity to break out of the line of questions that have been steering him toward responsibility for Dziekanski's death.

"How do you feel about the events as they unfolded?" Harris asks his client.

"This is a tragic thing that happened and it saddens me any time I have to look at them," Robinson answers. "This has been the hardest last couple of months to go through this. And, you know, this should not have happened. No one should have passed away. It's not where every day doesn't go by where I think about this and replay this through my head. And then having to sit here and go through the video, yes, it's one of those things that's just really hard to keep together."

Robinson is telling the inquiry that you can be involved in someone's death as a police officer, but that doesn't make you guilty of misconduct.

"Is there anything that you did, from your perspective, that contributed to this event that you can see?" Harris asks.

Robinson slips back into the say-as-little-as-required mode. "No," he says.

When it comes time for Poland's lawyer to fathom the depth of Robinson's credibility, Don Rosenbloom is characteristically sharp tongued. "I'm going to suggest to you," Rosenbloom says as he launches his assault, "that a contributing factor in how this incident unfolded and in Mr. Dziekanski's death was how you and your fellow officers handled the events of that evening. Are you willing to agree with me about that?"

Robinson is adamant. "We handled it consistent with our training."

Rosenbloom takes the combined testimony of four officers over the past month and lays it at Robinson's feet. "I've been struck by the consistencies with the errors that each of you, meaning the four officers, have made during your testimony." Rosenbloom produces a list. "I'm speaking of the raised stapler; I'm speaking of the yelling; I'm speaking of the advance movements of Mr. Dziekanski; I'm speaking of the second Tasering while still standing, when in fact he was down; I'm speaking of the officers having tackled him to the ground."

172 | BLAMED AND BROKEN

Robinson's lawyer interrupts. "My friend has given a laundry list of things that are not the same in all the officers' statements nor the same in their evidence, and he's lumped it together like it is consistent inconsistencies," Harris protests.

It's not an insignificant point. Much will come to be made of how similar — even identical — the officer's statements are, when in fact they are unique enough that if the four intended to describe the same false version of events, they did a lousy job of getting their story straight.

It is Braidwood himself who questions the point of putting the theory of collusion to Robinson, "We all know exactly what the Corporal is going to say to your question."

Braidwood's guidance from the bench sounds less like a defence of Robinson's position, and more like an admission that, as commissioner, he's not interested in anything Robinson has to say about the matter.

Rosenbloom pivots swiftly. "I am going to suggest to the Corporal that you and your fellow officers collaborated to fabricate your story in the expectation that it would justify your conduct the night that Mr. Dziekanski died. Do you deny that?"

Robinson is calm. "I deny that."

Rosenbloom doesn't let up. "I am going to further suggest that you and your fellow officers were fast at work at the scene cooking up the story and you continued your collaboration at the detachment office."

Rosenbloom has either forgotten or simply disregarded the evidence that the four officers were never together at the detachment office prior to giving their statements.

"I deny that," Robinson says, without explanation.

"And lastly, officer," Rosenbloom sums up, "I'll be less charitable. I'm going to suggest to you that you and your fellow officers intentionally misled IHIT investigators and you continued to lie under oath before this commission. Do you deny that?"

Rosenbloom's roll is stopped short when Robinson's lawyer points out he's just asked two questions at the same time, forcing Rosenbloom to ask them again, separately.

Robinson answers, exactly as Braidwood might have expected.

18 | DIRTY QUESTIONS

IT HAS BEEN DIFFICULT for Zofia Cisowski to endure police testimony that her son was a threat, and that they acted according to their training. Surely her son did not deserve what happened to him, let alone to die under the conditions captured by the Pritchard video? The notion that the Mounties had no intent or belief that their actions would precipitate Dziekanski's death is meaningless to Cisowski. Her response to the officers' explanations has been to weep in the inquiry gallery or to flee the room, especially when the video is played ad nauseam.

The office of B.C.'s attorney general acknowledges the police testimony at the inquiry has prompted an upsurge of letters and email demanding another look at laying criminal charges.

"I think they want to save themselves," Cisowski declares. "They want to cover, because at first day they start lying."

As the inquiry heads into its final weeks, the public remains focused on the role of the Mounties in Dziekanski's death, in large part because of the media attention on their testimony. There are, however, details that emerge that pose nagging questions that are never fully answered. The theory adopted by some to explain Dziekanski's wildly erratic and threatening behaviour is that he succumbed to either alcohol withdrawal or hunger or both. A medical expert testifies that perhaps he picked up the stapler with no real intent because he was delirious.

Putting aside the fact that the police would not have known that in the split second they used what they believed was a relatively safe method to subdue Dziekanski, the "delirious" theory presents a problem. It has been argued by Cisowski's lawyer and others that Dziekanski was actually co-operating and complying with everything the officers directed him to do. The inquiry never explains how Dziekanski could be both delirious and rational at the same time.

Further, if Dziekanski was starving, why didn't he eat the sealed strawberry Danish he had in his pocket? If he was dying for a drink, why not crack open the bottle of vodka in his luggage?

In an effort to explore why Dziekanski behaved the way he did, and what might have contributed to his death beyond the restraint used by police, Braidwood invites testimony from some of the last people to see him alive in Poland. They are the same people the RCMP investigators spoke to a year earlier in their controversial overseas trip to examine Dziekanski's background. Braidwood sees their testimony as vital to the job at hand. However, it is the lawyers for the police who carry the burden of asking tough questions about Dziekanski's mental and physical fitness, and who receive the condemnation for it.

The witnesses testify by telephone and web camera, and the first one on the line makes it clear she isn't about to say anything negative about Dziekanski. Iwona Kosowska is reluctant to say much, in fact, even when asked general questions such as, "How would you describe him?" and "How long did you know Mr. Dziekanski?"

Kosowska testifies through an interpreter that "he was a healthy man" and "I've never seen him drunk."

Bill Bentley's lawyer, David Butcher, asks Kosowska about the statement she gave to police that Dziekanski lived for some eight years with Elzbieta Dibon, whom she described as an alcoholic.

"I'm sorry," Kosowska says angrily, "we're here to talk about Mr. Dziekanski, not Elzbieta Dibon, and I'm really getting tired of these questions."

There is little doubt Dziekanski drank, and drank enough that his mother was concerned. IHIT investigators who examined his belongings found her handwritten note on the last page of one of Dziekaski's immigration documents. It was in Polish, and it urged Dziekanski to curb his excessive drinking. The note was never made public.

Whatever Kosowska knows, she insists Dziekanski's private life is off limits and regardless of what she told police and Polish prosecutors, she won't answer these questions for the inquiry.

Kwesi Millington's lawyer makes another attempt. Ravi Hira asks Kosowska about Dziekanski's cigarette habit, and whether she noticed he had started to sweat before his trip to Canada.

"Trust me," Kosowska says without answering the question, "he wasn't sick. He didn't have any illnesses. I think I know your intent."

Hira feels he has no choice but to press on. "You agree with me that in the video he appears to be acting aggressively?"

Kosowska disagrees.

"In the video, you'll agree with me that he throws a computer onto the ground?"

Kosowska refuses to answer.

"I'm sorry. I'm losing it," she shouts down the phone line in Polish. Kosowska insists she would have behaved exactly the same way as Dziekanski did, leaving little doubt that her testimony is completely unreliable. "You guys made a mistake. Now you're going to turn everything around," Kosowska rails. "For me, my friend got killed in front of my eyes."

Hira's apologies do nothing to stem Kosowska's anger as he continues. "Would you agree that he, that is Mr. Dziekanski, had a drinking problem, an alcohol problem?"

There are audible catcalls in the gallery directed at Hira as Kosowska replies, "You are trying to make a bad person out of him, which means that you can kill a bad person but you cannot kill a good person. I'm fed up. I'm not going to answer any more questions."

As distasteful as the questions may sound, they are legitimate and integral to the mandate of the inquiry, which is to find a complete and comprehensive explanation for why Dziekanski died. The autopsy and the opinions of a number of expert pathologists go only so far.

Dziekanski's actual habits when it came to alcohol and cigarettes are relevant. So is any history of Dziekanski's temperament and involvement with police.

"Now, you were aware that he had served a period of time in jail?" Hira asks.

This brings Kosteckyj to his feet and Braidwood puts the brakes on whatever Hira is trying to do.

"Just a moment now. What's this got to do with it?" Braidwood demands.

While there is nary an objection to questions about how Dziekanski played chess with his neighbour or what sort of affable and healthy fellow he was, those which probe whether there were aspects of his character or constitution that might help explain how the incident started, and why he might have picked up a stapler at the worst possible time in the encounter, are deemed irrelevant, unseemly, and self-serving.

The fact is that when Dziekanski was seventeen, he spent several years in a reformatory for a robbery conviction.

"Even if that's true, and I have no idea whether it is or not, that question is irrelevant," Braidwood instantly rules.

People in the gallery who've been verbally heckling Hira as he does his job — indeed the job of the inquiry — now erupt in applause. In a court, these people would be immediately ejected by the judge. Braidwood doesn't even acknowledge the disruption, let alone chastise it.

Before Kosowska is excused, she is asked about the cellphone Dziekanski had when he left Poland. She testifies the plan was for him to call her as soon as he landed. She testifies she never received a call, but that Dziekanski may have phoned his uncle in Poland once he got to Vancouver.

The inquiry never pursues it, or makes the connection with what Cisowski's friend Richard Hutchinson said. Months earlier Hutchinson had testified that after they returned to Kamloops without Dziekanski, Cisowski came to his apartment asking him to listen to a voicemail message. Hutchinson thought it was in Polish and he couldn't understand it. That call, its contents, and the larger question of why Dziekanski never called his mother, or vice versa, when he allegedly had a cellphone, is treated by the inquiry as if it didn't happen, or at the very least was irrelevant.

It is undoubtedly difficult to pursue, because of the decision not to hear first-hand evidence from Zofia Cisowski. Instead, Cisowski makes statements outside the hearing, to journalists who have an insatiable need for clips of the grieving mother. It doesn't matter that what she says is often the product of manipulation — intentional or otherwise — by journalists using leading questions to elicit the sound bite: "Do you believe the officers are lying?"; "What do you think of the questions about your son's drinking?"; "Do you believe another mother will suffer?"

When Cisowski steps forward to read a prepared statement calling on the premier and attorney general to reopen an investigation into the Mounties' actions and appoint a special prosecutor, some journalists want to know more about Dziekanski's background. They ask about his criminal record.

"C'mon," says Cisowski's Polish friend who has been prompting her.

"I'm so tired," Cisowski says, refusing to discuss it. Journalists oblige, turning instead to her call to put the Mounties back under investigation.

Speaking to the CBC, Attorney General Wally Oppal says that "we're getting more and more evidence being elicited on a daily basis, so it may well be, at the end of the day, the people in the Criminal Justice Branch could re-examine this."

It's an extraordinary statement, given that Braidwood hasn't finished hearing the evidence, let alone drawn any conclusions, at least not publicly. Three levels of management at the branch examined all the police statements, the Pritchard video, and an eighteen-hundred-page investigation report. It also had the benefit of a report by the Ontario Provincial Police which independently reviewed IHIT's investigation and found it was both "thorough and conducted in an unbiased manner."

Yet Oppal, as the top cop in the province and the man who also appointed Braidwood, delivers what sounds very much like an opinion that the Mounties may be convictable. "The fact that a lot of this evidence is now being tested in a different light may result in something different happening."

Oppal's equivocation notwithstanding, his comments could be seen by some as at least an appearance of conflict of interest. They also come before key expert witnesses challenge the notion of "more and more evidence" that somehow suggests there's a criminal offence in what the police did.

Vancouver Police sergeant Brad Fawcett looked at all the evidence and concluded that while he might have handled the situation differently, the Mounties' use of force was reasonable, even considering Dziekanski fell to the ground and wasn't wrestled. Corporal Gregg Gillis, the officer who trained the Mounties, acknowledged that after viewing the Pritchard video, "there's certainly some other options that could have been used to resolve that situation." However, Gillis is clear he would not use hindsight and a tragic outcome to blame them. "The actions they took are consistent with what I would expect to see with similarly trained police officers."

On the very same day Gillis is defending the four Mounties in Vancouver, the RCMP's second-in-command is seen to be throwing them under the bus. Deputy Commissioner Bill Sweeney appears before the Senate Committee on National Security and Defence in Ottawa, ostensibly to speak about how the RCMP is responding to the controversial Brown report on governance and cultural change in the force.

When it's Senator Grant Mitchell's turn to question Sweeney, the senator, like most committee members, makes a statement, and it's a doozy. "Almost as discouraging as the Robert Dziekanski death," Mitchell declares, "was what can be construed as the explicit lying that occurred after the event to cover it up." In a separate thought, Mitchell allows what he just said is only an allegation, "currently." He then adds to the suggestion that the Mounties are, in fact, lying. "Currently, we have the sense that there is a conspiracy."

In one fell swoop, a representative of Canada's chamber of sober second thought has damned Robinson, Millington, Bentley, and Rundel.

Sweeney does not challenge the good senator's characterization of his officers as lying conspirators. Instead he offers a half-hearted sentiment of regret. "We are very sorry for Mr. Dziekanski's death and we are committed to learning as much as possible from this terrible event."

One interpretation of Sweeney's reply is that he is being prudent and doesn't want to be seen to be taking a side in an issue viewed internally as an albatross around the force's neck. However, some media jump on Sweeney's words and parse them as an admission of guilt.

True to form, the RCMP doesn't deign to clarify.

Sweeney's perceived apology comes on the heels of another admission from the officer in charge of Dziekanski's homicide investigation. Superintendent Wayne Rideout testifies at the Braidwood Inquiry that he made the decision to shut down any release of information about what happened to Dziekanski because it might compromise a criminal investigation.

Rideout's edict meant that errors by media spokesperson Sergeant Pierre Lemaitre went uncorrected. In an interview two days after the incident Lemaitre had insisted the Taser was fired only twice at Dziekanski, contrary to a claim by witness Sima Ashrafinia, who heard it go off at least four times.

"I don't disagree that interview shouldn't have taken place," Rideout testifies, adding that's why he shut down any communication about the Mounties' use of force.

Rideout contributed to public mistrust, however, when he appeared to lift his own media blackout. At the time, everyone from the commissioner on down had been concerned about an imminent media blitz based on a report by firefighters that the Mounties did nothing to monitor Dziekanski's vital signs. Rideout authorized a statement from IHIT to counter it, saying the officers had been checking on him.

Testifying at the inquiry, Rideout was brought to admit that "with the benefit of hindsight" he would do things differently.

Lemaitre doesn't get off quite as easily when it's his turn in the witness chair. He is asked to explain and account for every single error he made in the two days he was the media contact on the incident. Why did he insist Dziekanski had been Tasered only twice?

"Because at that time that is the information that I had obtained from that morning," Lemaitre testifies.

Why didn't he volunteer that the RCMP had a bystander's video of what happened?

Lemaitre says he wasn't authorized to reveal that.

Lawyers on the hunt for evidence of a conspiracy to cover up what happened press Lemaitre to divulge who told him to say what he said. The answer is unsatisfying to those who still believe Lemaitre is a lying spin doctor: Corporal Dale Carr told him what information he could release.

Carr himself testifies that he can't remember giving Lemaitre some of the erroneous details in the early hours of the investigation. Lemaitre came to know he made mistakes, but he didn't have the authority to go rogue and start making statements to the media on his own without approval, as much as he wanted to set the record straight.

"You didn't feel like you could bring up to a superior, 'My personal reputation has been besmirched here?'" Kosteckyj asks.

"You know what," Lemaitre replies, barely containing his contempt and frustration, "being a police officer — and I think you were at one time — you grow a thicker skin. What was of greater concern was that a man had lost his life, that an investigation had to be conducted to get to the bottom of it. Whether my feelings are hurt or not had absolutely nothing to do with it. I can live with that."

Before Lemaitre is excused he asks Braidwood if he can put something on the record. "I know Mrs. Dziekanski ... is not here, but I've never had an opportunity to do this since this incident occurred. But I would like to extend my sincere condolences for her loss, and I can't begin to imagine the pain that she's gone through, and that is my personal opinion, not that of the RCMP."

As Lemaitre leaves the inquiry, another RCMP spokesperson delivers a prepared statement to the assembled media. "During the course of the investigation we found there was some information that was provided and made public that was not accurate," Corporal Tim Shields says, "and for those inaccuracies we apologize and we are sorry."

The apology does nothing to explain why the RCMP appears at times to withhold information unless specifically asked about it. It is also far short of an official exoneration of Lemaitre, or even an acknowledgement of the bullet he took for the RCMP's mishandling of the communications strategy.

Lemaitre made a grave error in his testimony: his skin isn't as thick as he let on. The hurt Lemaitre suffered runs far deeper than his feelings. He won't be able to live with what happened, after all.

What follows at the inquiry is a dense, dizzying, and often contradictory stream of testimony from no less than fourteen medical and scientific experts, who offer their opinions about what exactly caused Dziekanski's death. The autopsy finding is generic and vague: sudden death during restraint. Each expert gives a view of the role Dziekanski's health played, whether his state before the police arrived was a factor, and to what extent both the Taser and the struggle caused Dziekanski's heart to suffer an irregular beat, which led to cardiac arrest.

Every step of the way interests at the inquiry compete to tease out details from the testimony that will either finger the police for having caused or contributed to Dziekanski's death, or dispel the connection.

After months of hearings, it appears as if Braidwood will retire to write his report using evidence that pits the credibility of four Mounties against the indelible sight and sound of Dziekanski's unintended death.

With almost no time left on the inquiry's clock, Bill Bentley's lawyer makes a Hail Mary pass to put the blame ball in Dziekanski's zone. David Butcher springs a report by a forensic video analyst on Poland's lawyer, Don Rosenbloom, suggesting that the new evidence is game over for those arguing Dziekanski didn't pose a threat. Grant Fredericks is a former TV reporter, and former police officer, who now makes his living analyzing crime scene video. Butcher believes Fredericks will say that Dziekanski was clearly moving toward the officers before Millington fired the Taser. Rosenbloom now sets about trying to find his own expert in a science known as photogrammetry.

It turns out Fredericks has no degree in the science, and has made errors in his calculations, which involve counting pixels on the grainy

Pritchard video in order to determine whether Dziekanski is moving toward the officers at the critical time. Rosenbloom unearths bona fide specialists in the techniques Fredericks is using, and they testify Fredericks's conclusions are wrong. Braidwood delivers a number of impatient and terse comments about the whole matter. Butcher's pass has been a fumble. It does nothing to boost the credibility of the officers.

It becomes clear, however, that for some time now Braidwood has been considering a harsh condemnation of the officers. A month earlier he issued confidential notices to the four RCMP officers that he might level findings of misconduct against them. Specifically, Braidwood advised the Mounties that, in his view, they failed to react appropriately in confronting Dziekanski, that their statements afterward were deliberate attempts to justify their actions, and that at the inquiry their testimony was "self-serving and misleading."

The Mounties' lawyers reveal Braidwood's intentions when they launch a legal challenge in the B.C. Supreme Court to stop Braidwood from condemning their clients. They argue he has neither the jurisdiction nor the mandate to make what are tantamount to criminal charges. Millington's lawyer, Ravi Hira, suggests Braidwood is perilously close to accusing the officers of obstruction of justice and perjury.

While commission counsel Art Vertlieb says nothing has been decided and the notices are merely legal warnings of what "might" be in Braidwood's final report, no one who has sat through the inquiry believes it. It appears the Mounties' legal challenges to save what's left of their reputations may stall the beginning of closing arguments at the inquiry, but then the B.C. Supreme Court rules against them.

Fate has another surprise in store, too. Just as Braidwood is ready to begin hearing final arguments, there is one more stunning blow to the credibility of the four Mounties. Lawyers for the Government of Canada discover an unopened CD in its files that had been turned over by the RCMP a month ago. The disc contains internal RCMP documents that were supposed to be disclosed to the inquiry. Buried among the files is one email from Dick Bent, the chief superintendent of criminal operations, to Assistant Commissioner Al McIntyre. It was written just a couple of weeks after Dziekanski died, but before the Pritchard video was released. In it, Bent tells McIntyre that Superintendent Rideout told him that the four Mounties planned to use the Taser on Dziekanski before they even got to the airport.

"The members discussed the response enroute," Bent wrote, "and decided if he did not comply they would go to the CEW."

If the email is accurate, it's clear evidence the Mounties lied. It's hard to understand how it could possibly be true, however. The officers drove to the terminal in separate cars and there are no recordings of them discussing anything over their radios. On arrival, Bentley did an equipment check and asked his partners if anyone had a Taser. Why would he ask that if they'd already discussed they were going to use it?

In her scramble to mitigate the damage to the Mounties' already battered credibility, Department of Justice lawyer Helen Roberts asks the people involved in the email chain to explain it. She tells Braidwood that their belief is that the reference was based on a misunderstanding. They're willing to testify to that effect, Roberts says. It is, however, an indication of just how bad this development is, that as Roberts addresses Braidwood, she is on her feet, crying, apologizing for a mistake that some could see as part of a pattern of deceit on the part of the RCMP. Roberts, who a year earlier confidently assured the Mounties they had nothing to worry about, and didn't need their own lawyers, is uttering her last words at the inquiry through tears and sniffles.

One by one, lawyers for the officers rise to state their clients' denials about any such premeditated plan to Taser Dziekanski. They sum up the consequences of Roberts's grave error.

Millington's lawyer, Ravi Hira, says it means "reputations are being damaged."

David Butcher tells Braidwood "there is now a dark cloud," over his client, Bill Bentley.

"I'm obviously appalled and I'm going to need a little time," Braidwood announces before adjourning briefly. When he returns, he has decided to follow the advice of Art Vertlieb, and postpone the rest of the inquiry until every paper and electronic record generated by the

RCMP since Dziekanski died has been turned over and analyzed. It will take three months, but it is a prudent and necessary decision given the tone of some internal RCMP communications that have already been made public. Early on, Commissioner Bill Elliott himself staked out the force's position on public scrutiny by referring to journalists in one email as people asking "dirty questions."

Eighteen thousand new documents are dumped on Braidwood. Not one of them contains so much as a hint that the Mounties lied or tried to mislead anyone. Though Roberts is shown not to have misdirected anyone or otherwise altered the outcome of the inquiry, this verdict comes only after many months spent defending the actions of the four officers. All of this serves as a catalyst: Roberts, unhappy with how the government and the DOJ handled the inquiry, resigns from the Department of Justice. She retires from practising law altogether.

If indeed Roberts's oversight helped to create a dark cloud over Bentley, as his lawyer pleaded, the absence of any evidence of collusion in the trove of RCMP files signals a change in the weather.

Bentley starts to think he will be back at work by the spring. He allows himself to believe that life will return to normal. That sign of good things to come may be when he meets Makayla Lefebvre through an internet dating site just before Christmas. Lefebvre hasn't gone on a single date with anyone who's contacted her online, but Bentley seems different. She knows Bentley's an RCMP officer but she doesn't realize he's *that* Bill Bentley. Lefebvre doesn't have cable. She doesn't follow the news closely. On their second date, she jokingly asks if he rides a horse. Laughter ensues. As a follow-up, she wants to know if Bentley's ever Tasered anyone.

"Why are you asking me that?" Bentley says.

"I'm curious," Lefebvre tells him.

Bentley puts everything on the table. In a few minutes he lays out what happened, and who he is. He tells her that everything is okay now, and he expects to be going back to work.

During a Christmas visit with her parents, a TV news story about the YVR incident, complete with scenes from the Pritchard video, blasts into the household. Lefebvre's mother and father start to riff at the dinner table about how horrible those Mounties are for what they did, and why they should be punished. Without giving away that her new boyfriend is one of the stars of that notorious video, Lefebvre becomes defensive. "You don't know all the details," she argues.

19 | LIARS AND COWARDS

THE LEAVES ARE BEGINNING to change colour as the second anniversary of Robert Dziekanski's death draws near. A memorial bench bearing his name, tucked behind some shrubs near the international terminal building at YVR, sits largely vacant, except for the flowers and candles occasionally placed there by his mother.

Over the summer, Braidwood released his findings for the first phase of his inquiry, dealing with Tasers. No one is surprised when he concludes there needs to be stricter rules for their use, and that the provincial government has, until now, failed to set the standards. Police and Taser's manufacturer had become the de facto arbiters of what's appropriate and what isn't. However, Braidwood decides a ban on the weapon wouldn't be prudent. That being said, he recommends that Tasers never be used to deal with petty infractions like jaywalking or evading a transit fare. They should only be used, he says, to respond to serious incidents. Even then, Braidwood believes the weapon should be drawn only when someone is about to cause bodily harm and when no other less-harmful means will work.

The B.C. government agrees.

Now, however, Braidwood is listening to lawyers take one last kick at the can to make the case that the Mounties are either the malevolent monsters some have made them out to be, or victims themselves to a degree, having performed their duties as best as they could, only to be made notorious because of the tragic outcome.

Walter Kosteckyj does argue that the police aren't the only ones to blame. "In the aftermath of Mr. Dziekanski's take-down," Kosteckyj submits, "we are then left to wonder whether a petty turf war between officials at Vancouver International Airport prevented Mr. Dziekanski from receiving medical attention minutes earlier than he did." Kosteckyj describes Dziekanski as a "gentle soul" and "although he enjoyed alcohol from time to time he was not considered an alcohol abuser" by his friends.

However, Kosteckyj leaves no doubt that the ultimate responsibility lies squarely with the Mounties. "Even if it can be argued that Mr. Dziekanski was arrestable," Kosteckyj argues, "the force visited upon him by the four police officers was excessive." Going further, Kosteckyj says, "One is left with the further inescapable conclusion that the members collaborated between themselves" to mislead the investigation.

Not surprisingly, Don Rosenbloom puts forward Poland's position that the Mounties acted with gross misconduct and that "Mr. Dziekanski's death was totally unnecessary, totally unjustified. Put bluntly, Mr. Dziekanski was the victim of incompetence, misconduct, and a reckless disregard for his life."

Mitch Taylor, the lawyer for the Government of Canada, delivers a submission that is the product of more than a dozen people in Ottawa weighing in on its contents. Canada, Taylor says, adopts the position that Dziekanski did indeed take a step toward the police before he was stunned. Further, to the extent that there was a delay that kept Dziekanski from being able to reunite with his mother, that was Dziekanski's fault for disappearing for six hours. Taylor points out the inquiry heard no evidence to support a theory of conspiracy and collusion to cover up what happened at the airport. The Mounties readily admitted the mistakes in their initial statements at the inquiry.

For their part, the officers, through their lawyers, maintain they acted in good faith, without malice, and to the best of their ability at the time. Millington's lawyer says Dziekanski is at least partly responsible for his own fate. "The evidence establishes he was an alcoholic, a regular smoker, and had some heart disease and some blood pressure problems." Hira argues it's not fair to judge Millington in hindsight using frame-by-frame analysis of the video. The law, he says, doesn't allow his client to be held to a standard of perfection, just what's reasonable at the time.

It is on the very day Hira speaks that Dziekanski's mother sues everyone potentially involved in her son's death: the airport, the governments of Canada and British Columbia, and the four officers who were the last to deal with him alive. Their actions, she alleges in the suit, caused her to "suffer a psychiatric injury or psychological harm." Having to endure endless exposure to the Pritchard video, she argues, has been "horrifying, shocking, and frightening." It wasn't Dziekanski's fault he became lost, the claim says. It was the airport's fault. It was the Canada Border Services Agency's fault. As far as the RCMP is concerned, Cisowski alleges the Mounties had no grounds to arrest her son, restrain him, or use any force whatsoever. It was "cruel and unusual treatment or punishment" the suit claims. Dziekanski's Charter right to security of the person was breached, she argues. She claims a host of specific financial damages, including medical and funeral expenses, and loss of earnings. What's more, she says the actions of the four Mounties were malicious, and demands an award of punitive damages against them.

On the one hand, the suit is a wager with an uncertain reward. If the case is judged on the basis that Dziekanski's death was a wrongful death, it is unlikely to attract much in the way of a court-ordered settlement. Unlike in the United States, where pain and suffering from a self-inflicted paper cut could lead to a six- or seven-figure payout, Canadian courts evaluate financial loss more practically. In Dziekanski's case, his age, his questionable job skills, and his own expectation of support as a new immigrant could result in an award amounting to just a few tens of thousands of dollars.

Dziekanski isn't just anyone, however.

Braidwood has retired to write his final report, and no one thinks it's going to be kind to the RCMP, or to any of the other parties named in the suit. The Mounties, in particular, are motivated to put an end to the YVR incident once and for all. The image of the RCMP doing battle with a grieving mother in court would consume what little is left of public confidence in the force.

Walter Kosteckyj files the lawsuit just a few days before the two-year limitation period on civil claims expires, and says he believes the damages could be in the "millions." He redeems himself in the eyes of Cisowski and her supporters who had at one time considered firing him because they felt Kosteckyj wasn't aggressive enough. They had already produced a list of demands on Cisowski's behalf. They had delivered it personally to B.C.'s Deputy Commissioner Gary Bass at a secret meeting in Kamloops a few weeks earlier. Bass and his assistants showed up in conspicuous black SUVs.

Not only does Cisowski want a financial settlement, she wants a public apology and formal discipline for the Mounties. Bass had yet to publicly support the Mounties involved. He also knows that any settlement implying guilt, however informal, will not fly at HQ or the Department of Justice in Ottawa.

There are incentives, however, for the RCMP to conduct negotiations as quickly as possible. On December 1, Monty Robinson is charged with attempting to obstruct justice for leaving the collision with Orion Hutchinson and drinking vodka before submitting for a Breathalyzer test. It's not impaired driving causing death, as the Delta Police had recommended. While that removes the potential of a life sentence for a conviction, the charge of attempting to obstruct justice reinforces the popular belief that Robinson and his former fellow officers tried the same thing in Dziekanski's death.

A week later, the head of the RCMP's watchdog delivers critics of the force an early Christmas present and releases the findings from his own investigation into what happened to Robert Dziekanski. Paul Kennedy, the chair of the Commission for Public Complaints Against the RCMP, appears to steal Braidwood's thunder, by producing a report that damns virtually everything the four Mounties did except show up when they were called. Kennedy even opines they were so inept, one of them might have drawn a gun.

It is a statement that completely misrepresents the facts. Kennedy isn't immune from making mistakes himself. His report includes a finding that it was inappropriate for the Mounties to have met alone at the YVR subdetachment after Dziekanski's death. The trouble is, they never did. Kennedy never corrects the error, leaving it to foster the misapprehension of willful misconduct and conspiracy.

A month later, the RCMP is rocked again when it's revealed that two members of IHIT working on the Surrey Six murder case that opened just a few days after Dziekanski's death have been taken off the job. One officer is charged for submitting fraudulent overtime claims. Far worse for the RCMP, though, is the revelation that Sergeant Derek Brassington has allegedly been having an affair with a witness. As a corporal, Brassington led the investigation into the YVR homicide. He had taken statements. The optics are devastating for senior officers who just want to get Dziekanski's death off the front burner. The allegations will eventually mount, forcing Brassington and other members of IHIT to resign in disgrace.

Through all of this, negotiations toward an apology and financial settlement for Cisowski continue in secret — at least as far as the public is concerned. Dozens of people within the RCMP and Department of Justice are involved. Lawyers from the DOJ float the idea of a settlement of a couple of hundred thousand dollars. Cisowski rejects it. The haggling ends when 1.1 million dollars is put on the table. That's when Cisowski balks. When she first hired her lawyer, she signed an agreement to give him 40 percent of any future settlement. Given Kosteckyj has already been paid close to a quarter of a million dollars through the inquiry for his work representing her, Cisowski feels turning over another four hundred thousand dollars isn't equitable. Deputy Commissioner Bass is the point person in British Columbia for the negotiations and an addendum is struck that Cisowski will receive a settlement of eight hundred thousand dollars and Kosteckyj will get three hundred thousand. With Braidwood's final report looming, Kosteckyj is persuaded to accept for the sake of his client. It's likely far more than any Canadian court would have awarded.

By mutual agreement, the terms of the deal will be kept confidential. In many ways, getting the RCMP to say it was sorry was more difficult than getting a seven-figure cheque. A large part of those negotiations takes place via email, using private, not government, addresses. It is a deliberate strategy to make many parts of the candid back-and-forth invisible to future freedom of information requests. It's likely most of the material would be exempt from release anyway, but Bass isn't taking chances. That is not to say there aren't hundreds of pages of RCMP and government email generated by scores of people anxious to settle Cisowski's case.

On the eve of what will be a public apology delivered by Bass, he writes to an RCMP staff relations representative who wants to know how the apology is going to be expressed. "Even though the word 'apology' worries some," Bass writes, "we are not apologizing for the actions of specific members or saying anything about specific actions. I am apologizing for the loss of her son and where the Cmmr [Commissioner Bill Elliott] says we could have done better, from my perspective, that relates to the fact that we had to revise our policy and training."

Bass clearly hopes rank and file members of the RCMP understand that the apology isn't an admission of wrongdoing. The four Mounties involved wish Bass would actually say that publicly. Instead, they are handed copies of the apology, already signed by Bass and Cisowski, and told that if they don't sign, the RCMP will settle without them, and Cisowski will be free to sue them individually. They don't like that it suggests they are guilty of wrongdoing. They don't like the dollar figure they see. They feel bullied into signing, because they have no choice.

There has been some tweaking of the apology from its original form. Initially, Bass was to go before the microphones and cameras with Cisowski and say, "Your son's death is a tragedy, and for the role the RCMP played in this tragedy, the force offers its sincere apology."

RCMP and DOJ wordsmithing pares it down to "I want to apologize for our role in the tragic death of your son." Another line — "There are no words to express how sorry the RCMP is about your son's death and the pain this has brought" — is simply removed.

Assistant Commissioner Al McIntyre leaves little doubt that the payoff for the RCMP has got to be a boost to its image. Before the big day, McIntyre writes to Bass suggesting he stand with Cisowski while delivering the scripted sorry. "I think hearing you say it in front of her will demonstrate the compassion/caring/acceptance of responsibility," McIntyre advises Bass, "and to seal it with a handshake/respectful embrace would be appropriate."

The next day, an RCMP plane carries Cisowski from Kamloops to Vancouver for what is supposed to be a secret announcement. The RCMP strategy is to invite media to an event without telling them what it will be about. Once again, the RCMP's ham-fisted attempt to control public perception fails.

As a journalist who has covered the case since the morning of Dziekanski's death, I have developed my sources, and they alert me to the plans before the big day. It troubles Bass and others in the RCMP when they get news of their carefully planned apology and settlement from CBC Radio and TV courtesy of yours truly. They want to know where the leaks are. They fail to realize the scoop only adds to the public interest in the development. Along with the words of regret and a dollar amount they keep secret, the RCMP also cough up twenty thousand dollars for a scholarship fund in Dziekanski's name at Thompson Rivers University in Kamloops. Cisowski accepts the fund, the money, and the apology in an emotional and teary speech that has also been carefully scripted by the architects of the settlement.

"I am not angry," she tells reporters who want to know how she feels about the length of time it's taken to gain even this admission from the RCMP. As for the four officers themselves, Cisowski is unequivocal. "I do not want them charged criminally. That's no help to me at all."

It is the first, and last, time Cisowski will allow that there should be a limit to the retribution for her son's death. However, while she has signed away her right to sue the Mounties, when it comes to her feelings about them she is bound only by her own animus and hostility. Both are soon to be reawakened.

Unbeknownst to Cisowski and her lawyer, the RCMP has tried to cover its bases insofar as the conduct of the four Mounties is concerned. While talks to settle with Cisowski out of court are in full swing, the RCMP enlists the expertise of a preeminent legal authority to take a hard look at whether the evidence supports the idea that the YVR officers lied about what happened. Lawyer Len Doust is an expert when it comes to perjury. As a special prosecutor, he successfully argued the case against Air India bomb-maker Inderjit Singh Reyat. After considering all the evidence, Doust hands the RCMP an eleven-page report concluding that the errors in the Mounties' notes and statements — "evidentiary discord" in legalese — don't meet the bar for perjury. "It is far from clear that the discord stems from any intention or recklessness on the part of any of the Officers to mislead the Inquiry."

Doust's reasons are not unfamiliar to those who know the facts: "Human memory is not perfect," Doust writes, especially when held up against an event that is "finely dissected and parsed with the aid of video recordings and many days of questioning by skilled examiners and cross-examiners."

Doust finds the Mounties' testimony at the inquiry was actually consistent with the video recording and the memories of other witnesses. Was it self-serving to try and rationalize the mistakes they made? Possibly. But Doust maintains that does not meet the bar for criminal perjury. Doust delivers his report in confidence to the RCMP just over a week after the deal is sealed with Cisowski.

There is little doubt Braidwood's interpretation of months of evidence comes from the same source as his first impression of what happened before he was appointed: the Pritchard video. "It was necessary for me to watch poor Mr. Dziekanski die a number of times nearly every day," Braidwood says on the day he releases his four-hundred-and-sixty-page report into Dziekanski's death.

Braidwood finds there were many who played a role in what happened, but Dziekanski himself is blameless. "Mr. Dziekanski in no way brought this on himself," Braidwood declares, summarily discounting anything Dziekanski did as contributing to the events leading to his unintended death. Braidwood doesn't ignore the fact that Dziekanski picked up the stapler in the critical moment before he was Tasered. It doesn't take more than a couple of viewings of the Pritchard video at normal speed to clearly see Dziekanski grab the stapler, and hold it at what appears to be chest height while facing the officers. However, Braidwood rules, on the basis of no evidence, that Dziekanski wasn't brandishing it.

In determining a cause of death, Braidwood acknowledges that Dziekanski struggled with police, adding to his adrenaline levels, which were likely spiking before the Mounties even showed up. Combined with the effects of the Taser, Dziekanski's struggles precipitated his fatal cardiac arrest. Yet Braidwood finds Dziekanski is not responsible for his own struggling.

As Braidwood knits his findings into a straightjacket for the police, he draws subjective conclusions from the evidence. He makes it clear that if the airport hadn't screwed up, Dziekanski would be alive. Yet, rather than apportion blame on the airport authority, he congratulates it for making "extensive changes."

There is criticism of some of the other actors in this tragedy, including Immigration officer Tina Zadravec. Braidwood calls her "cavalier" for telling Cisowski her son wasn't in the airport without actually looking for him. However, Braidwood says, "You can't put the whole thing on her shoulders … It wasn't her that discharged the weapon."

The Mounties are the real culprits in Braidwood's eyes, as they were before he even began hearing the evidence. They had no right to use the Taser, he says, and couldn't possibly have believed Dziekanski had intended to use the stapler as a weapon. While never offering a plausible alternative for why Dziekanski picked up the stapler in the first place, Braidwood leaves readers to infer the police were cowards. Sure, they admitted in testimony to making mistakes. They acknowledged what they got wrong. However, Braidwood paints their admissions as "self-serving" and "patently unbelievable."

His is a scathing condemnation that for the most part hangs the tragic ending to Dziekanski's ten hours in Vancouver on the four people who saw him for the least amount of time. Despite having gone to court for the right to level charges of misconduct against the officers, Braidwood never once uses the term in his report. He also never uses the word *lie* to describe the Mounties' testimony. This is not accidental. While some may say it's splitting hairs, a blunt accusation of lying or misconduct could open the door to a legal challenge that Braidwood is overstepping his authority and mandate. The words he chooses, or at least those chosen by the author who penned the passages that Braidwood put his name to, get the job done.

Braidwood's conclusions are not without errors. He describes the officers approaching the incident as if it were a "barroom brawl," the effect being to portray them as cowboys. The evidence actually shows the officers were calm and measured on arrival at the airport. A far more troubling mistake in Braidwood's findings is his reference to all four Mounties having made the same false claim that they wrestled Dziekanski to the ground. This is simply not true, though by dint of Braidwood's repetition of the notion, it becomes a powerful myth with drastic consequences for the officers.

RCMP Commissioner Bill Elliott amplifies the damning effect of Braidwood's report when he steps up to the microphone to address it. It's not clear whether Elliott has read the report. It seems unlikely he's even spoken to the lawyers he helped secure for his own officers. What is certain is that Elliott is utterly ignorant of the evidence his own organization marshalled for their defence. While he acknowledges the RCMP's training was deficient, Elliott goes beyond the carefully crafted settlement with Cisowski and identifies the individual officers as being responsible.

"We acknowledge that the actions of our members who dealt with Mr. Dziekanski also fell short."

It is arguable that Elliot's statement is a direct contradiction of the RCMP's own experts who testified the officers had acted within the scope of their training. Now, thanks to Elliott, the four officers who had hoped to get back to work and put the traumatic incident behind them have the wheels of a very large bus on their backs.

196 | BLAMED AND BROKEN

One of Braidwood's recommendations is for the provincial government to set up a civilian agency to take over any criminal investigation of a police officer involved in death or serious injury. The inference is that in this case there was bias. At least, the public perceived bias, even though the Commission for Public Complaints Against the RCMP — a civilian watchdog — was given unfettered access to the investigation, and all of it was then examined by the Ontario Provincial Police. At the end of the day, three levels of management of the Criminal Justice Branch looked at all the evidence and determined no charges were warranted. It is unimaginable that Braidwood's civilian agency, had it existed when Dziekanski died, would have forwarded any information to the Crown prosecutors that the prosecutors didn't have anyway. Indeed, had the agency already been in place, the result likely would have been that no charges would be laid, and that would have been the end of it. No inquiry.

That's not what happened, however.

It is eminently obvious that Braidwood's view of the Mounties is the same one that seeped into the offices of the Criminal Justice Branch, long before the release of Braidwood's findings and perhaps before his completed report was even submitted to the government. Before Braidwood even speaks publicly about his findings, B.C.'s assistant attorney general hires a prominent Vancouver lawyer and drafts his mandate to serve as a special prosecutor. Richard Peck will not only review whether the initial decision not to charge the Mounties was the right one, he will also mine evidence from the inquiry to see if there are new avenues to hold them criminally responsible.

When the results of Len Doust's analysis of the evidence is shared with the four officers in an effort to boost their optimism, they remember the comforting assurances they got two years earlier from government lawyer Helen Roberts, when she told them they had little to worry about over testifying at the inquiry.

20 | RED SERGE AND SILENCE

ON THE ONE HAND, the RCMP's deal to end Zofia Cisowski's lawsuit before Braidwood all but accused the officers of killing her son for no good reason was probably a shrewd financial move. If, however, the RCMP thought it would make the YVR incident go away, they were very wrong. In fact, as it turned out, the deal with Cisowski would end up ranking as one of the force's dumbest decisions.

Fresh from that painstakingly plotted public apology in April, Zofia Cisowski insisted she didn't want to see the officers face criminal charges. Now that Richard Peck is on the case as a special prosecutor, however, Cisowski has changed her mind.

"I hope, I hope Mr. Peck will decide to charge them criminally. I think like that. I hope."

The Mounties have some protection under the provincial Inquiries Act. The content of their testimony cannot be used as evidence in a prosecution. There is one exception, however: evidence given that is deemed to have been deliberately false and misleading can result in a charge of perjury.

There is also the reality of the four Mounties being convicted in the court of public opinion. Even when they don't say or do anything, events still conspire against them. When Taser International tries and fails to convince B.C. courts to strike down Braidwood's finding that the weapons can cause death in some exceptional circumstances, the judge hearing the case called Taser's complaint "self-serving." The net effect is to subliminally link, in the public's mind, the motives of a profit-driven weapons maker with the actions of four officers who thought they were doing their job.

Don Rosenbloom is raised to the status of national hero in Poland, for having so deftly made the case against the Mounties. Radosław Sikorski, the country's foreign minister, had been in regular contact with Rosenbloom throughout the inquiry. In the fall of 2010, Sikorski bestows the Order of Poland medal on Rosenbloom in a ceremony in Krakow.

The media moves on from the Mounties, but the officers are never allowed to leave behind the blame for Dziekanski's death. The RCMP, which once stood by them, now turns on them. Assistant Commissioner Bob Paulson, who will eventually take over as the top cop, determines that, all the other reports notwithstanding, the findings of Paul Kennedy and Thomas Braidwood demand that the officers be disciplined. Writing to Commissioner Elliott, Paulson says it makes the force look bad if the Mounties aren't sanctioned.

He admits the RCMP's own "loose" Taser policy and "less than ideal training practices around use of force" are partly to blame, but so, too, is "the conduct of these members."

Paulson lashes out at the senior officers in British Columbia for failing to recognize that the appearance of the Mounties rushing to use the Taser, and then making similar errors in their statements, would bring discredit on the force. Paulson concludes from Braidwood's findings something that Braidwood himself either couldn't or wouldn't: the Mounties committed assault and obstruction.

"How can it be that a retired court of appeal Judge can find as he has," Paulson writes, "while the Force seems to have reviewed the same facts and determined there was not even the appearance of a violation of our code of conduct?"

Paulson intends his question to be rhetorical, but there is one real, and opposing, answer: there was ample evidence that supported the conclusion that the tragic outcome was not the product of intentional, let alone criminal conduct. Those investigations included findings from the Criminal Justice Branch on down.

Another answer, however, could be that Braidwood made up his mind about the officers before he actually heard the evidence. Judges, even experienced, revered, and well-meaning ones, are human and susceptible to biases. So are police officers, for that matter. Is that so hard to believe, if most of the people you deal with throughout your career are guilty of a crime?

Whatever the answer, Paulson is concerned with the appearance of doing nothing to discipline the officers, and the message it sends about whether the force can ever investigate one of its members for misconduct. As a result of Paulson's analysis, each of the officers is issued a formal notice of poor performance known as a ten-oh-four (1004). Not surprisingly, the Mounties grieve them.

Renny Nesset, the officer in charge of the Richmond detachment, who was ordered to sign the notices, removes them from the files and shreds them. Nesset has never believed the officers were guilty of misconduct and it's his small way of saying to the RCMP brass that they are wrong.

The 1004s, however, are the least of the Mounties' problems. Each, to a certain extent, has retreated from the world. They are dealing with varying degrees of depression and PTSD, both of which can be traced back to Dziekanski's death and both of which have been amplified by non-stop public excoriation.

None of them are working. Bentley's boyhood dream of being a police officer is now a nightmare, although Makayla Lefebvre is one ray of hope in his life. By now Bentley has met virtually everyone in her family, and they think the world of him. That's when Lefebvre confesses to her mother that Bentley has been involved in some events she can't discuss. After Google offers to fill in the blanks, Lefebvre's mother calls up her daughter to tell her two things: She knows who Bentley is, and her opinion of what happened, which had been shaped by media coverage, has changed. The Bill Bentley portrayed in news stories and Braidwood's report isn't the Mountie they know.

Inside, however, Bentley is barely keeping himself together. When an email arrives from Peck's office suggesting he is looking at laying charges, Bentley is inconsolable. Lefebvre becomes so worried she calls Millington and asks him to come over to help calm Bentley down. Bentley is distraught and moved to tears when he calls up Robinson and Rundel by phone.

Robinson, who is already facing a trial for his actions the night Orion Hutchinson died, tells Bentley not to worry.

Their lawyers have Doust's expert analysis, which makes it clear that perjury charges won't hold up in court. Peck has a copy, as well. Bentley's division rep, Staff Sergeant Mike Ingles, is also telling him not to worry, nothing's going to happen.

Believing everything will be fine, Bentley and Lefebvre get engaged in April. The plan is for them to move in together at Bentley's place when they're married. His tiny Toronto home is a barren bachelor wasteland, however. Lefebvre is furniture shopping at IKEA when she gets a text from Millington's girlfriend.

"Have you heard?" reads the text.

"What?" Lefebvre asks.

"They've been charged with perjury."

Lefebvre, stunned, texts Bentley, telling him to call his lawyer. Bentley's greatest fear has become a reality, and Lefebvre doesn't want to be the one to tell him.

Robinson and Rundel also learn they've been charged in the same haphazard, informal way. It doesn't come from the RCMP. It doesn't even come from their lawyers. It's on the news.

Peck has indicted each of them separately with one count of perjury a piece. However, contained within each count are a number of discrete examples, called *averments*, which Peck has chosen from the testimony at the Braidwood Inquiry. The averments vary from one officer to the next, but each is based on the same allegation that, even though the officers admitted they were wrong about various details, their explanations for why they were mistaken, were lies. In essence, Peck is alleging the Mounties lied about lying.

The strategy of loading up a single charge of perjury with as many as ten separate averments, as in Millington's indictment, means that all Peck has to do is convince a judge that just one of those explanations is a lie, to secure a conviction. It's a little like placing a box bet at the horse races. A more colloquial comparison is that it's like throwing a whole pot of spaghetti at the wall to see if one noodle sticks.

There are challenges with Peck's reasoning. There is no proof the officers' original notes and statements were lies, as opposed to mistakes. If there was, Peck could charge the officers with perjury for what they said to investigators about what happened. Yet he doesn't.

There is another potential weakness in Peck's case, which is made clear by what the indictments don't say. Peck re-examined the Crown's original decision not to charge the Mounties related to their use of force. Yet he isn't confident there's enough evidence of excessive use of force to meet a legal standard of proof beyond a reasonable doubt. So, Peck's courtroom arguments will, by necessity, be contorted. He won't be able to say the officers did anything criminal the night Dziekanski died. Peck will, instead, have to convince a judge that they lied about their non-criminal actions anyway.

A number of lawyers familiar with the Braidwood Inquiry and the Mounties' testimony, even some who feel the Mounties are guilty, shake their heads when they read Peck's indictments.

Each of the officers takes the news differently. Bentley tells Lefebvre he doesn't want to get married anymore. He begins to shut down, spending entire days on the couch or sleeping. He's physically fit and has been a long-distance runner since he was a kid. Now he's weak and has no energy to do anything past noon on any given day. Bentley goes through with the marriage at Lefebvre's urging. Millington, who has become a close friend since the incident, is best man at their wedding.

Rundel eventually goes back to work in September, nearly four years after the incident that is still dragging on. He is put on desk duty, and struggles with the feeling that some officers in the Nanaimo detachment see him for what the media and even the RCMP brass have suggested he is: a liar who's brought discredit on the force.

Millington is off work, struggling with PTSD, the symptoms of which include flashbacks and nightmares about the incident. He's been diagnosed with clinical depression.

Meanwhile, Cisowski is frequently quoted by media, which have long since abandoned any critical thinking about the case. She says, for example, that the Mounties who "murdered" her son are on an indefinite paid vacation. Nothing could be further from the truth, as the calendar flips into the fifth year since Dziekanski died.

———————

For several days in February, Robinson shows up at the B.C. Supreme Court in New Westminster to stand trial for his actions the night Orion Hutchinson died. Robinson's penchant for wearing a pinstripe suit, dark sunglasses, and at times a serene smile as he walks to and from the courthouse, earns him no public sympathy.

At his trial by judge alone, Robinson is represented by a new lawyer, David Crossin, one of the sharpest and most respected criminal defence counsels in the province. Robinson's inquiry lawyer has moved up the ladder and become a judge of the B.C. provincial court. Robinson tells Crossin that he wants to raise the fact that it was Hutchinson who hit *him*, at high speed, and that the twenty-one-year-old motorcyclist's intoxication was far worse than his own. Crossin tells Robinson he can't raise Hutchinson's culpability for the crash: Hutchinson is not on trial. The charge relates to Robinson's decision to leave the scene and drink vodka before returning to deal with police. Even if he could bring up Hutchinson's speed and intoxication, Crossin says it would win him no points with the judge.

The Crown's final witness in the trial is a woman who testifies that months before the crash she overheard Robinson at a party share his technique for avoiding drunk-driving charges, which turns out to be exactly what he did the night in question: give someone your licence, leave the scene, drink alcohol to render the Breathalyzer useless in a prosecution, and return.

There's no question Robinson left the scene, telling a bystander, "I've got to get my kids out of here, this is gross," before thrusting his driver's licence at the man, and there's no question that the technique described is one that Robinson would have been taught as part of his own RCMP training in accident investigation. However, Robinson denies the conversation at the party took place. An independent witness from the party also challenges the story. The judge has doubts, too, given the Crown's witness is also a friend of the dead man's mother, and she came forward with the story only after reading about Robinson's actions in a local paper.

Robinson testifies that he can't recall a single thing about the accident and his only goal that night was to get his kids away from the accident scene. The Crown prosecutor is disbelieving. "What would your kids have seen? A Police officer helping an injured person? Would that have traumatized them in your opinion?"

Robinson is taciturn. "Potentially," he says.

In Robinson's defence, Crossin brings forward a doctor with an expertise in addiction diagnosis and treatment. He testifies Robinson's alcoholism is severe. Robinson has used alcohol throughout his career as an RCMP officer to dull the pain and self-medicate following critical incidents like the fatal encounter with Dziekanski.

It all rings hollow to Hutchinson's mother who, like Dziekanski's mother, believes there's only one possible conclusion. "The true crime," Judith Hutchinson says outside the courtroom, "is the utter lack of responsibility and basic humanity shown by the accused at the scene."

In reality, Hutchinson was likely killed instantly. In many people's minds, that changes nothing.

In her decision, B.C. Supreme Court justice Janice Dillon discounts the story about Robinson regaling people at a party with his tips on how to beat drunk driving. Nevertheless, Dillon concludes Robinson knew the technique and knew it would throw off investigators. She pokes holes in the doctor's assessment that Robinson is an alcoholic, largely because he appeared to function just fine for years. Dillon finds Robinson guilty.

204 | BLAMED AND BROKEN

Those who know Robinson are completely convinced he has an alcohol problem. Even though he's been suspended, Robinson has regular meetings with staff relations representatives, Staff Sergeants Mike Ingles and Scott Warren, along with his commanding officer Superintendent Renny Nesset. All of them realize Robinson is an alcoholic. To cover the smell of the alcohol on his breath, he shows up to meetings chewing gum and wearing too much aftershave. They agree he needs help. Ingles puts Robinson on the ferry to Vancouver Island. Warren picks him up and drives him to Edgewood Treatment Centre, where he is forced to face his addiction.

There is no question Robinson's conduct around the crash is incompatible with being an RCMP officer.

As treatment starts to have an effect, Robinson sees the writing on the wall, and decides to quit. Publicly, Craig Callens, the new deputy commissioner for British Columbia, tells reporters he wanted to fire the disgraced officer, but that the RCMP process for doing so was "absolute madness." It creates the impression Robinson beat Callens to the punch. Callens doesn't reveal that, privately, he actually approved an amicably worded medical discharge for Robinson. Robinson gets to keep his badge as a memento for his years of service. His red serge uniform, never to be worn again, hangs in his closet, still.

Although Robinson wasn't tried or convicted for Hutchinson's death, Justice Dillon orders him to write an apology to the man's family, and hands him a twelve-month conditional sentence. Hutchinson's parents are devastated, and continue to hold Robinson directly responsible for their son's death.

Robinson's legal troubles ignite fresh publicity that blows back on his former fellow officers facing perjury trials. Bill Elliott is gone from the job as head of the RCMP. His successor, Bob Paulson, writes an open letter to Canadians, protesting that the problem with the RCMP isn't its senior managers, or its training, it's "the few rotten apples you hear about on the news who demonstrate unacceptable behaviour." There is no doubt among the officers involved in Dziekanski's death that Paulson is talking about them.

21 | TESTING THE EVIDENCE — BENTLEY'S TRIAL

RICHARD PECK IS KNOWN as a lawyer's lawyer. Without a doubt, he is one of the most revered and distinguished criminal defence counsels in British Columbia — he is often described by his peers anecdotally as someone who advocates in court for clients who don't stand a chance. Peck's skill helped acquit Kamloops sawmill worker Ajaib Singh Bagri of conspiracy and mass murder in connection with the bombing of Air India flight 182.

His reputation has helped to put him on the list of lawyers to work as special prosecutors, even beyond B.C.'s borders. Some of those cases have run into trouble.

One has some eerie parallels with the YVR incident. In 2009, cyclist Darcy Allan Sheppard died after getting into an altercation with the driver of a car on a Toronto street. The driver, former attorney general of Ontario Michael Bryant, claimed Sheppard had been trying to attack him when he sped away, knocking the man into a fire hydrant. A bystander captured some of what happened in twenty-eight seconds of video.

Peck, serving as a special prosecutor in the case, dropped the charges, which included criminal negligence causing death. "Mr. Bryant had been attacked by a man who unfortunately was in a rage," Peck told reporters. He said the case was unwinnable because, essentially, it was the cyclist's fault.

In British Columbia, Peck is known for his controversial decision not to lay charges of polygamy against two leaders of a Mormon sect in the small town of Bountiful. Peck had been asked to look at the case by Attorney General Wally Oppal, a long-time friend, despite that the role of a special prosecutor is partly to remove any appearance of conflict in cases that may be coloured by politics or personal connections.

It is Oppal's successor who hires Peck to re-examine whether criminal charges should be filed against the Mounties in light of Braidwood's findings and the language he used to describe the police officers. There is a peculiar aspect to the appointment of special prosecutors in British Columbia, of which most people aren't aware. He's not only the person who decides whether to launch a criminal case, which could span years, he's also the person who argues the case in court. Peck's bill to the provincial government will run close to two million dollars by the time he's finished. It is at least an appearance of conflict built into the system that some in the legal profession believe should be changed. No one suggests Peck is looking to rack up billable hours, yet he decides to move forward knowing convictions are less than certain.

In his own clear statement on announcing the indictments against the four Mounties, Peck reiterates the charge assessment guidelines established in British Columbia: there must be a substantial likelihood of a conviction, and, if there is, a prosecution must also be in the public interest. The implication from the indictments, then, is that Peck has met the bar for having enough evidence. Yet, privately, Peck isn't sure he has enough.

This seems apparent when Robinson is contacted by his lawyer, David Crossin. "As a result of communications with Mr. Peck, I am obliged to pass something on to you," Crossin writes in an email. "As you may know, the Crown believes that the strongest case they have is against you. This is particularly in relation to the knee on the neck allegation. In any event, as a result of that view, they have asked whether you would be interested in entering a plea in return for giving evidence in the other trials against your fellow officers. In this event, the Crown would agree to a conditional sentence. Please call me."

Robinson, if he is guilty, knows he has little to lose by admitting guilt. He's already left the RCMP under a cloud. He would be able to move on with his life rather than having to spend the next couple of years waiting for a trial that might end in prison. A man who knows he's guilty might take the deal. Robinson declines.

Peck has also decided to pursue each officer in a separate trial, even though he amends the indictments to reflect a theory that the Mounties were joined together in a conspiracy. Peck adds new averments to each indictment to the effect that the officers lied when they testified they never discussed among themselves what happened. Conspiracy becomes the guts of the Crown's case. Normally, conspiracy cases are tried together, but prosecuting them individually can favour the Crown. Doing so gives Peck and his team of lawyers four judges and four chances to make the case that all four of the Mounties lied. If one case ends in acquittal, they can learn where the deficiencies are in their evidence, retool their arguments, and try again with the next accused. Publicly, the explanation is that Peck and his team are simply trying to avoid the problems that could arise in one big trial, with four defendants raising constitutional questions and using other trial-stopping arguments.

Initially, Bentley's lawyer, David Butcher, wants his client to be the last of the four to face trial. Butcher tells him that if the other officers are acquitted, it might mean Bentley's prosecution would be abandoned. However, because Bentley was indicted for testimony made while Butcher was his lawyer, Butcher decides his colleague Peter Wilson should take over the criminal defence. Wilson chooses a different strategy, preferring to go first in the trial order. Wilson meets his new client, who seems anything but the thug and bent cop that Braidwood, the media, and now Peck's team are making him out to be. Bentley is a clean-cut, all-Canadian kid who enjoys long-distance running and solitude.

The first few days of the trial do not bode well. Wilson applies to have Bentley's original statements to homicide investigators thrown out, on the grounds that Bentley was never given a Charter warning that his words could be used against him in a criminal proceeding. B.C. Supreme Court Justice Mark McEwan rules against him. In the courthouse lobby during a break, Bentley turns to his wife, Makayla, who has travelled from Toronto for the trial, and says, "We're losing. I feel like we're losing."

Peck has brought in a younger barrister from Ontario as part of his prosecution team. Scott Fenton does most of the heavy lifting at the trial, relying for the most part on the inconsistencies between the Pritchard video and Bentley's notes and statements. The Crown hangs much of its case on the argument that the police made strikingly similar errors in their descriptions of the event, which the lawyers argue can only be indicative of a conspiracy.

Fenton does not have an easy time of it, though. Several witnesses at the airport made similar errors when describing what happened for investigators. Some said they thought Dziekanski had indeed swung the stapler, that he did fight before going down, and that he had to be physically brought to the ground.

Once again, the media plays a role in shaping what the public believes about Bentley's guilt. When the Pritchard video is played for the first of many times at his trial, Bentley is sitting in the prisoner's box. His monitor is installed near his feet, and Bentley watches it the entire time the video is on. What gets reported is that Bentley "sat in court … with his head bowed as his perjury trial watched the now-infamous video of the confrontation" that left Dziekanski dead. The implication is obvious: Bentley was too ashamed to even look at the video.

After several weeks of evidence, closing arguments are given. As Fenton sets about explaining why the similarities between all four officers' versions of the incident must mean they colluded, McEwan interrupts him. "They don't have the exact same stories. I've compared them," the judge says. McEwan is alive to the fact that the officers used distinctly different language, even in describing the same event inaccurately.

Be that as it may, Fenton insists, they all described something that didn't happen. It must be a lie.

Wilson zeroes in on what he calls the lynchpin of the Crown's case, which is the notion that the four officers must have gotten together. The main problem with that theory is that there is absolutely no evidence they did. Bentley's time at the airport is accounted for down to the minute. While it's true he and two other officers eventually retreated to the subdetachment prior to giving statements, they sat in an open area with other officers around them. Robinson wasn't even there.

Fenton is forced to hang the case on an assumption that the entire coordinated plan to falsely describe a series of events was accomplished in the space of a minute or less. Not even Braidwood, who had the much lower bar requiring only a balance of probabilities, believed there was enough evidence of collusion.

Wilson argues what Doust concluded in his confidential report, namely that the mistakes can be explained by "the frailties of human memory."

"God help us if we all have to account for our lives frame by frame, because we're going to be in serious trouble," Wilson says.

As for motive, Wilson points out that Bentley had no direct involvement in using any force when dealing with Dziekanski. It was Bentley who called for an ambulance. "What on earth did he have to cover up?" Wilson asks rhetorically.

Justice McEwan sets a date for his decision in a month's time.

Wilson does not allow himself to feel confident in an acquittal, thinking it might jinx the verdict. Years of distinguished service, blending logic and reason as a defence lawyer and a prosecutor, and superstition still creep into the mix. Certainly McEwan's comments from the bench have been encouraging. This case, however, has the intangible element of being rooted in public outrage, fuelled by missteps and mistakes by the RCMP, and a media freight train moving in one direction. Dziekanski has been transformed into a character that is almost saintlike. Although Bentley isn't on trial for anything to do with Dziekanski's death, his ghost is summoned frequently by the Crown to be a silent witness who can never be cross-examined. Wilson is naturally apprehensive.

McEwan has scheduled his decision for two o'clock on a Monday in July. Every seat in the gallery is taken. Makayla has one. Her husband sits in the prisoner's box. At two, the judge's chair is empty. McEwan is not here. Two-ten, two-fifteen, two-twenty and still no judge. Bentley is nearly out of his mind. What could this mean? Where is the judge? This must be bad. When McEwan enters the courtroom at two-thirty, he explains there was a printer problem.

Bentley is still not in the clear.

McEwan reads through his decision, as is the practice in most cases. In doing so, the verdict always comes as virtually the last thing to be said. Until then, even positive-sounding findings from the judge must be paired with the sober understanding that the next words out of his mouth could damn the accused. However, as McEwan reads his summary it gives Bentley reason to think it may all soon be over. Point by point, McEwan disassembles the Crown's argument that the similarities in the officers' statements can only mean they colluded. McEwan says it's a fact that Dziekanski was combative; that he picked up a stapler; that he gestured with it; that after he was hit with the Taser he appeared to fight through it; once on the floor he was difficult to subdue.

"I do not find it surprising that they occasionally use the same words," McEwan says. "'Combative' is obviously a form of 'cop speak' … it would actually be more surprising if some such terms were not found in common in the accounts."

McEwan realizes the Pritchard video doesn't show what the police saw and, due to obstacles and camera movement, it doesn't even form a perfect record from a bystander's view. "The video must be viewed with caution," McEwan says. "The accounts of others who had a different perspective are of some assistance in determining what occurred, or, at least, in casting doubt upon the proposition that if something cannot be seen in the video it didn't happen."

Perjury is a notoriously difficult charge to prove because of the need for evidence that the perjurer knew their statement to be false when they made it.

"The Crown has advanced a suspicion based largely on circumstantial evidence," McEwan concludes. "There are other explanations, inconsistent with guilt of the accused" that can explain the mistakes. As for the Crown's lynchpin — the officers got together to create a false narrative — McEwan says he didn't see it. "About all that can be said is that the evidence does not foreclose the possibility of an opportunity for collaboration," McEwan summarizes," but there is no direct evidence as to how, or by what means Mr. Bentley and the other officers got together."

Bentley is acquitted. He bows his head into his hands, this time because he is truly moved. He is crying.

Makayla is crying, too. She feels like the weight of the world just came off their shoulders. Now they can move on with their lives.

They had discussed having children, but couldn't imagine it with the possibility of Bentley going to prison. In the two years she's been married to Bentley, it has been a struggle. There were regular arguments. The strain has changed the man she met. Makayla thinks he's mentally checked out. Bentley picks fights and says things like the thought of spending the rest of his life with his wife puts a pit in his stomach. Makayla understands that PTSD likely accounts for at least some of what is happening between them.

A month after his vindication, Bentley finds Makayla in their basement, running on a treadmill. "He's appealed," Bentley says after hearing from his lawyer that Peck won't let the case go.

Makayla collapses on the floor against the wall. "I can't deal with this shit anymore," she says. She's crying when she calls her mother, who tells her to hold on. Ride it out. After it's done, you'll be stronger for it, her mom says. Makayla only sees darkness and more delays before there's even a possibility that life will get any better for either of them.

Neither she nor Bentley know why Richard Peck thinks his case is now winnable.

22 | THE LAST HONOURABLE DAY

WHEN BENTLEY AWAKES on the morning of his acquittal, he has no idea whether his nightmare will end. Rising in his cousin's rented Vancouver duplex, he's immediately aware that whatever he eats for breakfast might be his last meal as an innocent man. Bentley is sick to his stomach, but he's a man of habit. He will confront the strangeness of the day with his quotidian comfort: a cup of coffee and Rice Krispies. Bentley finds a bowl.

———

At the same time, about an hour's drive east of Vancouver, Sheila Lemaitre grabs a bowl for a meal she will never eat.

Her morning routine these late July days is to amble to the bushes at the back of her three-acre property before breakfast, and gather enough blueberries for the day. The twenty or thirty minutes it takes is a brief respite from watching her husband, Pierre, drowning in depression. Anything can set him off, especially the media. So smartphones and other devices aren't allowed in the house: they could ambush him with headlines. TV news is all but forbidden.

Sheila has taken to sneaking glimpses of what's going on when Pierre is either in the basement or outside. A month earlier, during Bentley's trial, the media regularly reported the evidence that often

THE LAST HONOURABLE DAY | 213

followed the Crown's narrative of lying police officers, cover-up, and conspiracy.

This morning before Sheila heads out the door for her daily blueberry harvest, Pierre is in another part of the house. She turns on the TV and mutes the sound. There's hardly any point to being secretive. Her husband is depressed but he's not dumb. Sheila's certain Pierre knows the judgment in Bentley's case is being handed down today. The headlines confirming that news appear silently on the TV screen as Pierre walks into the room. Sheila isn't sure whether he sees it before she can turn it off, grab her bowl, and head into the yard.

Pierre is a shadow of the man Sheila married nearly twenty years ago. Before they met in 1994, the scuttlebutt about his arrival at the Prince George detachment where Sheila was posted was favourable. Pierre's reputation as an experienced, respected, and affable Mountie was widely known. After Pierre's three years of service in Bella Coola, the Nuxalk First Nation so approved of him that the band made him an honorary member.

Rewards went hand in hand with regrets, however. Pierre had married his Montreal hometown sweetheart right after training. In the years since, as Pierre went from one detachment to another, they had two daughters. After a move to Cranbrook, the marriage broke down. When Pierre's ex-wife began a relationship with another Mountie there, Pierre requested a transfer.

When Pierre walked into the Prince George detachment radio room where Sheila was working to introduce himself, Sheila had a good feeling. Here was a man with laughing eyes, gap teeth frequently on display from a persistent boyish grin, and a confidence that couldn't have come from a chiselled physique because Pierre didn't have one. It would be a couple of weeks on the same watch together before that confidence would surprise her. Fresh from making an arrest and placing a midnight mischief-maker in one of the detachment's cells, Pierre displayed his trademark forthrightness: he asked Sheila out to a movie. The oddly timed proposal drew embarrassing laughter from the guard who overheard it but in no time Pierre and Sheila were poring over a newspaper to see what was playing.

What Pierre didn't know at the time was that Sheila's journey through the RCMP had been nothing like his. It was 1985 when Sheila was accepted into training, just ten years after the force minted its very first female Mountie. Sheila's recruiter appeared to set a trap for her by asking what she thought of affirmative action. Driven to be a police officer, and just twenty-three years old, Sheila answered the only way she could: she just wanted a chance. Sheila had no interest in raising the flag for her sex in an organization that seemed openly hostile to these new female members.

While at Depot in Regina, Sheila went on a weekend sailing excursion with a fellow female recruit. The woman's father, the head of training for the RCMP, was also on board. As his daughter looked on in silence, he angrily lectured Sheila about why women had no business being police officers. Sheila's own father, who was a former sergeant in the Canadian Air Force, thought as much, too.

Despite enduring that blatant animosity to women in the RCMP, Sheila hadn't expected, once she made it to training, the depth of antipathy and loathing that came with official sanction. Male officers at Depot would single out individuals for harassment and humiliation and command Sheila and her troop mates to shun them. Many new recruits would willingly oblige by taking the victim's kit trunk containing all their personal belongings and dump it in the parade square. The male officers endorsed the harsh treatment as a means to test whether the women could be relied upon when needed to provide stone-cold backup to the men.

Sheila wouldn't participate, nor would she retaliate against fellow cadets when she was the brunt of the intimidation.

The intense indoctrination to undermine fellow recruits played out even on graduation day. Red serge uniforms, pomp, and pride didn't discourage some members from shoving and threatening others during celebrations in front of proud friends and family.

It didn't end there. At Sheila's first posting in Roberval, Quebec, some of her files went missing. When she discovered another constable shredding them, she confronted him in French. He replied coldly that's what he learned to do in Depot: stab the other person in the back before they stab you.

In Prince George, a drunken lumberjack who'd gone off the road in the middle of a rainy night fought Sheila's attempts to subdue, handcuff, and arrest him for nearly half an hour. It would have been clear from her laboured breathing on the radio call that she was single-handedly bringing in a difficult subject. Other officers would normally be expected to be ready waiting to help get the prisoner into the detachment elevator and up to a cell. Instead, when Sheila arrived, covered in mud, her male co-workers watched on closed-circuit camera as she fought again to get the man behind bars.

Over the years, there were other incidents, insults, and sexual harassment — the sorts of things that many women in the force endured. Sheila had made friends, good friends, to be sure. But it wasn't until Pierre arrived at Prince George, nearly a decade into her career, that Sheila met the person who made her feel accepted.

As Pierre heard about her experiences, he couldn't understand it. His time at Depot was memorable. He had made wonderful friends. "You just had a bad troop," he insisted.

They had settled on a movie for what would be their first date: *Schindler's List.* In Prince George you take what you can get. Sheila was impressed with how moved Pierre was by the film. They talked about it afterward at the local White Spot — a B.C.-based restaurant chain as ubiquitous there as McDonald's. Sheila sipped her hot chocolate. Pierre drank his coffee. They were so engrossed in conversation that eventually they were interrupted by an employee mopping the floor around them. He was sorry, he told them. The restaurant had closed fifteen minutes ago. Still talking, they went to Sheila's apartment for coffee. As they sat together, Sheila's German shepherd, Tiger, silently went to the door, picked up one of Pierre's shoes, and dropped it in his lap.

"Seriously?" Pierre said with a laugh, before saying goodnight.

As friendship blossomed into romance, Tiger kept his role as chaperone. On one of their first drives out along the forest roads for a hike, Pierre took one hand off the steering wheel and placed it on

Sheila's, beside him. Tiger wedged his snout under Pierre's hand and lifted it off.

"What is it with this dog? Do you pay him to do this?" he laughed.

A year later, when Pierre and Sheila married, Tiger approved. They held their wedding in the backyard of the house they shared. At the sound of music during the ceremony, Tiger retrieved the ring basket from the matron of honour, carried it to Sheila, then laid at her feet during the vows. When Sheila assumed Tiger would stay behind in Prince George while they went for a short honeymoon on Vancouver Island, Pierre insisted the dog join them. It was just one of the ways Pierre showed his heart, his willingness to accept and adapt, and his do-right attitude.

Sheila had seen how Pierre treated people as a police officer. Almost nightly, Pierre had encountered Esther, a First Nations sex trade worker. She had a mental disability and was clearly being taken advantage of. Sheila had a necklace from childhood she never wore. Pierre convinced her to part with it. He gave it to Esther and watched her face light up at receiving such a rare gift on the streets that had taken so much. During Prince George's bitter winters, Pierre enlisted Sheila in their off-duty hours to distribute coats, mitts, sweaters, and blankets to people like Esther who eked out a difficult existence downtown. Pierre didn't think of them as drunks and nuisance calls. They were just people having a hard time who needed help. This was the man Sheila fell in love with.

Years after he and Sheila had left Prince George for posts in B.C.'s lower mainland, Pierre's seemingly boundless optimism persisted. At the Tim Hortons drive-thru, it wasn't uncommon for Pierre to pay for the order of the driver behind him. He'd do the same at the grocery store if he saw someone at the checkout who looked like they needed help. Incredulous store clerks would ask why. Pierre would suggest they just tell the recipient to "pay it forward someday."

When Sheila eventually left the RCMP because of a persistent spinal injury from the musical ride years earlier, she developed a skill in guard dog training. Pierre became interested in dog breeding and

Pierre Lemaitre with his dog, Isabelle, living his dream as an RCMP officer before the YVR incident.

showing. He settled on the Shiba Inu: a fox-faced dog that many would recognize from the ubiquitous internet Doge memes. Despite the fact that Shiba Inus are known as hard to train, Pierre and Sheila did train them, then donated the dogs free as service animals to people with MS or hearing and vision impairments.

One of them, named Coco, would become Pierre's own canine helper when he developed PTSD. Coco was born in the middle of a blizzard, when Pierre and Sheila were living out of a trailer on their property because a cordless drill battery charger had overheated and set fire to their cedar deck, destroying their house. Living in a remote corner of Abbotsford all but assured that first responders would arrive too late to make a difference. Pierre understood that.

The dogs became Pierre's "Zen," as he put it, as he was promoted to corporal. He would need it.

Working at headquarters media for E Division in Vancouver, Pierre was approached by a journalist who alleged a pattern of sexual harassment by Pierre's direct supervisor. Pierre reported it. The next day the supervisor berated him and used his authority to transfer Pierre to Chilliwack, two hours away by car. Pierre was relegated to menial police work on a nightshift. It was a profound betrayal by his beloved RCMP. Anxiety, stress, and sick leave followed. Even after the harassing superior was discovered and disciplined and Pierre was offered an apology, it would be several years before his ambitions were restored.

Pierre won a competition for a promotional transfer to become the sergeant in charge of media relations for the RCMP at E Division. Effectively, Pierre Lemaitre was the RCMP's public spokesperson in British Columbia. It was 2007. Pierre was riding high again.

———————

His career was back on track when he got the call early on the morning of October 14 about an incident at the Vancouver airport. In the weeks and months and years that followed, the reservoir of faith in the RCMP from which Pierre had drawn his sense of purpose had evaporated. Stripped of his media relations job, he was transferred out of the public eye to a backwater detachment in Langley to handle traffic issues.

Anyone outside the RCMP and not familiar with the force's hierarchy and strata guessed it was a punishment. Internally, it was understood by most members that, while Pierre kept his rank, he had been demoted and sent to a dumping ground.

His testimony at the Braidwood Inquiry left no doubt he was innocent of any attempt to mislead the public. It was equally clear that at the time he'd been threatened with losing his job if he tried to set the record straight. But few in the media or those in the public outraged by Dziekanski's death had much interest in revising their misapprehensions about Pierre. At best, he became a gutless pawn in a cover-up. In some people's minds that made Pierre not much better than the worst people he worked with.

David Reichert saw first-hand what it did to Pierre. Reichert was a corporal in Traffic and knew Pierre as "a model policeman" and a "good guy" who "wouldn't bullshit you."

Reichert says Pierre was routinely berated by other officers, despite his rank. When Pierre approved a new uniform for Reichert because he didn't have one and needed one to attend a training course, the officer in charge of the detachment snatched it away when it arrived and then lit into Pierre. Pierre's authority to sign for anything was permanently revoked. Reichert says his bosses played a cruel game of psychological warfare with Pierre, ignoring his rank and decades of experience to hand plums, like filling in for the commanding officer, to more junior members. Reichert had known more than a dozen members who'd committed suicide. He'd come to recognize the despair that drove good cops to kill themselves. He saw it in Pierre's face.

Pierre was being treated by a psychiatrist and a psychologist for PTSD, anxiety, and depression. He went off and on sick leave. It was a comment between two officers that sent him home for the last time. "That's Pierre Lemaitre," one of them said. "He's redundant."

Pierre's decline was dramatic for Rose Johnstone. Rose first met Pierre when he walked into the small country veterinary clinic in Abbotsford one day, years before the YVR incident. Back then, Pierre was quick with a joke and laughed easily. They shared a good-natured but sardonic sense of humour and frequently swapped stories about some of the seemingly stupid things people can do. For Rose, it came from her observations as a veterinary technician of some people and their pets. Pierre drew on his wealth of experience just dealing with people.

"We were always laughing," Rose remembers. "He'd come into the clinic and it would be three minutes and we'd be rolling around laughing."

As Rose came to know who Pierre was and what he did, she'd ask him about the challenges of police work and how Pierre handled difficult situations. She came away impressed that Pierre believed most people he encountered were good people who made mistakes.

One day after the incident at YVR, Pierre had one of his dogs in for an X-ray and Rose quietly pressed him. "For God's sake, Pierre, what the hell happened?"

Pierre was uncharacteristically terse. "I can't say," Rose recalls him replying. "I can't talk to you about it."

Rose was convinced Pierre was withholding a bombshell about the guilt of the four officers involved in Dziekanski's death and over time she prevailed on her friend to open up.

"I'm not allowed to talk about it," Pierre told her. "I can't correct the press. I've lost friends in the press ... people who've had respect for me."

Rose says Pierre acknowledged his career had been destroyed. "All that ground I covered. All the gains I made are gone. I have no credibility."

After the incident, Pierre began to withdraw. He declined invitations that he and Sheila received to holiday parties or backyard barbeques. Sometimes Pierre would decide at the last minute he didn't want to go.

The man who once found it a happy privilege to pay for someone else's groceries at the checkout couldn't bring himself to even enter a store. He'd sit in the car while Sheila did the shopping because he was afraid of being recognized. If Sheila did convince Pierre to accompany her, a stranger's gesture in their direction became a finger of accusation.

"They're pointing at me," he would insist.

No amount of reassurance would allay Pierre's fear. It didn't help when he WAS recognized. Cashiers who saw the name on his credit card would ask if he was THAT police officer. Usually Pierre would suddenly bolt, and Sheila would make an excuse that her husband had forgotten something in the car.

It didn't help that every time the story came up in the news, Pierre's picture was frequently used as wallpaper. Not because he really figured in it anymore, but because every news outlet had his face in their files. TV used it as background visuals, or B-roll as it's known. Years after Braidwood absolved Pierre of any complicity in any alleged cover-up or conspiracy, his face was still dragged onto newspaper and web pages with headlines like "RCMP Spin Doctor." In the days leading up to the verdict on whether Bill Bentley was part of a conspiracy to mislead the Braidwood Inquiry, the media put up a fresh crop of images and reminders of Pierre and his role in it all.

So it is surprising to Sheila that Pierre suddenly seems not only unaffected by it, but his mood appears to have lightened. Sheila has been nagging Pierre for weeks to lay in a supply of five-gallon water bottles in the event of an earthquake. It seems prudent, considering they live in a rural area and they have ten dogs. Pierre had balked. He rolled his eyes. It led to an outright argument. But on the Friday before the verdict, Pierre surprises Sheila by announcing he's bought four of the bottles, and asks where she wants them.

A local farmer up the road is offering free manure. Sheila and Pierre have passed by the place many times on the walks Sheila forces Pierre to take. Her suggestions that it would be perfect for their blueberry bushes have, until now, been answered with sullen silence. Today, however, Pierre is anxious to take their utility trailer and wheelbarrow and bring home as much as Sheila would like. Then there is a trip to Costco for dog food. Pierre not only drives there, but he goes inside. He doesn't buy just one large bag. He loads a number of them onto the cart. When Sheila says they don't need so much, Pierre stops her. "No, you've been wanting to have some for emergencies ... for an earthquake or whatever." Back at home Pierre doesn't ask Sheila where they should put it all. He asks her where *she* wants it stored.

All weekend, Pierre seems like a man with a mission. He does a round of chores he's either put off, or that are too strenuous for Sheila to do on her own because of her spinal injury. The morning of Bill Bentley's verdict, as she makes the long walk to the back of the property for a bowl of blueberries, Sheila thinks the new medication Pierre is taking is finally working. For the first time in years, Sheila thinks she's getting her husband back. Pierre watches her go.

A stride or two before Sheila reaches the blueberry bushes, she turns back toward the house, expecting to see Pierre in the yard with the dogs. He's not there. Sheila is suddenly uneasy and walks back the way she came, empty bowl in hand. Walking through the door, Sheila calls out for Pierre. No answer. She walks down a hall to their bedroom. No Pierre. The house isn't that big, so her husband can only be in the basement rec room. It's where Pierre keeps his uniform and ironed shirts. Still holding the bowl, Sheila opens the door to the cellar and starts down the stairs with her heart beginning to race from a horrible notion that has begun to creep into her thoughts. At the bottom of the stairs Sheila rounds a corner. She drops the blueberry bowl to the floor, rushes toward Pierre, and begins to yell as if he can hear her. "No, no, no!" Sheila cries. "Why? Why?"

Pierre is silent. Unmoving. He is suspended in the air from the top metal bar of a home exercise gym. The noose of a thick rope dog leash grips his neck. The other end is knotted tightly to the home gym.

Sheila immediately begins to try to cut Pierre down. As a police officer, Sheila has seen many dead bodies. Her cop brain is telling her Pierre is dead. Against hope, against reason, she thinks if she can just cut him down, maybe she can get him to come around. *If only I can raise him up to loosen the noose,* she thinks frantically. *If I can just loosen the knot he tied.*

Sheila struggles. Pierre is heavy. Adrenaline isn't giving Sheila the strength she needs to raise him up. The knots Pierre tied are impossibly solid. Sheila scours the basement looking for anything to cut him down. Nothing. She runs to the next room looking for something sharp. As she let go of Pierre's body, it started to swing so that when she returns a moment later she has to stop his momentum.

Now armed with a pair of scissors Sheila tries cutting the leash, but the rope is too thick. Sheila opens up the scissors and uses the blades like a saw. She desperately cuts with one hand, while the other holds the rope steady. She expects that when the rope finally snaps she can lower Pierre to the floor and begin resuscitation. Just as she's through the last strands, Pierre falls away from her and his head hits the floor with a thud.

Sheila grabs a phone and calls 9-1-1.

When their house burned down in 2004, it took firefighters twenty-five minutes to arrive. There is no local ambulance service, and Sheila has to put her panic and grief aside, long enough to give the 9-1-1 operator detailed directions to the house. Sheila knows help will not arrive soon and she begins CPR. It's not easy. Pierre's airway is blocked by saliva and foam. The 9-1-1 operator is trying to keep Sheila calm as she works to get her husband breathing again.

Sheila pauses long enough to speak to Pierre. "I'm sorry," she repeats over and over.

Sheila is overcome with regret for not realizing Pierre was suicidal. For not knowing he had a plan to kill himself. For not being able to reach him in time.

"You're being recorded, Sheila! You're being recorded!" barks the operator, who assumes the tearful apologies she's hearing coming down the line are admissions of guilt and incriminating statements of culpability for Pierre's death.

Time stands still until the first responders arrive at her door and immediately ask Sheila what she's done to revive her husband.

"Everything I could, until you got here," she tells them.

The two paramedics move quickly, inserting a tube into Pierre's mouth while Sheila sits on the stairs watching the futile attempts to bring her husband back.

There are three Abbotsford police officers here now. Sheila is in shock. Grief is already taking hold.

"They killed him," she says to no one in particular. "They killed him."

A police officer at her side says, "I know."

After a time, one of the paramedics bent over Pierre's lifeless body makes eye contact with the police officer, and shakes his head slowly from side to side.

Upstairs, the female officer in the team that responded asks Sheila who she can call. As Sheila begins to think of family, she is suddenly aware that for years she was that officer who made the next-of-kin calls. Now she is the "victim." Knowing how this usually goes, Sheila wonders when the police might start asking questions to put to rest any concern about how Pierre died. It's routine, especially when the only witness utters things like "they killed him." But there are no probing questions to suggest the police have any doubts about what happened in Sheila's basement. Pierre's body is later removed and the coroner releases it that day without performing an autopsy. There is no doubt what happened.

The morning sun rises over the blueberry bushes and into the western sky. Sheila's confusion and despair at Pierre's decision to end his life sharpens with every new visitor who crosses her front door threshold. Sheila's phone begins ringing as word of Pierre's suicide reaches some in the media. One of her sisters, a neighbour, and Sheila's seventy-eight-year-old mother come to her side.

Sheila goes to the kitchen to make some coffee. Pierre loved coffee. So much so that when the level of the grounds in the ceramic keeper dipped to the halfway mark, it was imperative that he go out and buy more, without fail. Sheila opens the container and freezes. It's completely empty. It's now clear. Pierre knew he would have no need for coffee. The sudden effort to help Sheila stock up on dog food. The water and fertilizer. It starts to make sense. Pierre wasn't getting better. The meds weren't helping. Pierre had made up his mind to end his life and Sheila hadn't twigged. Pierre left no note. No explanation. Standing in her kitchen, an empty coffee container in her hands, Sheila is more alone than she's ever been.

You'd expect that at a time like this the RCMP would rush to Sheila's side to offer condolences and comfort. Sheila wants nothing to do with the force, but the RCMP officers come anyway and bring the force chaplain Jim Turner to the house for introductions. At first it seems to Sheila that the Mounties are focused on "doing the pretty" — holding a ceremony to give Pierre an official send-off while conveniently ignoring the hell her husband suffered. It doesn't take long for Sheila to become convinced that the RCMP isn't as interested in preserving Pierre's memory as it is protecting its own reputation.

Immediately, Chaplain Turner explains to Sheila that he will be taking control of Pierre's memorial service. He will pick the music, he tells her. He will vet any eulogy. He must have the name and phone number of anyone wishing to speak. Sheila is forbidden to deliver her own tribute to Pierre. Turner's explanation for the ban is that it's for her own good. She'll be too upset, he tells her. Media will be barred from the event, as well, he tells Sheila, in case journalists "pick up" on something she says.

In the days that follow, there are more calls and communications. There is the phone call from RCMP brass suggesting that if Pierre had only held on until he'd heard the Bentley verdict, he would never have killed himself. Sheila is infuriated. She knew Pierre well enough to understand that it would have made no difference. So the officers whose actions led to Pierre's pillory and humiliation are absolved in court? Pierre had no day in court. Sheila believes knowing Bentley was acquitted would only have deepened her husband's commitment to ending his life.

One senior officer making arrangements to secure a photo of Pierre in his red serge uniform tells Sheila that there will be other Mounties in dress uniform at Pierre's memorial. When Sheila suggests that she doesn't want anyone who attends forced to wear the red serge because it's a symbol of what drove Pierre to despair, she's astonished when the inspector from E Division tells her that "what was done to Pierre was done for the good of the force." The comment removes any doubt in Sheila's mind that her husband was a sacrifice. A deliberate sacrifice made in a bureaucratic, self-serving calculation to ease public criticism of the RCMP over the whole YVR incident.

As Sheila grieves, the pressure from the RCMP chaplain intensifies. Sheila wants to play music at the memorial that meant something to both of them. Back when they first started dating, Pierre would often put Jackson Browne on the car stereo as they drove. "Doctor, My Eyes" was a favourite. The lyrics are a poetic lament about having lived a life with the best intentions only to find regret in the realization about having seen too much. Sheila also wants another Browne song,

"Too Many Angels." The words allude to a dysfunctional relationship wrecked by lies.

Sheila is told the lyrics are subversive and could be misinterpreted as commentary about the RCMP. Both are banned.

Chaplain Turner wants to play a spiritual pop song by Josh Groban called "You Raise Me Up."

"Listen," Sheila tells Turner, "Pierre and I both love listening to Josh Groban but there's no way that song will be played at Pierre's funeral."

"I've used it before at other funerals and it goes over very nicely," the chaplain insists.

"You don't understand," Sheila pleads. "I couldn't lift Pierre up to loosen the knot at the top. In the end I had to saw him down and he fell with a thud. That will always stay with me. There's just no way 'You Raise Me Up' is going to be there.

"And I obviously didn't lift him up emotionally because he chose to leave me. There's no part of 'You Raise Me Up' that will be part of this ceremony. I can't listen to it."

The protests of a grieving widow make no difference. The chaplain is adamant. The standoff continues for nearly two weeks. Each day that passes he demands copies of the eulogies that will be read. Sheila refuses. He insists on speaking to the people who will deliver them. Sheila stalls. Sheila is forced into an unwanted conspiracy in order to overcome the wagons being circled by the RCMP around her husband's funeral. Sheila feigns memory loss, claiming that she can't recall the last name or the phone number of Rose Johnston, the vet tech who will read the main eulogy.

Saturday morning, the day before the service, Sheila is asleep in bed with her dogs when the phone rings. It's 7:30. Sheila is exhausted, dealing with pain from her spinal injury, and in desperate need of sleep before tomorrow's emotionally difficult day. She lets the call go to an answering machine. She can hear that the caller doesn't leave a message and hangs up. Sheila sighs and rolls over to go back to sleep. The phone rings again. The machine kicks in once more and the caller hangs up again. The phone rings again and again. Eleven calls in succession, back to back. All hang-ups and no messages. The twelfth time Sheila picks up the phone. It's Chaplain Jim Turner.

"It's you? You were the one that's been calling?" Sheila asks incredulously. "Twelve times at 7:30 in the morning?"

"It's really important that I talk to you," Turner says. The night before Sheila wrote him an email saying she wants to do a eulogy.

"We can't let you do that," Turner tells her. Sheila asks what he means by "we." He pauses briefly before answering. "You know who signs my cheques."

Later that day, Sheila's younger sister Shelley pulls her aside. "Sheila, stop fighting with him; he's not going to listen." The next day, an hour before the service, Shelley connects with the funeral director and switches out the songs.

Officers in red serge and in street uniforms stand guard at the entrance to the building at Fort Langley Golf Course where Pierre's service is being held. It's standing room only. A couple of reporters have been admitted on the condition they won't record anything and won't approach anyone to ask for comment, or "clip" them, as it's known.

Meanwhile, Sheila's friends and family work secretly behind the scenes to claw back as much of the stage-managed service as they can from the RCMP. In the end the RCMP's paranoia proves irrational and unwarranted. The eulogy the force wanted so desperately to vet refers to all police officers as people who often do thankless, dangerous, and emotionally difficult jobs. Pierre is lauded as a good and decent man. Perhaps too good and too decent for the jobs he had to carry out. It notes that both he and Sheila suffered scars from their years of service, but that neither complained. In some ways the eulogy is as much a tribute to the calling for which Pierre gave so much, as it is to Pierre himself.

Missing from the gathering is Lynn, another of Sheila's sisters. Lynn is nearly fifty years old, just a couple years younger than Sheila. She's been in care much of her adult life coping with a fairly profound autism. She didn't speak until she was twelve. From the time Pierre met Sheila, he warmed to Lynn and treated her like his own sister. There were invitations for her to visit in Prince George. There were trips. Pierre was often on the phone with Lynn to see how she was. The two bonded like siblings. But Lynn, childlike and easily upset, isn't invited to the funeral. Sheila's parents are afraid how she'll handle the news of Pierre's suicide. They end up telling Lynn Pierre died of a broken heart.

23 | POLITICAL PROSECUTION

JANICE NORGARD WEARS a Mona Lisa smile. Her face is dimly lit by the October afternoon sun bouncing off the building across the street into the boardroom where she sits. Norgard is by herself on one side of a long, wooden conference table that is so large there's space for little else in the room. She radiates an aura of confidence mixed with anticipation, casually tossing her shoulder-length brown hair, easing back into the leather chair, occasionally cradling a large coffee cup on the table in front of her. A coat to repel the creeping fall chill is thrown over the seat beside her. The sound of Howe Street traffic making its way through downtown Vancouver six floors below ebbs and flows through the open windows. Norgard adjusts her dark-rimmed glasses and shifts her gaze to the others in the room.

A tall, lean man with a brush cut in a suit takes a seat opposite Norgard. She sits up. Her back stiffens. She crosses her arms on the table in front of her. Vancouver Police detective constable Glenn Burchart picks up a pen and looks at his watch.

"Okay, so the video tape is on. It is approximately twenty-six minutes after two."

As any investigative journalist will tell you, in the course of working on a story there are "Aha!" moments when the discovery of one piece of information clinches a story. Those discoveries are seductive. They demand scrutiny to make sure the journalist isn't just seeing what they

230 I BLAMED AND BROKEN

want to see to fit some preconceived narrative. One of the first questions an investigative journalist should ask when dealing with a remarkable source is "Why are you telling me this?"

If you don't, you may find the horse you're betting on is really a unicorn. Detective Constable Burchart looks at the unicorn across the table.

"You understand that the door's closed but it's not locked and you can leave at any time ..."

Norgard chuckles. She has no intention of leaving. She's here to tell a story. A story that promises not only to resuscitate the withered perjury case against the Dziekanski four, but make it jump up and do a buck-and-wing in court. Right now — as Norgard sits with a half-smile ready to talk — it's on life-support.

The near-fatal blow came from B.C. Supreme Court justice Mark McEwan in his stinging decision to acquit Constable Bill Bentley just a few weeks earlier. McEwan found a critical flaw in the Crown's prosecutorial swagger: a theory that Bentley and the other three Mounties colluded to lie about their encounter with Dziekanski. It was weak tea. The Crown had no direct evidence Bentley said anything that he knew to be a lie. It was "suspicion based largely on circumstantial evidence," according to McEwan, whose ruling swung like a sledgehammer against the central pillar of the Crown's case.

As prosecutors ponder the way forward with the other cases, Norgard shows up at their door with the one piece of evidence they desperately need. Norgard's timing seems providential. The truth is there's nothing divine or lucky about it.

Burchart begins to unpack the gift Norgard has brought.

"So, what's gonna happen ... I'm going to just reflect back about the incident we're talking about here today and I'm gonna ask you to tell me everything ..."

"Okay," Norgard offers confidently.

While it's common for police to interview potential witnesses to a crime in their home, at their work, or perhaps at their lawyer's office, this spartan boardroom is nestled amid the offices of Richard Peck, the special prosecutor handling the perjury cases. Norgard and Burchart aren't the only ones in the room. Burchart's partner Detective Constable Ryan Smith sits nearby, for the most part just listening. Burchart acknowledges one more person for the record.

"Uh, Mr. Wally Oppal is in the room."

Burchart says nothing else to explain why the former British Columbia attorney general and past supreme court and appeal court judge is sitting in on a criminal investigation that doesn't involve him. Oppal himself is silent. He doesn't acknowledge his presence. He doesn't have to. Oppal is a legal legend in British Columbia. His name is familiar to anyone in British Columbia. Especially the police.

A couple of times a week Oppal can be found on a basketball court playing friendly games with a chummy group of cops and lawyers. Not bad for a guy who's seventy-three. The streaks of grey in his black, slicked-back hair give away some of his age. The lines on his face hint at

Wally Oppal, former judge of the B.C. Supreme Court, appeal court judge, and B.C. attorney general from 2005 to 2009. Oppal was a personal friend of Janice Norgard and sat in on her interviews with police and the prosecutor after she claimed the Mounties lied about meeting secretly before the Braidwood Inquiry.

the four decades Oppal spent in courtrooms as a lawyer, then a supreme court and appeal court justice.

Oppal's roots are as humble as his achievements are lofty. He's the son of Indian immigrants, and grew up in a logging town on Vancouver Island at a time when his parents didn't even have the right to vote. In 2003, then-premier Gordon Campbell lured him off the bench with a carrot: the job of attorney general. It lasted just one election cycle and Oppal lost his seat in 2009, but not before overseeing the province's involvement in key legal cases, often with a disregard for conflict.

When Oppal's special prosecutor wouldn't lay charges against the polygamists at the FLDS colony in Bountiful, Oppal appointed another prosecutor, then another. Until he found one who would. After serial killer Robert Pickton was convicted and sentenced for just a handful of the more than two dozen murders he was charged with, Oppal dismissed the idea of an inquiry. When Oppal's successor relented to public pressure, Oppal was appointed to lead the very inquiry he considered unnecessary.

Robert Dziekanski's death happened on Oppal's watch, too, though he had no publicly discernable role in the decision not to charge any of the Mounties involved. There's a good reason for that. There is supposed to be a firewall between an attorney general and the faceless lawyers involved in making the call, to prevent even the appearance of political interference. Oppal wasn't a typical minister, however. His experience as a lawyer and a judge made him feel confident that he sometimes knew better than the people deciding who should be prosecuted. There is a provision in the Crown Counsel Act that allows the attorney general to influence the conduct of prosecutions, by directing his subordinates to do something such as press charges in a case, or file an appeal. That discretionary power was rarely used by Oppal's predecessors. The previous attorney general never exercised it. Oppal did it multiple times.

It is inconceivable to think Oppal was kept completely in the dark about a case that carried the political implications and tested the integrity of the justice system in British Columbia the way this one did. Indeed, after his department's decision not to prosecute the Mounties, it was Oppal who launched the inquiry into what happened. It was Oppal who picked retired judge Thomas Braidwood to lead that investigation.

Now, out of office and no longer bound by any conventions of conflict — perceived or real — Oppal sits slouched in a leather chair at the special prosecutor's conference table. Oppal is acutely aware that Braidwood's condemnation of the Mounties as self-serving liars has fizzled in court, contradicted by a judge. More precisely, perhaps, special prosecutor Richard Peck and his team — hired by the province — failed to make the case for lack of evidence.

Peck and Oppal go back more than three decades as friends and colleagues. It's another relationship that remains unspoken and off-the-record as the interview with Norgard begins. Oppal turns to give Norgard his full attention.

"The reason why I'm here today," Norgard says while clutching her coffee cup, "is because my ex-common-law-partner's first cousin was Bill Bentley. There was coverage in the newspaper ... after Bill Bentley's trial ... statements made by the attorneys were that they had never found evidence of these four officers meeting ..."

Before Norgard even forms the thought and speaks it, Detective Burchart becomes a bobble-head. He's nodding so emphatically and approvingly as Norgard speaks, he could be mistaken for someone in the front row at a rock concert. Burchart leaves no doubt Norgard is telling him exactly what he wants to hear.

"I realized I had evidence to the contrary so that's why I came to Wally."

Two months before Norgard sat confidently smiling in the company of Vancouver Police detectives, she was angry. Norgard draws on a deep well of bitterness toward her ex-spouse, Brian Dietrich, a pilot for Air Canada. The two spent as many years locked in acrimonious separation talks as they'd actually been together as a couple. In mediation sessions to work out the financial details of their divorce, Norgard refused to look at or speak with Dietrich directly. They sat in separate rooms hashing out the terms while a mediator shuttled back and forth between them.

Now with their separation finalized, Norgard is forced to accept a financial settlement that is far less than she believes she is owed. It's bad enough the court threw out her application to have Dietrich pay child support for children that aren't his. Now the mediator rules she's not entitled to about $150,000 in rent from a property Norgard and Dietrich jointly owned. Norgard is furious at her ex, and there is nothing she can do about it.

Norgard reads in the news that Bill Bentley is acquitted of perjury. The startling verdict shakes loose a long-forgotten memory for Norgard. One that implicates her ex-spouse in a conspiracy to protect his cousin.

Norgard's decision to phone up Wally Oppal isn't altogether odd. Sure, Oppal had been a lawyer, a judge, and the attorney general. He'd also been Norgard's neighbour when her family and his lived on the same street in Tsawwassen. Their kids played together. Norgard was good friends with Oppal's ex-wife, Connie. Oppal was also familiar with Norgard's marital strife. But when Norgard calls Oppal in the days following her unjust settlement with Dietrich, she isn't interested in reminiscing about old times, good or bad.

It's early August and already the Vancouver summer has stepped aside for cool weather and cloudy skies. But when Norgard and Oppal meet in a downtown café, they move outside to get away from the bustling Saturday afternoon shoppers who might overhear their conversation. The two find a bench nearby, and Norgard begins.

"I think, you know, I might have seen something that was relevant."

Norgard then unwraps what could be a life jacket for the prosecution's foundering case. Norgard recalls a day when Bill Bentley and the other Mounties involved in Dziekanski's death sat around her kitchen table, talking and drinking coffee. Norgard tells Oppal her ex-spouse set up the meeting for his cousin. While her memory is fuzzy, Norgard believes the Mounties met just before they testified at the Braidwood Inquiry in 2009. Norgard tells Oppal she thinks it might be significant because of what she read in the paper, something about prosecutors losing the case against Bentley because they had no evidence the Mounties conspired to get their stories straight.

That last detail is certainly true. The main issue in Bentley's trial was whether he and his partners got together in the hours after Dziekanski died, hatched a plan to tell the same false story about what happened, and then covered up their conspiracy more than a year later when they testified at the inquiry. The Crown failed to prove any such collusion took place.

What was *never* part of the criminal case, however, was whether the Mounties had ever simply *talked* with each other about the incident *before* giving testimony at the Braidwood Inquiry. Each had been asked under oath whether they'd had any such discussions. They all denied it. It was a dead end for the special prosecutor.

Norgard's tale could change that. The indictments could be rewritten to include an allegation the officers had lied about having talked before testifying. It didn't matter that it had nothing to do with Dziekanski's death, nothing to do with colluding to mislead investigators. A lie is a lie. The Crown would be happy if they could convict the Mounties of lying about their favourite colours. Norgard was offering a bona fide "Gotcha!"

Oppal doesn't question Norgard about how she suddenly recalled this secret meeting from four years earlier, or, for that matter, how she forgot about it.

It's possible Norgard's preoccupation with her own vexing personal problems kept her from being aware that Bill Bentley had been at the centre of a high-profile perjury trial. Certainly Norgard knew Bentley was one of the four officers involved in the death of Robert Dziekanski. To Norgard, Bentley was more than a headline. He was family. He used to live in a condo within walking distance of Norgard's house. Bentley was a frequent dinner guest. Norgard would say Bentley was great with her kids. In better days, the Mountie house-sat for her. When Bentley's mom got married in Ontario, Norgard and Dietrich went back east to join the wedding party.

Yet as Norgard weaves her story for Oppal, a main thread is that she never paid any attention to the trial that could have ended with a prison term for someone she considered family, someone she was fond of. It was only when Bentley was acquitted, while Norgard fumed about her ex, that she remembered the illicit meeting he set up.

Oppal knows immediately that Norgard's hazy recollection could form the basis of a new indictment against the officers. Oppal says his goodbyes to Norgard and calls his good friend, special prosecutor Richard Peck.

When Oppal gets back to Norgard, he tells her Peck thinks her story is an important piece of evidence. Peck wants her to give a statement. A couple of weeks after sitting on that bench with Oppal, Norgard is in Peck's offices. Once again, Oppal is at her side, this time inexplicably.

Lawyer George Macintosh conducts Norgard's sworn deposition. Macintosh gently presses Norgard to narrow down the time of the secret meeting with Bentley and the others.

Norgard suggests that "somebody could pull his flight records, I'm sure."

It's a reasonable idea. The Crown never follows up.

Macintosh asks Norgard why she went to Oppal with her story. It's a good question.

Norgard sidesteps it. "I thought, well, after too much watching *Law & Order* maybe there is wire taps and these guys are — so I just said, well, you know, they did meet. I saw it. So I think I should probably do the right thing. I have no idea what they said, but I can witness that they have met."

Norgard never actually explains why Oppal was the person she contacted.

Macintosh moves on to other questions. None of them touch on Norgard's clear dislike for her ex-spouse, whom she calls a "buffoon."

As Macintosh tries to end the interview, Norgard squeezes in one more piece of potential criminal evidence. She thinks she remembers another meeting at her house between Bentley and "the black officer."

"He has got a weird first name."

Norgard can't remember much else about it and Macintosh thanks her. It's one of the last depositions Macintosh takes. A few months later he is appointed to the Supreme Court.

If Bill Bentley's acquittal struck a potentially terminal blow to the prosecution's theory, then Norgard's statement provides a seemingly miraculous recovery. It not only revives the Crown's moribund case against the Mounties, it injects the team of prosecutors with new vigour to go after the remaining accused. Peck and company trade their black lawyers' robes for deerstalker caps. They enlist the Vancouver Police to nail down the details Norgard has gifted them. Police wait until after the long Labour Day weekend to pay a visit to Brian Dietrich.

It's a weekday morning, just before ten when Dietrich hears the door. Two plainclothes police officers show him their badges and ask to speak to him. Dietrich is confused, but polite and invites them into his duplex. They all sit down.

Detective Glenn Burchart says little. His partner, Detective Laurence Rankin, does the talking. Rankin doesn't get to the point right away. He wants to record the conversation that's about to unfold. Dietrich has no problem with that. Rankin begins by using cop-speak. Dietrich is becoming rattled.

"I've explained to you that this is a non-custodial interview," Rankin says, moments after he turns on the recorder.

Dietrich interrupts. "What's a non-custodial interview?"

"You're not being arrested," Rankin states matter-of-factly. There is an implied "yet," in Rankin's tone. Dietrich is a witness, he says. "It's a serious matter that we're investigating. It's criminal in nature."

Dietrich is still in the dark about why the VPD is in his house. "Sure," he says. "I just don't think I've seen any criminal activity."

Detective Burchart breaks his silence. "I think it will make sense to you in a minute."

The police have caught Dietrich just as he's about to leave his house to get his hair cut. Dietrich doesn't work nine to five: errands like hair-cuts and grocery shopping get done when he has the time. The police still haven't told Dietrich what they want, but when Rankin asks if he can put off his appointment, Dietrich cheerfully obliges. He picks up the phone, calls the salon, and reschedules. Rankin thanks him for doing it.

"Yep, no worries," Dietrich replies. Little does he know.

The recorder running, and Dietrich now right where they want him, the detectives begin to back into an explanation for their appearance this morning. Rankin begins with a preamble that sounds like a veiled threat. "Whether it's looking at cellphone records, emails, there could be any number of things that the police can do. Where a witness is completely candid and forthright it allows us to investigate a matter without having to pursue those investigative avenues."

Rankin's implied promise would turn out to be false. The detective then launches into an accusation. "What we're here to speak to you about, Brian, is a meeting that you arranged with your cousin Bill Bentley at your former residence … in Richmond. We're here to clarify what transpired over the course of that meeting."

Before Brian can open his mouth Rankin warns him. "What you say here today may be used in evidence in court but you are most definitely a witness in this matter."

Dietrich is confused. "Okay, it was a meeting?"

"Yep. A meeting that you arranged at your residence. It would have been a couple of years ago."

Rankin isn't asking. He's telling. It's not an interview. It's a confrontation. Journalists employ the same tactic as a last resort when they've gathered all the facts, triple-sourced them, and the subject of the story refuses multiple attempts to respond to questions. Colloquially, it's called door-stepping, ambushing, or gooning. Rankin is gooning Dietrich on the basis of a single uncorroborated statement by his ex-wife. Dietrich thinks back to the last time he was at the home in Richmond he shared with Norgard.

"That's like four years ago you're talking about here. I have no recollection of any meeting four years ago. I'm not sure what you're talking about."

Rankin presses on. "It's the meeting that took place in your residence with Bill Bentley and other individuals before the inquiry occurred." Then Rankin turns it up a notch. He misleads Dietrich with a blatantly false statement. "We have other witnesses." In fact, there is only one witness: Norgard.

Dietrich is beginning to get nervous. He had always been close to his cousin. When Bill was posted to the YVR detachment right out of RCMP training, Dietrich took him in until the rookie got his own place. Even after that, Bill was frequently at Dietrich's house, sometimes with another Mountie or two, like Kwesi Millington.

Dietrich's divorce and Bill's transfer to Ontario affected that closeness, but not their affection for each other. When Bill flew to British Columbia to face trial, he stayed with his cousin. When Bill was acquitted, Dietrich was relieved. The whole extended family celebrated. When the Crown filed an appeal, Dietrich lamented at what he believed was a persecution, not a prosecution. Now a police officer is insisting Dietrich had played a role in some apparently criminal act involving Bill.

Dietrich is used to pressure, whether it's the pilots' old aphorism about landing and takeoff being the sheer terror punctuating hours of in-flight boredom, or his own experience of having engines shut down in mid-air. But this. Dietrich never trained for this. The interrogation unfolding in his living room is quickly becoming a nightmare at ground level. Dietrich is petrified.

"What can you tell me about the meeting that occurred between Bill and other individuals a short time before the inquiry, the Braidwood Inquiry," Rankin repeats.

"I couldn't ... I don't ... I don't even know what you're referring to." Dietrich then tries to explain that it wasn't unusual for Bentley to have colleagues over at the house *before* Dziekanski's death. "I think he met with them a couple of times, I don't know."

Rankin senses Dietrich is about to crack and feigns a connection with him. "Brian, I don't want to put words in your mouth. Do you remember a meeting?"

"I think a couple of times, it could be as many as four or as many as one," Dietrich says, adding that it's difficult to remember events from four years ago. Dietrich has no idea it's his ex-wife who is playing the role of the "witnesses" and suggests the police talk to her if they want details. "Janice would remember, she's good with stuff like this. I don't even remember it occurring or anything, I'm sorry but I don't."

For close to half an hour the detectives pick away at Dietrich's imperfect memory. He repeatedly tells them he has no recollection of the meeting they want him to talk about.

Detective Burchart either hasn't been listening to Dietrich or intends to trip him up. "Okay, so if we're understanding you right, it is possible that you call your cousin or your cousin asks you to somehow arrange this meeting?"

It dawns on Dietrich the police may have an agenda. "What? What I'm saying is that I don't have a recollection."

Rankin tightens the screws. "The problem we have, Brian, and I'm not going to suggest that you're lying —"

Dietrich cuts him off. "I'm not lying. And I'll take a lie detector. I'm not lying."

Rankin suggests that Dietrich may be trying to cover for his cousin.

"Well, I'll tell you right off," Dietrich says, "I think what's happened to Bill is ridiculous. It's a witch hunt; it's an absolute witch hunt and it should never be occurring." Dietrich adds that he thinks the Braidwood Inquiry was "ridiculous" and "horrid." Dietrich is now gaining his footing in this lopsided interrogation.

"I'm supportive of my cousin, there's no doubt, and, and I would not want to do anything to harm him, but I don't remember specifics about any meeting or even that the meeting occurred and that's not a lie, but if I did I'd be very hesitant to say anything, I'm not going to lie to you. I'd call a lawyer, you know, and I'd stop the interview. I don't have to because I don't actually remember it. You know, so I'm not trying to cover anything up because I don't have a recollection."

Dietrich announces he's going to call Bentley. "Unless there's a law against it, I'm going to do it. He's my cousin. I'm not going to lie to you guys. Is there a law against it?"

There is no law against what Dietrich intends, but Rankin suggests he could be charged "if this in any way obstructs with our investigation." When Dietrich says he'll call a lawyer, Rankin makes another implied threat. "We cannot stress how important this is that, you know, you are a witness and we would, we don't want to see anything like that change. We would hate to, you know, find out over the course of the investigation, if we're called upon to do additional work that you haven't been forthright."

Dietrich, now frustrated at being manoeuvred into this interrogation, speaks plainly. "You guys are trying to find evidence to prove that they colluded.

"I just think it's really sad. It's an unfortunate incident and the media got a hold of it.… They got six lawyers going after them and they couldn't get them, and now, like the resources being put into this, you know, it seems to be a witch hunt. You guys get orders. You follow them. That's your job. I get that, you know, and it's nothing against you guys but I don't think people should be going after them anymore."

Rankin knows he won't get any more out of Dietrich today and begins to wrap up the interrogation by getting him to absolve the detectives of their tactics. "Do you feel we in any way threatened you?" Rankin asks.

The detective has made it clear a number of times during the interview that the police have the power to make Dietrich's life unpleasant if he doesn't tell them what they want to hear. Dietrich believes his answers will also have a direct effect on his cousin's life, so he gives Rankin the answer he's expecting: "No."

Rankin is not appeased by Dietrich's capitulation.

"What I don't want to see, Brian, is fast forward six months from now and then have information that maybe we are not privy to at the moment that would indicate you *do* have a recollection of the event." Rankin leaves the consequence unspoken, the way a parent does with a disobedient child: "Don't make me tell you again."

But Dietrich is barely listening. He's more interested in putting something he *does* remember on the record. "You know, Bill, since he was a young child, wanted to be a police officer. In high school some of his friends started smoking marijuana and stuff and he changed all his friends 'cause, you know, he didn't want anything to impede his career as a police officer. He's been wanting to do that his whole life and it's ruined. You know, a guy with six months experience. He's just a kid and

242 | BLAMED AND BROKEN

he's been going through hell all these years and it's still going on. I mean it's just ridiculous and he would never intentionally do anything wrong for the police. He's always wanted to do this and his career is practically destroyed and it's just a shame. I think the people prosecuting him should know that."

Rankin doesn't respond. He notes the time and turns off the digital recorder.

24 | TUNNEL VISION

THE POLICE TREAT Dietrich's ex-spouse very differently when they sit down with her in the special prosecutor's boardroom that crisp fall afternoon. Then again, Dietrich didn't have Wally Oppal at his side. Norgard does. Her confidence is apparent.

"No detail is too small," Detective Burchart explains as he begins to get Norgard's version of events. Burchart offers an example of what he means by holding up his pen. "So if I was to ask you to describe this pen, how would you describe it?"

"Black, white markings ... I get it," Norgard says with a dismissive tone.

Oppal is also afforded deference. In the midst of a key police examination for a "serious criminal" allegation, Oppal is freely allowed to receive and send emails on his iPhone, which chimes a number of times throughout the interview. Rankin says nothing about the distraction or Oppal's activity. He doesn't give Oppal the same "keep-this-confidential-or-risk-obstruction" warning Burchart and his partner gave Dietrich.

As Norgard describes the meeting around her kitchen table, her eyes dart back and forth to Oppal, as if looking for affirmation.

"Anything else you can remember?" Burchart asks.

Norgard stares at Oppal as if looking for the right answer. Oppal is busy thumbing his phone.

"That's it," she says.

244 | BLAMED AND BROKEN

"In my estimation you've done a very good job here," Burchart rewards her.

Norgard continues, speaking as if the room is on her side. "Brian was addicted to games and spent a lot of time in the games room …"

She breaks out in a wide grin and a laugh and connects with Oppal's gaze. He responds with a smile and a chortle.

"It is what it is," Norgard says, the way a stand-up comedian asks rhetorically, "Am I right?"

Oppal is now chuckling.

All of the merriment, including the smile on Burchart's face, goes undocumented when the interview is transcribed for the purposes of evidence in court. Neither the humour Norgard employs to dig at her ex-husband, nor Oppal's participation in the joke, is noted. All that's written in the transcript is a generic and unattributed "laughter." Burchart gets the interview back on track.

"You recollected this period as January or February of 2009."

When Norgard first went to Oppal, and then the Crown, she wasn't positive. Something has happened in the past two months to sharpen her memory.

"I'm certain it's January or February of 2009. I remember them thanking me for letting them meet around my kitchen table."

Norgard turns to Oppal with an expression as if to say, "Can you believe it? Thanking me when they're conspiring!"

Oppal stretches his mouth into a grin of acknowledgement.

There's something else Norgard recalls. "I remember going down-stairs and making a joke about who had a gun. Like … it would be faster."

Norgard snorts and laughs and looks at Oppal as if it's a joke they'd shared before.

"I know it's a terrible thing to say but it's the truth. I can't lie." Norgard raises her hands in a who-can-blame-me? gesture. Oppal is laughing now. Burchart thinks it's funny, as well. "He was the only guy I was mad at in the house," Norgard concludes. It's the kind of punchline you might hear if this were a cocktail party.

Burchart moves on, and asks Norgard if she can remember the individual officers.

She has no trouble with Bentley and Robinson, the "native" officer. What the transcript doesn't show is that when she appears to struggle to remember Kwesi Millington's name, she looks straight at Oppal. She also draws a blank on Gerry Rundel.

When Dietrich claimed his memory was faulty, he was met with suspicion and threats of a subpoena. Norgard's imperfect recall elicits sympathy. "I know it's a long time ago," Burchart sympathetically reassures. "So the fourth fellow that you don't know the name of … you don't think you would be able to recognize him?"

"No, no. I … I … I can't." As she stammers, Norgard looks to Oppal, but he's back on his phone and doesn't see her silent call for help.

Burchart moves a white piece of paper across the wooden table toward her. A colour photograph is printed in the upper left corner. Norgard removes her glasses. It's Bentley. Burchart pushes another sheet her way. Millington. Norgard doesn't even let the third page get to her side of the table before immediately sending it back. "That's Monty," she says, barely looking at it.

Burchart is pleased. "Okay. Good. You've done [a] really a good job about painting a picture and talking about Brian's role here."

Once more the detective leads Norgard to confirm — *not recall* — that the four Mounties met *before* the inquiry.

Norgard obliges. "I don't know if it was three days before … or the week before, but it was quite close to whenever he would have come out."

Norgard looks straight at Oppal as she answers. Oppal, now patently participating in the police interview, nods at Norgard in agreement. If Burchart sees Oppal's gesture, he ignores it.

"That totally makes sense," Burchart says.

Oppal is now fixed on Norgard as she hammers the point. "I'm certain it was just before … I do remember distinctly that it was a weekend."

Burchart wants to know whether Norgard and Dietrich ever spoke of this odd, secret, and potentially criminal get-together. There is zero corroboration for what Norgard is saying, and a conversation between the two might help establish that it actually happened.

"No," Norgard replies. Then, without missing a beat, she fires off a bombshell with a smug smile on her face. "After he threatened to have me killed, I stopped talking to him."

In a room with two police officers, and a former judge and attorney general, you might expect the reaction to an allegation of a death threat to be one of concern or, at least, curiosity.

Oppal and Burchart laugh. "Okay, that makes sense," the detective chuckles as he puts his hand up to stifle any more details.

But Norgard continues with the punchline. "That's where the damn good communication broke down."

Once again the official transcript would fail to reflect the entire exchange. Norgard's final comment is recorded as "unintelligible." What makes it into print is Burchart's endorsement. "Okay, everything you're saying is making sense," he says.

Detective Ryan Smith, who's been largely silent so far, isn't so sure. As Norgard tells the story, she thinks Bentley was the last one to leave her house, because she said he could have "walked home" to his condo. But Ryan notes that at the time Norgard says the meeting happened, Bentley had long since moved to Toronto. He couldn't have walked home.

"Oh sorry, no, he wouldn't have been able to walk home," Norgard admits, "because he was coming in. I'm confused on that. That's my mistake."

It is a mistake that clearly raises a question about Norgard's certainty about timing. It points to a need to investigate the movements of the officers, perhaps by looking at the travel itineraries of the two who no longer lived in British Columbia. The police would never bother.

Burchart takes the reins once more, asking Norgard about her ex-husband's old email addresses and cell numbers.

"I found out he hacked into my email," she offers. "I think that was before he threatened to kill me. Yeah."

Norgard is now talking entirely to Oppal as she answers Burchart's questions. Once again, neither the police nor the former attorney general appear concerned with the criminal complaints Norgard is tossing out about her ex.

While Norgard hasn't spoken to Dietrich in years, she rattles off his cell number without hesitation. Burchart laughs the way someone laughs at a magic trick, and shoots his partner a look of amazement.

"You said you weren't going to have a good memory at the beginning of this. I can't remember my own ... now."

Norgard has a look of achievement as she and Oppal lock eyes.

———

As soon as the police leave Dietrich's house, he picks up the phone and calls his cousin, just as he said he would. When Bentley answers, he thinks Dietrich sounds shaken and hyper as he describes what's just happened.

A meeting? What is his cousin talking about? Conspiracy? *That's insane*, Bentley thinks to himself. Then Bentley remembers he stayed with Dietrich at the house his cousin shared with Norgard the entire time he spent testifying at the Braidwood Inquiry, contrary to what Norgard told Oppal, the Crown, and the police. It's only after the two hang up that Bentley guesses this has something to do with the time all four officers got together in May 2009, months *after* they'd finished testifying.

But the development is unsettling. The Crown has already indicated they are going to appeal Bentley's acquittal, and now it appears they've got a new allegation to throw at him. Bentley calls his lawyer, Peter Wilson, who is just as surprised, and advises Bentley to sever all communication with his cousin, who now appears to be a witness. The two won't speak to each other again for more than a year.

Bentley alerts his former partners. They have been counting on the verdict in Bentley's case to set the tone for their trials. When Gerry Rundel reads Bentley's email about the new conspiracy allegation, his jaw drops.

It would take some time for Dietrich, Bentley, and the others to learn the source of the new allegation is Janice Norgard. Bentley takes it the hardest.

"That really hurt me," Bentley recalls, searching for the words. "It really cut me deeply. This was a lady I thought I knew. I liked Janice regardless of her differences with Brian. I thought we were friends. So when she came out with these allegations, it really hurt me. Big time."

When Detectives Burchart and Rankin pay Dietrich one final visit in November, he isn't as welcoming. Dietrich invites them in, but only after the police assure him they are not there to ask questions. They just want to relay some of the "important changes" that occurred in the investigation. They tell Dietrich that Norgard's "memory had improved to the point she was certain about the date and timing." Dietrich tells them he isn't surprised, because his ex-spouse was "emotional but organized."

As the detective duo begin asking questions, Dietrich becomes upset that they've misled him about their intentions again. Dietrich gets up and motions them toward the door. Dietrich refuses to allow the police to record their interaction without a lawyer present. Burchart's notes of the discussion indicate when the subject of a court order comes up to troll Dietrich's email and cellphone records, Dietrich allegedly tells the officers he deleted everything anyway.

"That's not true," Dietrich would later insist. "I said I routinely empty my mail box. It makes it look like I intentionally went back and deleted the emails from four years ago when I hadn't."

The police had promised Dietrich they wouldn't invade his private communications if he told the truth. Dietrich had been honest. The police would get a court order to comb his email and phone records anyway. Search warrants would allow them to seize and forensically examine seven of Dietrich's electronic devices, including an old broken PC found stuffed into a closet.

Rather than yield evidence of what police suspected — that Dietrich was lying to protect his cousin — the computer's old hard drive surrendered emails suggesting Janice Norgard was either mistaken or lying.

25 | THE MEANING OF "HIGH" — MILLINGTON'S TRIAL

PUBLICLY, SPECIAL PROSECUTOR Richard Peck and his team appear confident in the case against the four Mounties. Peck is not only intending to bring forward Norgard as a witness against the officers who've yet to go to trial, he wants to introduce her testimony as fresh evidence at the appeal he filed in Bentley's acquittal. Confidentially, however, Peck appears less than certain in obtaining any convictions, even with Norgard's rock-solid claim that the Mounties are lying. As 2013 nears an end, Bentley's lawyer conveys an offer from the prosecutor. If Bentley will agree to testify against the other three, the Crown will drop the appeal. It's a bizarre proposition that would essentially require Bentley to perjure himself. There's nothing to think about.

Millington faces the new year knowing it could be his last as a free man. The past six years have been difficult, to say the least. While his friendship with Bentley has been a bright light, Millington battles depression. There have been days spent in bed, with the blinds closed. Therapy helps. Antidepressants do some good. Until this, Millington has been ambitious and goal driven, in his professional and personal life. He has always been focused on his physical fitness. Now that he is not at work, there is more time for that. He starts working as a trainer and decides to get involved in what appears to be a monumentally ironic hobby: public speaking.

His spirits are lifted when he meets Cindy Sztejner, a friend of his brother's wife. Sztejner is certainly aware who Millington is, though she hasn't followed the ins and outs of everything that happened at the airport the night Dziekanski died. She is not entirely clear about Millington's legal troubles when they meet. Sztejner is drawn to his personality. He seems gentle, which is something of a surprise to her, knowing he is a cop. Especially since he's *that* cop.

After a few dates, Millington invites Sztejner to ask anything she wants about what happened and where things stand. She comes away from the discussion feeling sympathetic toward Millington and believing that he did what he was trained to do. Sztejner can't imagine what it's like to wear the shoes of a police officer. She doesn't make a judgment about whether Millington should or shouldn't have used the Taser. She just knows that while the outcome was tragic, the lead-up to it was not simple, and it makes no sense to hold Millington responsible for Dziekanski's death.

As she falls in love, Sztejner comes to accept that their relationship for the foreseeable future will be defined by it, and their future together will be governed by it. There is so much about their lives that are completely out of their hands. One of those things is who the judge will be for Millington's trial.

———————

So much of the justice system is cloaked in arcane ritual, protocol, and rules of respect that it can be intimidating for the average person, especially those who've never been in a courtroom. The black robes, the hushed tones, the church-like decorum all contribute to elicit an acceptance that the edicts issued from the bench, which is physically higher than everyone else in the room, are based on wisdom beyond question. It's human nature to look at something that is the product of something mysterious and imbue it with almost magical properties — impossible to comprehend let alone challenge.

Just as the decisions about a case that are made inside in the courtroom can seem mysterious, so, too, are some of those made outside of it.

One of the biggest of these mysteries is how judges in British Columbia — the high priests of the church of law and order — are assigned to hear a given case. It falls to the chief justice of the Supreme Court to connect a judge with a trial. Just exactly how that is done is not made public. Whether the choice is made by lottery, or whether consideration is given to a particular judge's interest in the matter is unknown to the public; they are not entitled to know. Any questions to the chief justice and associate chief justice regarding that process, posed in the interests of promoting a transparent and accountable justice system, are rejected. One is not permitted to speak directly with the province's top jurists to explore such matters.

Questions to them are handled by Bruce Cohen, a former judge who has taken on the role of media liaison for them. "It is not a matter of them withholding information about the assignment process," he writes in reply to queries about the matter. Interrupting their work of assigning judges to explain how they do it will "make any further general comment by the chief justice difficult and most likely unhelpful."

Unfortunately, the response makes it impossible to weigh the merit of opinions from some in the legal profession who privately confide that upon hearing the name of Millington's judge, they were certain he'd be found guilty. The exact phrase used by several people independently on the condition they won't be quoted is "He's fucked." The general sense is that Justice William Ehrcke, who as a lawyer had only ever served as a prosecutor, is unlikely to put himself in the shoes of a police officer, let alone one who has been accused of being a dirty cop.

Millington is facing just one count of perjury, but it contains ten separate averments. The special prosecutor added one after hearing Janice Norgard spin her story of the secret meeting. Even if the four Mounties had met at that point, it's hard to imagine why it would be significant. By then, the Mounties had long since given their statements, which were already at odds with the Pritchard video. That was the issue at the Braidwood Inquiry. A meeting some sixteen months afterward couldn't change what they did the night Dziekanski died, nor would it change what they said at the time. The new allegation, however, is like another piece of spaghetti thrown against the wall: maybe this one will stick with the judge, even if the others fall limp.

One of the first things Millington's lawyer does when he goes before Ehrcke is to argue one of the allegations should be stayed, namely that Millington discussed the incident with the others before talking to investigators. Ravi Hira points to Bentley's acquittal. The judge who issued that verdict already looked at the Crown's evidence of collusion. Hira believes that applying the same arguments against Millington would amount to a retrial and an abuse of process.

Peck has hired lawyer Eric Gottardi as part of his prosecution team. Gottardi argues Bentley's judge never said collusion didn't occur, just that the evidence didn't support it. In any event, Gottardi says, the cases are different.

That is a matter of debate. Many of the individual perjury averments against the officers are either identical or — to use the prosecution's pet phrase — strikingly similar. There is also no doubt that the underlying theory of the prosecution is that all the Mounties acted as one. It's the very basis for their case that each officer is guilty of perjury: they knowingly lied at the Braidwood Inquiry after getting their stories straight. The Crown needs the officers to be linked. However, when the similarity between the cases threatens to undermine the prosecution, as in Hira's argument to stay one of the averments against his client, the Crown says they are different. What matters to the prosecution is preserving the collusion theory, even if Bentley's judge didn't buy it. It's why Norgard's story is so attractive to Peck and his team. "If the accused are prepared to get together to coordinate their version before the Braidwood Inquiry," Gottardi tells the judge, "surely they're prepared to do the same thing before being interviewed by homicide investigators."

Justice Ehrcke agrees with the prosecution that the cases are different, and "there is no evidence before me of any past, present, or potential egregious abuse of Crown power in connection with the prosecution of this case."

The trial is adjourned until later in the year.

In a matter of days, however, two of Millington's former colleagues who've yet to get their day in court allege the evidence against them has been tainted by witness tampering. Robinson and Rundel file grievances with B.C.'s police complaint commissioner, alleging Vancouver Police officers asked Norgard "leading questions" to produce answers intended to incriminate the Mounties, while they used intimidation tactics with Norgard's ex-common-law partner. The Mounties also question why the former B.C. attorney general was permitted to be present for their interview with Norgard, because he "has a vested interest."

Stan Lowe, who prior to leading the commission spent nearly twenty years working in B.C.'s Criminal Justice Branch, rejects the Mounties' complaints without making any effort to substantiate them. Lowe says police have broad discretion to ask questions the way they see fit, and while Oppal's involvement "is by no means common practice," it wasn't against the law.

———

It isn't until late November that Millington is back in the prisoner's box, now more than seven years since those few seconds altered so many lives, including his own.

Among the first witnesses to be called are those first heard by Braidwood. Airport security guard Sidharth Arora testifies that, from what he saw, Dziekanski was hostile and uncooperative with the RCMP. He thought he saw Dziekanski swing the stapler, just as the Mounties did. Limo driver Lorne Meltzer tells justice Ehrcke he saw Dziekanski "lunge forward" at the RCMP officers with the stapler held above his head. While both observations can be said to be false, what's important to Millington's defence is that they are similar to the errors all four officers made. Lance Rudek, another YVR security guard, shows the court how Dziekanski held the stapler toward the officers, squeezing off staples before he was Tasered. The re-enactment causes Dziekanski's mother, who's sitting in the gallery, to cover her face while she cries.

Bob Ginter, the airport response coordinator who chose not to call in his own first responders, testifies Dziekanski was a danger to the public. Asked if he was scared to approach him in the International Arrivals lounge, Ginter replies, "I wasn't going in there."

At this point, Ehrcke, who seems less interested in the evidence than something he spots in his courtroom, interrupts Millington's lawyer mid-sentence. "Just a moment," Ehrcke says, stopping the trial, "someone has entered the courtroom apparently with audio recording equipment. Does anyone have a concern about that?"

Ehrcke looks down from his bench, staring at a journalist who's been at the trial since it began. Ehrcke appears unaware of his own court's rules, which allow accredited media to record proceedings for note-taking purposes. The journalist identifies himself as such, expecting that will be satisfactory. However, Ehrcke isn't satisfied. "Nobody has any concern about that?" he asks the prosecutor and defence lawyers. The question hangs in the air. Ehrcke has effectively opened the door for lawyers with vested interests to decide whether the media can do their job in his courtroom. Fortunately, there is no objection.

When Norgard appears as a witness, her disdain for Dietrich is palpable. In order to establish her story, the Crown has to establish he was no longer living with Norgard in February 2009 when she says Dietrich called her wanting to hold the secret meeting at her house. When Norgard is presented with records such as phone and cable bills that cast doubt on that, she doesn't agree. When it's put to her that she provided the bills to the Crown, she testifies she doesn't know what she handed to prosecutors because it was in an envelope. She even refuses to examine her own personal emails that contradict her story, because she says Dietrich could have forged them. When it's put to her that the meeting happened, but it was months after the officers had finished testifying, she refuses to accept she might be wrong.

The next day, the Crown acknowledges to the court that the Vancouver Police seized and conducted a forensic examination on seven of Dietrich's electronic devices, including several computers, an external hard drive, an iPhone, and a BlackBerry. The police got a warrant to force Dietrich's internet service provider to comb through his emails. As well, investigators scanned as many as five hundred of his text messages. Anything made of paper in Dietrich's possession that might be used to arrange or record or mention the meeting Janice Norgard says happened before the officers testified, was also swept up by police. They found nothing. Shaky as it appears, the Crown rests its case, giving way for Hira to mount a defence of his client. Before doing so, he tries to have the case tossed out of court. Technically, it's a motion of "no evidence," which, if successful, would result in acquittal. It's a long shot, but one worth trying given the evidence is circumstantial and all but one of the allegations of perjury relate to what Millington really thought but wouldn't admit.

"It is questionable whether there's any evidence capable of establishing what Constable Millington believed, saw, realized, and or thought during the events surrounding Mr. Dziekanski's death," Hira argues. "Human memory and human perception does not operate like a video camera."

One by one, Hira runs through each of the averments, arguing they are suspicions, with nothing to back them up. But it's at this point Millington begins to think Ehrcke will not let him leave his courtroom an innocent man.

During the Braidwood Inquiry, Millington had been asked to account for why he told homicide investigators that Dziekanski raised the stapler "high." He testified that he never said Dziekanski held the stapler above his head or shoulders, just that it was high. Depending on the circumstances, that could mean above the waist. Millington testified that, as a police officer, if he told someone to raise their hands "high," that person would be compliant if they held their hands at chest level, as long as he could see their palms. The perjury allegation is based on only one of Millington's exchanges during three days of testimony, in which he just says "high" can mean above the waist but below the shoulders.

As Hira attempts to explain why the indictment doesn't actually reflect what Millington said at the inquiry, Ehrcke cuts him off. "It's not *Alice in Wonderland*," Ehrcke says, sounding frustrated. "Or Humpty

Dumpty, who says words can mean whatever I want them to mean. That isn't the way it works. Words have a meaning."

Hira argues Millington can't be convicted for his own thoughts about how high a suspect should have their hands when so ordered.

"It's patently implausible," Ehrcke says, before he rules against the motion.

Cisowski, who has been in the gallery, loudly calls out "Murderer!" as she glares at Millington in the prisoner's box. She is stopped by the sheriff, who ushers her out.

It is during her son's trial that Cynthia Hewitt meets Dziekanski's mother. On a break, the quiet, graceful woman slips out of the courtroom and finds a bench in the carpeted waiting area beneath the glass roof of the building's atrium. Cisowski walks by, half speaking to herself and half to whoever might be near. Hewitt isn't sure who the woman is at first, when Cisowski looks her right in the face and says, "Seven years and I have no son."

Hewitt introduces herself as Millington's mother. Cisowski goes quiet and then declares that Hewitt's son and the other three officers killed her child and she will never forgive them. Cisowski is angry. Hewitt, a Christian who considers herself a woman of faith, does her best to be compassionate, telling Cisowski that no one can live without forgiveness. "I'm sorry," she says, one mother to another. Cisowski repeats that she can never forgive Millington, and walks away.

Prosecutor Scott Fenton provides forty-five pages of written submissions as to why Millington should not be acquitted. "The answers given by the accused are in the category of the absurd," Fenton says about Millington's use of the word *high*. "They are on the face of them preposterous answers." Fenton does, however, appear to back away from his star witness, Janice Norgard, telling Ehrcke that what can be said about her testimony is that she says a meeting happened.

Ehrcke says he needs time to consider whether the trial should proceed, though there's little doubt among those who've heard him so far. The trial is adjourned again. It is early in the new year, 2015, when Millington returns to Vancouver once more from Toronto for what he hopes will an acquittal. It is not to be. Ehrcke rules the trial must continue.

Hira has anticipated the result, and months ago came to the conclusion that Millington should testify on his own behalf. It is an unexpected decision for those just learning of it. On one hand, it's a risk. None of the other officers will testify at their trials, for good reason. It's easy to get tripped up in the witness chair. It can be frightening, especially when the lawyer doing the cross-examination is both capable and has a point to prove. There is often an enormous intellectual gap between lawyer and witness. It's not an even playing field. It's like giving your client the ball and telling them to score a touchdown when they don't even know where the end zone is.

In Millington's case, however, there is a danger of the judge forming an impression of him based on the Pritchard video and what Ehrcke has already said he believes are implausible, *Alice in Wonderland* rationalizations. If Millington can demonstrate he is calm, thoughtful, and sincere, that might raise enough doubt in this case made up entirely of circumstantial evidence.

Sztejner has come to Vancouver with Millington to offer moral support. The night before he sits in the witness chair is tough. There is no sleep. Cisowski is once more in the courtroom, as Millington is taken by his lawyer through the events of Dziekanski's death. She dabs her eyes with tissue as Millington recalls what happened. He admits that his memory is "based on the video at this point." Yet he recalls that Dziekanski "had a stapler in one hand and a fist in the other … at chest height." Millington testifies he thought Dziekanski was going to attack them.

Hira gives Millington an opportunity to describe how shocked he felt by what happened. "It was a traumatic incident. I'd never been to a call where someone passed."

He testifies he has no memory of talking to his partners about the details and doesn't think he did, because he was trained not to. Millington destroys Norgard's claim that all four met prior to testifying, when he uses bank debit card transactions to prove he was in Toronto when Norgard said he was in Vancouver. As for trying to mislead the

258 | BLAMED AND BROKEN

inquiry, Millington repeatedly insists that's not the case. Millington is coming across as relaxed and confident.

Prosecutor Scott Fenton wastes no time trying to rattle Millington's calm exterior when he gets the chance. Fenton puts it to Millington that his statements after Dziekanski died were intended to make him sound "like a bear of a man" and "superhuman" in order to justify his use of force and to fire the Taser more than once. Millington disagrees, admitting he made a mistake about whether Dziekanski was standing when he pulled the trigger a second time. "I was trying to recollect as good as I can, but I guess I made a mistake," Millington replies.

"I'm going to suggest to you that as you sit here today, you realize that this answer is very problematic for you," Fenton counters. "It suggests your testimony at the Braidwood Inquiry is therefore false." Fenton presses, "I'm going to suggest you weren't confused at the time, and I'm going to suggest you're not confused right now and I'll spend all afternoon on this if necessary."

Fenton acknowledges the obvious when he concedes that Millington is not on trial for his use of force. Yet during the trial he spends more than a day focused on Millington's use of the Taser. It is during this grilling that Millington is asked whether he was aware at the time Dziekanski died that he would have to justify his use of the Taser. He is also asked if, at the time, he understood that if Dziekanski was already on the ground he wouldn't have been justified in firing the Taser a second time. In both cases, Millington gives honest answers, indicating that of course he knew what his duty to account would be and what his training suggested. Those admissions will come back to haunt him as sufficient evidence for a motive to lie.

During one of the breaks, as Millington and Sztejner exit the courtroom, Cisowski makes a beeline for them, a smile on her face, and in her hand a tiny novelty stapler, no bigger than a few centimetres long. She tries to offer it to Millington as a "gift." Millington says nothing as he moves quickly away. Cisowski is reminded again by the sheriffs to refrain from making a scene.

In his closing arguments, Fenton scoffs at Millington's explanation that his mistakes were the product of what his lawyer said was a "fast-moving, novel, and traumatic situation." He then invites Ehrcke to watch the Pritchard video in slow motion, stopping it every few frames to highlight what was happening, apparently unaware of the irony. "Slowing down the video certainly enhances one's ability to see what's happening between each of the seconds," Fenton says. Fenton offers no evidence that the officers did collude, telling Ehrcke it isn't needed to find that they did.

At times Ehrcke appears unsure of the evidence. "Do we know that he did not fire any staples?" Ehrcke asks Fenton about Dziekanski wielding the stapler.

At least one witness had seen Dziekanski squeeze the stapler and staples fall to the carpet. A police investigator photographed the staples on the carpet. "I believe the evidence is he did not fire any staples," Fenton quickly answers. It's not true.

"I have to be careful about not making any statements of fact," Ehrcke confides to the prosecutor. "Looking at the video … people are not running for the exits. It doesn't appear as though the civilians on the public side are fearful for their own safety."

Ehrcke's statement reveals his almost complete reliance on an interpretation of the video put forward by the Crown that Dziekanski posed no threat. The statements of people who were actually there, which Ehrcke should be aware of, tell a different story.

When Hira makes the incontrovertible statement of fact that Dziekanski "acquired the stapler to use as a weapon … a reasonable inference by the officers," Ehrcke disagrees. "None of us knows what was going through his mind," he says of Dziekanski.

Hira addresses Ehrcke's *Alice in Wonderland* analysis by successfully arguing to allow the testimony of Vancouver Police Sergeant Brad Fawcett, an expert in the use of force. Fawcett not only says Millington's actions were justified, but also that his use of the word *high* in the sense he meant it was reasonable.

Hira also counters with what sounds like common sense. Why would Millington lie when he knew the whole thing had been videotaped?

The officers knew the stapler would be defined by the Criminal Code of Canada as a weapon, so there was no worry about justification for their use of force. Hira also maintains that Millington's claim that he thought Dziekanski was still standing when he fired a second time is consistent with someone telling the truth. "Is the Crown alleging that Constable Millington for some reason wanted to repeatedly Taser someone to death?" Hira asks. "There is no allegation that Millington was 'a trigger-happy cop.'"

There are, however, ten allegations that he lied, and Ehrcke has only to decide that one of them is valid to send Millington to prison. Weeks before the trial ends, Ehrcke sets the date for his decision. Millington thinks the judge has a verdict in mind when Ehrcke tells him to come back in a month to hear it.

26 | TWELVE STEPS – ROBINSON'S TRIAL

RATHER THAN RETREAT into retirement, Monty Robinson finds a new career in documenting as much as possible ahead of his own trial for perjury. A casual observer might conclude Robinson has traded alcohol for paranoia as he methodically leverages freedom of information laws to examine the usually darkened back channels of the RCMP, the Criminal Justice Branch, and other agencies. Robinson, the central figure in what special prosecutor Richard Peck argues was a conspiracy to mislead investigators, becomes an investigator himself in his own case. When he invites a reporter to his house in Delta because he says he wants to show them something, there's a half-expectation that upon opening his front door, the floor and walls will be found covered with plastic because he intends a messy end for one of his media critics. Instead, Robinson opens his life to scrutiny, answering questions about the good and the bad, because at the end of the day he believes the truth of what happened the night Dziekanski died will be understood and he and the others will be exonerated. He is wrong.

In the days leading up to his perjury trial, Robinson becomes increasingly anxious to detail for the judge hearing his case why he thinks the perjury charges against all four Mounties amount to a political prosecution to hold someone responsible for Dziekanski's death. He emails his lawyer, David Crossin, asking him to make that case at trial. "It's all there to call it out as political, you just do not want to,"

Robinson writes. "The three constables were at the Sub Detachment with S/Sgt Mike Ingles and I was with IHIT. Crown still charged me with colluding with the other three at the Sub Detachment that night. How is that not political?" Robinson wants Crossin to play the video of Norgard's police interview with Oppal in court. "This may not be the time or forum but what is?"

Crossin is diplomatic, but as a seasoned criminal defence counsel, he knows he wouldn't get five minutes into a speech about trumped-up charges before he was shut down. "You want me to somehow raise the issue that these charges are political," Crossin writes. "I'm not sure what you mean by that but I assume you mean that the Crown did not approve these charges in good faith nor are they proceeding to prosecute these charges in good faith but are motivated by improper or political considerations."

Crossin acknowledges he is bound to do what Robinson instructs him to do, but it "must be based on evidence or circumstances that are reasonable and not speculative. I simply do not appreciate how I can properly raise this issue at your trial." Crossin is at a crossroads. "In fact, if I am not of the view that there is a proper foundation to do this I am ethically obligated not to do this. You must make a decision in this regard."

As for alleging that Oppal is somehow involved in witness tampering, knowingly or otherwise, Crossin is reluctant to even consider it. "These would be of course very serious allegations indeed," he tells Robinson. "I cannot pursue this without firm evidence; as opposed to speculation and suspicion."

Robinson decides to take his lawyer's advice and let the trial unfold as planned.

Robinson appears to have only one suit when he appears in court. Dark pinstripe. It is worn consistently with one pair of dress shoes. Tan lace-up Oxfords. The ensemble was his suit of armour during his trial for obstruction in connection with the death of Orion Hutchinson. Then, Robinson had yet to really seek help for the severe alcohol addiction that haunted him through most of his career as an RCMP officer.

The crisp creases and pressed lapels brought him no good fortune. Out of the closet they came for his daily appearance at his trial for perjury, three years later. The outfit would be equally unhelpful now.

Unlike Millington, Robinson chooses not to testify on his own behalf. Robinson is relying once again on Crossin, on one of the smartest criminal defence lawyers in British Columbia. When the trial begins in October 2014, while Millington's is also underway, people jam into the courtroom on the first day to get a look at Robinson. Many filling the seats are local journalists who, like cats, are attracted to things dangled in front of them. Robinson on trial for perjury. This will be a story today. Tomorrow the seats will be empty because few reporters if any have either the time or the interest to actually listen to the evidence. They will return again when the judge issues a verdict and dutifully report it, without any real ability to weigh the judge's wisdom. Staff Sergeant Mike Ingles is by Robinson's side before he takes his seat in the prisoner's box, a subtle smile on his face at what he believes is a process that has already been decided.

After Robinson enters a plea of not guilty to one count of perjury with eight separate averments, Fenton pops up to outline a case that is fundamentally the same as the ones marshalled against the others. The specifics of Robinson's perjury may be unique, but once again, absent any direct evidence anyone lied, Fenton must sing the same song for Justice Nathan Smith as has already been played for Ehrcke and McEwan before him: Robinson and the others lied to cover up their use of force on the night Dziekanski died, and they lied at the Braidwood Inquiry to try to explain those lies as mistakes.

Fenton focuses on an allegation he thinks will be a slam dunk for the Crown: that Robinson lied when he testified at the inquiry that his knee was "nowhere near" Dziekanski's neck. Fenton tells Justice Smith that the Pritchard video will show "beyond any doubt" that statement is false. He also assures Justice Smith that Janice Norgard will testify that all four Mounties met at her house before they appeared at the inquiry. If either one of those things is found to be true, Robinson will go to prison.

264 | BLAMED AND BROKEN

As Fenton begins playing the Pritchard video and all of Robinson's testimony at the inquiry in real time — all three days of it — the courtroom gallery empties out. On the second day of this, Justice Smith can be seen yawning, propping his chin up with his hand while he listens. When it's all done, Fenton brings out his star witness.

Once Janice Norgard is sworn, she is taken through her story. "I remember being in my kitchen and Bill introducing me to the other three officers," she testifies. She has no idea what they discussed, but she remembers she made "a light hearted wise-crack" about needing a gun to speed up her separation from Bentley's cousin, Brian Dietrich. Although it's acknowledged she only came forward after first going to former Attorney General Wally Oppal with the story, Fenton tells the court he won't be asking any questions about that or the discussion she had with Oppal.

When Crossin gets a chance to question Norgard, he begins to point out the holes in her story, and suggests that she's mistaken. The meeting she says occurred in January or February actually occurred in May.

"No," Norgard says, "that's not true."

Norgard ties her certainty to a major event going on in her life, namely writing a separation agreement with her ex. Crossin places an email in front of her dated in May, which talks about writing the agreement in May, not January or February. Norgard refuses to even look at it, because she alleges Dietrich had access to her email account at the time and could have forged it. "I don't know if I wrote this," Norgard tells Crossin.

"Well it might be familiar to you or not familiar to you," he says.

"Sir, I don't even know if this is a real email."

Crossin persists. "I'm asking you to look at it and assist us."

Norgard refuses. "I can't verify that I wrote this email."

Crossin keeps trying. "Well, you haven't read it."

This ridiculous back-and-forth continues for ten or fifteen minutes, with Norgard's only contribution being a number of attacks on the character of Dietrich.

Crossin won't give up. "It's possible it's a legitimate email," he urges.

"I have no idea," Norgard replies.

"Ma'am," Crossin says, sounding frustrated, "I'm simply asking you this — it may be phony or it might be legitimate. One way to know is to read it and tell us what you believe."

After several more minutes of stonewalling, Norgard relents, and appears as if she's reading it. It's a very personal email to a friend. The kind most people would remember writing if they'd read it, or conversely, would know they had not written. She puts it down.

"Does that assist you in any way?" Crossin asks.

"No, sir. I don't recall writing that email and I cannot verify it."

There are a slew of other records that also debunk Norgard's story of a secret meeting. Phone records and internet bills suggest her ex was still living at the house when it allegedly happened, and so therefore he wouldn't have called her asking to use the house as she maintains he did. Norgard's own cellphone records suggest she wasn't even home when she claims she saw the four Mounties sitting around her kitchen table. Norgard seems unfazed, and uses her spot in the witness box to hurl insults and venom at the man she used to live with. It has nothing to do with the allegations against Robinson, but from the first time she told the story she has seemed more interested in making Dietrich's life difficult than in anything else.

Crossin has a truckload of evidence to show it simply couldn't have happened the way Norgard says it did. Flight records show Bentley wasn't in British Columbia when Norgard says he was. Rundel's own lawyer testifies that on the weekends Norgard insists the meeting must have taken place, Rundel was with him on Vancouver Island.

When Dietrich gets into the witness chair he flatly denies tampering with his ex-partner's email. He denies the meeting took place before the inquiry. It happened in May, months after they were done. Fenton points to what Dietrich told Vancouver Police detectives when they showed up unannounced on his doorstep and began accusing him of aiding and abetting the four Mounties. Dietrich had said he couldn't recall any meeting. "I was confused," Dietrich testifies. "I wouldn't have misled the police. I was trying to be careful."

The Crown's only witness in the case has been shown to be, at best, spectacularly wrong. It has accounted for days of court time, led nowhere, and could potentially have resulted in a wrongful conviction. At no point did the Crown do the work of verifying and testing her claims. They left that to the defence. At its worst, however, Norgard's testimony is an effort rooted in deep-seated spite to get back at her ex, aided and abetted by the Crown and police.

Special prosecutor Richard Peck has been an infrequent participant in the trials thus far, leaving the heavy lifting to other members of his team, such as Fenton. However, Peck shows up to help deliver the Crown's closing arguments against the Mountie he believes is the easiest to convict. Peck tells Justice Smith that Robinson's claims at the inquiry, which have resulted in the allegations of perjury, "rest on the notion of absurdity." Notions are pretty much all Peck has, given there is no direct evidence to which he can point.

The strongest allegation, he believes, is Robinson's contention at Braidwood that his knee was "nowhere near" Dziekanski's neck. In an agreed statement of facts, the Crown admits Dziekanski suffered no injuries at all to his neck. Crossin points out that in his testimony at the inquiry Robinson himself frequently conceded his knee was on Dziekanski's shoulder, so his words "cannot be construed literally."

Fenton holds to a view that it is "plainly false," based on what he says can be seen in the Pritchard video, which he calls "clear and high quality."

To make his point about the video, or to at least make one more gratuitous reference to the night Dziekanski died, Fenton plays the Pritchard video again. It is unnecessary, given Justice Smith has seen it and can view it any time he needs to when making his decision. It's "a silent, trustworthy, unemotional, and unbiased witness," Fenton tells Smith. "It's clear beyond any doubt that his knee is on Mr. Dziekanski's neck for a substantial period of time."

Smith, however, isn't convinced that when Robinson said it at the inquiry, he expected it to mean literally "nowhere near" Dziekanski's neck. "When the accused makes a statement about what happened,"

Smith asks, "and knows the commissioner can see the video, how do I infer an intention to mislead?"

Fenton doesn't concede. "Because it was manifestly absurd and non-sense," Fenton replies.

As Dziekanski's painful cries on the video resonate in the court-room, his mother, who has been sitting in the gallery, quickly gets up and bolts outside.

With no actual proof that Robinson lied about anything, Fenton compares his case to that of convicted liar and bomb-maker Inderjit Singh Reyat. He was convicted of perjury in 2011 after he faced trial for his involvement in the Air India terrorism plot. Reyat was found to have lied dozens of times during the trial for the two men ultimately acquit-ted of mass murder. Fenton acknowledges there is no direct evidence for any of the allegations against Robinson, just as there was none in Reyat's case. Therefore, no corroboration is needed here. In the process of making his analogy, Fenton equates the misstatements by a Mountie involved in a rapidly escalating arrest with those from a man who helped kill 331 people. Fenton also fails to mention that Len Doust, the law-yer who crafted the successful case against Reyat, is the same one who looked at the evidence against the Mounties and concluded it likely didn't amount to perjury.

The Crown has consistently clung to the idea that because the offi-cers did not wrestle Dziekanski to the ground when they said they did, they are lying when they explain the false statement by calling it a mis-take, or a "blending" of various parts of what occurred. Long forgotten, or perhaps ignored by the Crown, is the evolution of that phrase "wres-tled to the ground."

Bentley never used it. And a day after he said it, Rundel changed his mind and said accurately that Dziekanski fell. Millington and Robinson didn't correct their statements until the inquiry. Yet, not even Robinson's lawyer points out that originally Robinson did not think that was what had happened. When he was first asked by a homicide investigator, Robinson said Dziekanski "was put to the ground or wres-tled to the ground or struggled on the ground or whatever." It was only when pushed to make a choice that Robinson settled on "wrestled." Not exactly what you'd expect from someone who had conspired with his cop buddies to lie.

Crossin argues it would make no sense to concoct a story because all the Mounties knew the incident had been captured on video and there was no incentive to lie about what happened. "There is no evidence the response at the airport was in any way unlawful or unreasonable or unjustified or improper or was otherwise outside the bounds of police training and policy," Crossin tells Justice Smith. "That is buttressed by the fact that many of these civilian witnesses also saw the same thing."

"But they're not trained to accurately observe and report," Justice Smith challenges.

"These police officers were in the eye of the storm," Crossin says, noting the bystanders were not. "They made exactly the same errors as the police officers."

Rundel, who's following Robinson's trial in anticipation of his own, is angry. "When is enough, enough?" Rundel writes in an email. "For Crown to come out and compare Monty (essentially all of us) to the Air India bomb maker, Reyat, is offensive. Fenton has crossed both a professional and an ethical line."

Staff Sergeant Ingles, who's been in the court most days, agrees it appears the Crown is throwing everything it can at the case to earn a conviction. "Gerry, getting wound up over what Crown says in a trial is only making you sick," Ingles cautions. "Monty is doing great, even though it is tough going. His lawyer is one of the best and I have complete confidence in an acquittal. My feelings are the same for Kwesi."

Watching her son die all over again, thanks to the Crown, has been traumatic for Cisowski. "I will never be happy again," she says outside the court when both sides rest and Justice Smith adjourns. "Even I cry today … it's a bad day."

It is easy to see why every day is a bad day when you are told by so many people that the Mounties have gotten away with killing your son, and lying about it. Now, seven years on from her son's death, she is absolutely committed to a doctrine of hate. "They lied because they protect themselves," she says.

Even Cisowski can tell, however, that the Crown seemed to falter in its mission to put Robinson away. "I prepare myself for the worst," she says. She has at least that in common with Robinson.

27 | MAKING THE FACTS FIT — RUNDEL'S TRIAL

WHILE MILLINGTON'S PERJURY trial is still underway, Gerry Rundel takes his seat in the prisoner's box in a courtroom on another floor in the same building. Of the four Mounties involved in Robert Dziekanski's death, Rundel was the least involved. He didn't wield a weapon. He wasn't in command. He had nothing to do with monitoring Dziekanski's vital signs after he was handcuffed. His main role was to confiscate Pritchard's video once he was aware it existed.

After Rundel enters a not guilty plea to a count of perjury containing six alleged lies he made at the Braidwood Inquiry, the trial before Justice Miriam Gropper proceeds identically to the others. All of the testimony Rundel gave at the Braidwood Inquiry more than seven years ago is played into the record, in real time.

Several days later, Norgard is once more the Crown's witness, alleging Rundel and his former partners all got together at her house before they testified. Once again Norgard is argumentative, refusing to read her own emails that tend to undermine her story, because, she says, they could be forgeries. It is hard to understand how anyone would be unable to tell whether a multi-page email to a friend was genuine or fake just by reading it. Yet that is what Norgard insists. However, there remains a trove of evidence that Norgard is at least mistaken about the secret meeting, including her own cellphone records that appear to show she wasn't at home when it allegedly took place. It's apparent that anyone with eyes and ears watching the trial can see that Norgard's story, and the Crown's hope that she can help convict the Mounties, is collapsing.

In order to bolster the case against Rundel, the special prosecutor puts Delta Police constable Craig Baltzer in the witness chair. Baltzer is a veteran police trainer who has witnessed hundreds of uses of the Taser and has been stunned himself more than thirty times. Prosecutor Tony Paisana expects Baltzer will put the lie to Rundel's claim from the inquiry that he was simply mistaken when he told investigators he thought Dziekanski had been standing when he was Tasered a second time.

"At the beginning of the second deployment was Mr. Dziekanski already on the ground?" Paisana asks.

Baltzer pauses for several seconds before replying. "It's right at that moment where he's going to the ground or just about at the ground where the second Taser deployment came into play."

It's not the answer Paisana is expecting and he asks Baltzer to look at the video a second time.

"You agree with me at the time of the second deployment Mr. Dziekanski is on the ground?" Paisana asks.

"Yes. Going to the ground," Baltzer repeats.

This is not going well for Paisana.

Paisana tries a third time by freezing the Pritchard video on the exact frame when the Taser is fired for the second time. "You agree he's on the ground at this point in the video?" Paisana leads, and Baltzer finally agrees.

It looks bad for the prosecution's argument that the Mounties must've been lying, because they made the same mistake in real time. It looks even worse when Baltzer suggests that a second stun was reasonable.

Meanwhile, in Millington's trial prosecutors opposed the defence attempt to hear expert police testimony, arguing that Millington isn't on trial for misusing the Taser and any use-of-force witnesses would be irrelevant in a perjury trial. Rundel's judge is unaware of the apparent contradiction by the same prosecutor in another courtroom. The law wouldn't have allowed her to consider it, anyway.

Given the stakes and the effort involved in mounting a criminal defence, Rundel has hired a new lawyer. When the evidence is presented and the Crown rests its case, Glen Orris argues immediately that Justice Gropper should punt a number of the perjury allegations out of the trial. Orris tells her Rundel has no motive to lie. It was Rundel who seized the video and knew full well their actions had been caught on camera. "If you say these people are gonna get together to cook up a story when Mr. Rundel already knows there's a video of the whole thing … it doesn't make any sense," Orris tells her.

There's also no evidence Rundel was concerned about any use of force. All he did that night was try to get Dziekanski in handcuffs. Regardless, Paisana maintains Rundel and the others lied to exaggerate Dziekanski's threat because they had to have believed they would be scrutinized for their actions. It's a theory that by now is starting to wear thin. In the end, Justice Gropper declines to dismiss any of the allegations and the trial must continue to closing arguments and ultimately a decision.

In one of the strongest submissions yet, Orris lays out a list of convincing arguments why Rundel, and by extension the other Mounties, shouldn't be found guilty of perjury. The Crown's theory, Orris argues, goes like this: "The four of them could get together and say, 'Look, we're in a lot of shit here,'" Orris says about the night Dziekanski died, while apologizing for his language. But why?

"It basically says the Crown is of the view the RCMP generally are an immoral and likely-to-lie organization," Orris continues. "The Crown is saying these officers were prepared to form an unlawful conspiracy, to lie to their superiors, and to lie whenever necessary thereafter to cover themselves. In other words, to commit crimes and put their careers, their families, and, in fact, their lives, their livelihoods, in jeopardy."

The Crown's only witness, Orris insists, is vindictive and angry at her ex-spouse, who is the cousin of one of the other officers. "Norgard is unreliable," he says. Her surprising recall about a meeting that allegedly happened years earlier came just a few weeks after a bitter court battle with her ex-spouse ended with a separation agreement in which

Norgard lost her bid for child support. "Ms. Norgard was dissatisfied, very unhappy and frustrated," Orris tells Justice Gropper. "It's a reasonable inference to draw that she came forward not as a result of any selfless concern, but rather as an attempt to damage or get back at Brian Dietrich through causing difficulties for his cousin."

Orris doesn't fault Oppal for becoming involved. At least not directly. Instead he implicates Norgard for bringing him into it. "Her desire to have Mr. Oppal present … was simply a misguided attempt by her to use him to enhance her credibility."

During the trial, unable to ignore the reality of how unreliable Norgard is, even Peck was forced to concede his star witness might be wrong. Perhaps the meeting happened on a weekday and not a weekend. It is an admission that is never made in any of the other trials, because Peck isn't forced to make it.

Orris says in Rundel's case that it guts any value Norgard has to Crown's theory. "They would then be inviting the court to say 'our witness is unreliable,'" Orris said, "and in fact she was being dishonest."

Justice Gropper sets a date in April for her verdict. It's two months away. In the meantime, the world will change for all of them. Rundel goes home to Nanaimo, bitter and angry at the ability of the Crown to simply change evidence in order to make it fit. As he retreats back into a PTSD-fuelled state of isolation and loneliness, Rundel is flung into a deep depression.

———

In late February, Millington flies back to Vancouver and takes his seat in the prisoner's box of Justice William Ehrcke's courtroom. Ehrcke begins his verdict with an explanation as to why some of the allegations against Millington have not been proven. That doesn't take long. Ehrcke has decided to base his analysis on the Pritchard video, just as Braidwood did. "I consider the Pritchard video to be the most accurate, independent, and unbiased evidence of what actually transpired at YVR on the morning of October 14, 2007," Ehrcke reads.

274 | BLAMED AND BROKEN

"As this is a judge alone trial, it falls to me to make findings about what is actually shown on the Pritchard video," he says, adding he is not bound by any other evidence that raises doubt about what it actually shows. That being said, Ehrcke finds Millington guilty of six of the ten allegations against him. What's more, Ehrcke concludes that all four Mounties were involved in a conspiracy, not just the accused sitting in front of him. "There is no reason why any one of the four officers should have imagined that they wrestled Mr. Dziekanski to the ground when manifestly nothing of the sort occurred," Ehrcke says. It could only have been by colluding. As for Norgard's claim about the secret meeting, all Ehrcke finds is that her story is "in direct conflict" with the mounds of evidence refuting it. He actually finds the idea of the four meeting *after* the inquiry to be "dubious," but he doesn't feel he can convict Millington for lying about it.

It is a blow, to be sure, but Millington's lawyer immediately files an appeal and the possibility still remains he will be acquitted at some point. In the meantime, however, Millington will be sentenced in three months time while the appeal works its way through the courts.

A month after Millington is found guilty, so, too, is Robinson. While Justice Smith rules most of the Crown's case against Robinson isn't proven, Smith is convinced that when Robinson described Dziekanski as being wrestled to the ground, he was lying then, and he was lying at the inquiry when he said he had been confused.

"Coincidence becomes even more unlikely when the error is made not by two declarants but by four," Smith reads, as Robinson looks on solemnly.

"I have already said that I cannot accept that the most senior police officer involved would have made such a crucial error. I find it inconceivable that four trained officers would have made the same mistake at the same time by pure coincidence," Smith says, discounting that many other witnesses made similar errors. "The fact that not even one of them got this important fact right leads in my view to an inescapable inference of collusion among the four officers."

Robinson has been itching to make a public statement about his ordeal and what he thinks of those who've been working to put him in prison. He has one written out and plans to read it for any reporters who care to listen. Staff Sergeant Ingles, who's come to hear the verdict, sidles up to Rundel to make it clear to him that if Robinson opens his mouth, he can kiss any funding for an appeal goodbye. The RCMP will use Robinson's comments as an excuse to bail from any obligation to defend his actions while he was on duty.

Ingles's entreaty is timely. Robinson is full of fight and anger. He speaks of wanting to "expose them all. I don't care if I lose my funding," he says. "What'll it cost? A hundred thousand? I'll eat it. I did in the obstruction case." The peak of his ire passes, however. He folds up the piece of paper on which he's written his statement, and puts it back

Criminal Justice Branch spokesperson Neil MacKenzie takes questions outside the B.C. Supreme Court in Vancouver from reporters who missed Monty Robinson's perjury trial but came for the guilty verdict, March 20, 2015.

in his pocket. He will discover, however, that his silence has bought him nothing.

The convictions are especially troubling for Robinson and Millington. Just a month later, the B.C. Court of Appeal issues a strongly worded rejection of the Crown's appeal of Bentley's acquittal. Two days after that, Rundel is acquitted by Justice Gropper. She is careful to point out that despite the similarities between the cases, her decision should not be taken to be "inconsistent" with those of the judges who issued convictions. Gropper is equally kind to Norgard in her ruling, calling her evidence "contradictory," rather than plainly false. Justice Gropper's disclaimer notwithstanding, the decision only serves to underscore how absurd the findings are when compared to one another.

Zofia Cisowski offers her condemnation of Monty Robinson to reporters outside the B.C. Supreme Court in Vancouver, after Robinson was found guilty of perjury, March 20, 2015.

On the day Millington is sentenced, he is in court, about to take his seat in the prisoner's box, when he makes one last trip to see his wife, Cindy, sitting in the gallery. "Are you okay?" he asks, taking her hand before resuming his seat.

Millington's lawyer had asked for a conditional sentence based on a number of reasons including psychologists' reports outlining the mental struggle Millington has endured the past number of years while his case dragged on. Ravi Hira had also pointed out what is obvious to anyone who has read a newspaper in the past decade, namely that Millington has already been the subject of much public derision for nearly a third of his life. However, in a bizarre ruling, Justice Ehrcke disagrees. "While it is undoubtedly true that this case has been widely publicized," Ehrcke says, "I do not agree that the publicity generally cast the accused in a bad light, at least not prior to his conviction."

It is an astounding claim that bears no resemblance to reality. Ehrcke makes another ruling that will have some bearing on Millington's sentence. He allows Dziekanski's mother to submit a victim impact statement. While there is no question Dziekanski's death was tragic and regrettable, it did not form any part of the charges against the Mounties. They were neither charged, nor found guilty of any crime connected with Dziekanski's death. If there is a victim in the perjury case, it is the inquiry, or more broadly, the public process. Yet, Ehrcke maintains Cisowski is somehow a victim of the perjury, and reads a statement attributed to Cisowski into the record. "These police officers had the opportunity on many occasions to correct the lies they told and to take responsibility ... for the stories they told which were false, but they never have." It's clear Cisowski has not actually written the statement, but Ehrcke never questions its sincerity. Parts of it are simply untrue, and suggest it was indeed written by someone not entirely familiar with the evidence. "They have never expressed any remorse," Ehrcke continues reading, apparently unconcerned this is false. Ehrcke gives Millington thirty months in prison.

Zofia Cisowski sits in solitary contemplation at the Sacred Heart Cathedral in Kamloops, in May 2016. Nearly a decade after her son's death, Cisowski struggles to reconcile the teachings of her Catholic faith to forgive with her desire to see the Mounties punished.

Bill Bentley (left), flanked by his lawyer Peter Wilson, walks away from the B.C. Court of Appeal in Vancouver a free man on June 5, 2015, knowing two former partners have been convicted of the same alleged conspiracy.

When it is Robinson's turn to go before Justice Smith, he is given a more lenient punishment: two years less a day, which means he will serve his time in a provincial jail, barring any successful appeal. Both men are concerned that, with their history as police officers, even a day behind bars will be difficult.

Zofia Cisowski, with Walter Kosteckyj, who was her lawyer during the Braidwood Inquiry, shows reporters the portrait of her son from Braidwood's report. "Nothing will bring my son back," she tells reporters outside the B.C. Supreme Court in Vancouver after learning Monty Robinson has been sentenced to jail for two years less a day.

28 | GUILTY IF PROVEN INNOCENT

"HE'S RUNNING HIMSELF to death."

Gerry Rundel utters the words quietly, like a secret, with a hint of sadness. He looks toward a group of people nearby to gauge if he has been overheard. Rundel stands alone by a potted plant away from the cluster of people outside the courtroom. It makes him more noticeable than if he'd joined the others in suits, lawyers' cloaks, and street clothes. They shuffle about the carpeted terrace outside the room where arguments are being made about how long to lock up Kwesi Millington in prison. But Rundel isn't talking about Millington this morning.

It's a sunny day in May. The blue sky pours through the glass roof that covers most of the building housing the law courts. The light sustains the plant Rundel uses for limp camouflage. The brilliant rays feed the forest of potted trees and the ivy that drips from the atrium balconies.

Renowned architect Arthur Erickson intended the glass roof to be an obvious symbol of openness and transparency, of the courts' welcoming attitude toward the scrutiny of the often inscrutable and intimidating justice system. The courtrooms, however, where the serious and mysterious business of innocence and guilt is divined, are cut off from Erickson's airy vision, hidden behind heavy doors that swing shut when court is in session.

Rundel's conspiratorial tone continues. His eyes widen as he talks.

"Bill's not doing well. He's dropped twenty pounds. He's thin. He's running all the time."

Rundel explains that Bill Bentley frequently can't sleep as he paces alone in the Toronto house he once shared with his wife, Makayla. Often in the wee hours of the morning, Bentley picks up the phone and calls Rundel at home in Nanaimo. Bentley has reason to be anxious. It will be another month before the Court of Appeal reveals whether his acquittal will stand or the prosecutors will get a do-over. Prison is still a possibility.

What Rundel doesn't know is that Bentley's obsession with running is likely helping him to cope. Some recent studies have shown improvement in otherwise intractable PTSD symptoms for those who pound the pavement. Bentley may be practising a form of self-medicating, but it might be a good thing. The truth is Rundel's concern for his friend and former partner is as much a reflection of the anxiety he feels about his own situation. Although Rundel was acquitted days earlier, he is not in the clear. The special prosecutor has thirty days to appeal the verdict, and in Bentley's case, it came on the last possible day.

As he speaks, Rundel absent-mindedly fidgets with a sheet of paper in his hands. He says he's not ready to go back to work just yet, and anyway, he plans to be with his son Brodie next week when Brodie graduates from the federal government's fisheries officer training program. All along Rundel knew the ceremony would be held at the RCMP Academy in Regina. Of all places. He had dreaded the event until his acquittal.

"I didn't know how I was going to do it if I'd been convicted," Rundel says wistfully. "Now I can hold my head high."

Head high, yes, but Rundel's shoulders remain slumped. As an RCMP officer, Rundel has every right to wear his red serge uniform at his son's graduation next week. He won't. He says he can't. Eight years spent as one of the four poster boys for everything that's wrong with the RCMP makes putting on the scarlet jacket just too painful right now.

Rundel has no idea just how much more difficult it's about to become.

He descends the stairs to the street entrance of the building where a huddle of reporters with cameras and microphones wait. Rundel nervously unfolds the paper in his hand and begins to read from it.

"I'm here today to support a fellow officer," Rundel speaks of Millington.

"A person who I know is innocent and I'm having a difficult time understanding his conviction."

Rundel is sticking his neck out.

"I would like to know why judges are permitted to convict on a mere theory."

Rundel's bare throat now might as well be tattooed with the words *chop here.*

As he reads for the gaggle, Rundel praises the judges in his and Bentley's trials for acquitting "based on evidence," and slams Justices Ehrcke and Smith for convicting "on a theory ... that defies common sense.

"Agendas have become more important than the truth."

Every word in Rundel's statement is a blunt condemnation of the special prosecutor and his team of lawyers, the judges who convicted, and even his own bosses. "The RCMP needs to publicly back their officers when they act according to training, policy, and procedure, in order to prevent falsehoods from spinning out of control and influencing the processes."

Rundel reaches the end of the printed statement in a minute. He pauses amid a flurry of questions from reporters, then turns and walks away without saying another word. Moments later his voice has a twinge of shakiness.

"My mind was a blank after I read it. Did I say everything? How'd it sound," he presses, looking for reassurance.

"I thought afterward I missed a whole paragraph." Rundel ponders a possible mistake. There's no doubt he made one.

Out of courtesy and caution, Rundel emails a staff representative to inform him of the statement.

Sergeant Brad Szewczok is supposed to be an advocate of sorts. He is not happy. "Probably not your best decision!!" Szewczok writes, using not one but two exclamation points. He warns there "may be fallout."

Gerry Rundel risks discipline when he breaks his silence at Millington's sentencing, outside the B.C. Supreme Court, May 7, 2015, to publicly criticize the RCMP and the judges who convicted Monty Robinson and Kwesi Millington of perjury.

The fallout comes just a few minutes later from Rundel's commanding officer, Superintendent Mark Fisher. He dials Rundel's cell to order him to stop talking. Rundel isn't answering and Fisher is forced to plead with the constable's voicemail. "I wasn't aware you were going to be making a statement on the steps of the courthouse," Fisher speaks with a tone of exasperation in his voice. "Not a good idea ... you're still a serving member, and you're subject to the Code, Gerry, and I don't want to see you go down that road."

As Rundel listens to the message, anxiety wells up. "The Code" is the RCMP Code of Conduct. Mere mention of it is a threat that levers are already being pulled to launch an investigation that could result in punishment, ranging from the loss of a day's pay to being fired. The Code of Conduct is clear and absolute: RCMP members must not make public statements criticizing the government or the RCMP because they are sworn to be loyal to their masters.

Fisher lets out a long sigh, exhaling in frustration.

"You can't be going out in the media like that, and criticizing the Crown despite what your thoughts are."

Rundel is stunned. He'd run what he wanted to say past his lawyer. While Orris tweaked Rundel's script a little, he told him he was fine to criticize the Crown and the judges. It was Rundel's chance to say what he felt. Rundel also shared the statement with confidante Renny Nesset, the superintendent of Richmond detachment, where Rundel and his notorious former partners had all worked. Nesset's response was simply "Well said, my friend." Wasn't that an endorsement from someone who understood RCMP policy?

Fisher fires off an email to make sure Rundel gets the message. "Do not make any further statements of this nature to the media," he writes.

When Rundel calls Fisher back, he breaks down in tears. Rundel sobs about being silenced for eight years. He argues that he was only doing what the RCMP should have done. Fisher isn't unsympathetic, but there is no negotiation. "I'm ordering you not to speak on the YVR matters."

Rundel asks where the order is coming from. Fisher says it's from him.

A few days later, Rundel agrees to meet for an off-the-record chat over coffee at a White Spot restaurant in Nanaimo. Fisher talks about everything except Rundel's embarrassing public comments. As they head to the door, Fisher can no longer put it off. "I've taken a lot of heat for this," Fisher says, just before he heads back to the detachment. Upper management has been clamouring to put Rundel through a Code of Conduct hearing.

Fisher warns Rundel that when he gets back from his son's graduation in Regina he needs to come in for an official meeting.

When that day comes, Rundel shows up, unsure of what's going to happen.

With a staff representative present and his lawyer listening on the phone, Fisher tells Rundel he has run interference for him and negotiated a deal of sorts. The Code investigation will be dropped if Rundel accepts and signs an admonishment for violating the Code of Conduct and RCMP policy. It's a 1004. Rundel's admission of guilt will simply be tucked into his personnel file and then disposed of after two years. The paper he's asked to sign makes it clear, however, that should he utter another word about the criminal trials — even his own — there will be no second chance and his insolence would be considered an aggravating factor in determining his punishment.

Rundel argues that everything he said was true and came from personal experience. He challenges the notion that somehow his comments had any adverse impact on his ability to perform his duties. He feels bullied.

In the end, Rundel holds his nose and signs, to make it go away. The alternative is a Code investigation that would allow the RCMP commissioner to fire Rundel, regardless of the findings. The next day, Rundel is already regretting the decision and thinks he should have called the RCMP's bluff.

The thought doesn't have time to fester. A new worry takes its place. The Crown has until May 29 to appeal his acquittal. That's just a week away. As he did with Bentley's decision, prosecutor Richard Peck waits until the last possible day to tip his hand. Except Peck isn't willing to let Rundel walk, nor is he ready to show his cards.

In a last-minute letter delivered to Rundel's lawyer, Peck pleads he is in "a difficult position to make an ultimate decision regarding whether there is a question of law to be appealed." Peck says his problem is that he doesn't have Justice Gropper's decision, to acquit Rundel, in writing.

Yes, Gropper read her reasons why the Crown failed, in open court. They were clear, detailed, and precise. However, a month later, her decision is still not available in printed form. While anyone in the courtroom heard Gropper dismantle the Crown's case, apparently no one at the prosecutor's table bothered to record her decisive dismissal. So, for the past month while Rundel sweated, the best the prosecutor's team could manage was to identify "potential issues that may give rise to an appeal."

Peck then mentions what is arguably the real reason the prosecutors are stalling for time: they have no idea whether their arguments to claw Bentley back into court will fly with the appeal judges who are still deliberating. Peck says as a result he is filing a "pro forma notice of appeal." In Rundel's mind, Peck's action seems a declaration: *I might keep you tied up in court, I might not. I haven't decided yet, but I'm not giving up my shot at retrying the case.* It's in "the public interest," Peck writes. It's out of "fairness" to Rundel.

Rundel doesn't see the fairness in being caught in a process that has already robbed him of eight years of his life. Peck's manoeuvre is all perfectly proper in the legal realm. Even if it is a bit like playing craps and waiting until the dice have stopped rolling to place your bet.

A few days later, Peck gets the Bentley decision. It isn't what he wanted. The appeal court's ruling is an unambiguous take-down of the Crown's case. Justice Anne MacKenzie guts their arguments. She characterizes them as mere complaints by the Crown that the case didn't go

A long run lifts Bill Bentley's mood in May 2016. A year after his acquittal the RCMP has still not put him back to work.

their way. There was no error in law. The mighty binders and bankers boxes on which the prosecutors hoped to build the foundation for a prison sentence for the Mounties are now just so much dead weight they must drag from the courtroom.

Two weeks later the typed judgment in Rundel's case is finally in Peck's hands. Peck had said it was critical. Peck had said it contained potential issues for an appeal. Peck had said that until it arrived, it was only "fair" to let Rundel twist in the wind. However, there are no recalcitrant facts hidden mysteriously in the text of what Justice Gropper said viva voce more than a month earlier. Peck and his team don't reveal this to Rundel. He finds out quite by accident.

Dressed in street clothes, with some papers in his hand, he waits outside the courtroom where Kwesi Millington is being sentenced. Rundel has come to offer moral support. A man in a suit strikes up a conversation and it becomes clear he thinks Rundel is a reporter. When Rundel twigs to the misunderstanding, he clears up the confusion by offering a handshake, and announcing his name. The man appears puzzled. Rundel continues, and says he's *that* Gerry Rundel, one of the four Mounties who have been put on trial for perjury. Awkward. The man in the suit reveals he is Gordon Comer. Comer is the media spokesperson for the B.C. Criminal Justice Branch. His job is to speak authoritatively to reporters about the case and its outcome. As Comer begins to physically retreat from the accidental meeting, he blurts out that Rundel should be pleased. The prosecutor has decided not to appeal his conviction. Rundel is left standing alone, stunned.

"Bill called me the other night." Monty Robinson speaks with a mixture of dread and the sound of confession in his voice, like a father who's about to reveal some bad news about his child. It's November, and for the first time in eight years Bill Bentley has marked the anniversary of Robert Dziekanski's death as a free man. Yet five months after Bentley was vindicated by the B.C. Court of Appeal, it's as if he had been found guilty.

"He's scared," Robinson says, his tone changing to one of simmering anger. "He wants to go back to work. They won't let him."

There's no doubt who "they" are. Robinson sits in his kitchen, pounding his fist on the table for punctuation.

"All the work I've done in the RCMP to see bad people are put away ..." Thump.

"The people that are my bosses," thump, "at the top of the organization," thump, "are worse than anybody I've ever put away." Thump.

The papers and file folders laid out on the table tremble with every knock. Robinson regains his calm.

"I am so thankful I went to Edgewood," he says of the alcohol treatment facility in Nanaimo.

"If I did not have acceptance of how corrupt this is, I would have driven myself crazy by now. The RCMP bullied Lemaitre to death but not me."

Robinson has stayed busy waiting for his appeal since his conviction. Most of his time is taken up with creating and curating an expanding number of files that document even the most trivial and tangential development in his case. Any email or phone call or comment from anyone about what's going on is likely to end up in his archive.

The childhood home where he was confined following his conviction for attempting to obstruct justice remains a prison. Robinson is reluctant to leave the house, afraid of being recognized in Delta. He ventured to take a diving course over the summer with his teenage son, "but the class was small and not everyone can connect the dots." His home is his gym, and Robinson appears lean and fit. He walks the neighbour's pug at least once a week. The stubby-legged animal is one of the few contacts Robinson has that doesn't judge him.

"I'm so task-driven that this helps slow me down. I go at the dog's pace and that breed meanders."

Robinson uses the walks and the perpetual paperwork as a kind of therapy — a brain bleach to erase the Pritchard video from his thoughts. It's still rolling in Robinson's mind months after the Crown had it played over and over again in court.

"I hope to Christ I never have to watch that fucking thing ever again. I don't do well after it. Good God. It's like torture. I was telling Gerry, what a headache. You feel victimized; you feel shitty."

Right now, though, a more pressing concern is pushing the past from his plate. Months after his trial and conviction, the RCMP still hasn't paid the legal bill. Robinson's lawyer, David Crossin, is demanding $192,000. Failure to pay will scuttle Robinson's appeal. Crossin isn't going to work for free, and unless he gets six thousand dollars immediately, he won't meet the deadlines set by the court to submit the appeal documents. If that happens, Robinson will have to surrender himself immediately and begin his sentence. Robinson believes the holdup has to do with the lack of seriousness with which the RCMP is treating his case. In his more cynical moments, he believes that the delay may be due to the fact that there are those in the chain of command who want to see Robinson behind bars.

Robinson is angry and his anger extends to virtually everyone in the force who has dealt with him and his three compatriots. It extends to Mike Ingles, the RCMP staff sergeant who has backed the four members since the early morning hours after Dziekanski died.

It was Ingles who advised each of them they didn't need to give statements right away. It was Ingles who worked to make sure they each had a lawyer going into the Braidwood Inquiry. It was Ingles who successfully made the case to RCMP brass to pay the bills for the criminal trials. Now, Ingles barely contains his contempt for Robinson's lack of appreciation.

"I don't work for you," Ingles writes in a lengthy email. Some of the best RCMP staff reps in the country and a number of senior officers who believe Robinson is innocent have gone well beyond what they were expected to do and Robinson's tone is threatening to alienate his only allies.

"Throwing in the odd 'thanks' or 'could you help with this' wouldn't hurt. Everyone is not against you."

Ingles could have simply explained the RCMP's legal funding policy and let Robinson fend for himself. Ingles warns Robinson that he would likely fail. The small stuff isn't an issue. While Robinson resigned in disgrace more than three years ago, the public might be surprised to learn the RCMP automatically cuts him a cheque every time he is in court. It's classified as duty pay. His appearance and brief incarceration for his sentencing hearing in July netted Robinson more than three hundred dollars.

It's not so simple a matter, however, to secure approval for tens of thousands of dollars in legal fees. The case has to be made Robinson was acting within the scope of his duties. Now that he's been convicted, the arguments Ingles has to make to convince his superiors to endorse Robinson's appeal become more elaborate and delicate.

"Monty, I don't want you to be saddled with the cost either; however, it isn't as simple as just me asking for the money and them sending over a suitcase with the cash."

Ingles's strategy is to get RCMP bosses to green-light Millington's appeal first, then press for Robinson on the same basis. The reason is simple: Robinson is tainted and damaged. He was convicted for attempting to obstruct justice. Deputy Commissioner Craig Callens hung Robinson out publicly as the guy Callens wished he could have fired. Robinson is saddled with baggage the size of steamer trunks. Ingles knows it may not be fair, but it's a fact.

Forcing the public safety minister to make a decision now, Ingles says, "is not without risk. If you want me to go against my judgment and begin poking around ... I will, as long as you know that there is no appeal against the decision of the minister with the exception of a Federal Court review, and that would also require both time and money. Just understand that if you don't get the answer you are looking for the consequences impact you not me."

Ingles's warning is intended to get Robinson to take it down a notch. It doesn't work. Instead, Robinson continues to plot, bitterly concluding that "Mike has never been right in eight years."

———

Robinson's plans don't include the officer he commanded the night this all began so long ago.

"Kwesi ... how to put it?" Robinson searches for a word. He hesitates only for a moment. "He's like an ostrich. A long time ago he just put his head in the sand and said I'm just going to try to survive it. That's fine," Robinson says with a tone suggesting otherwise. "I won't keep you in the loop."

There is no doubt Kwesi Millington is doing all he can to avoid thinking about the future. As he waits for his appeal, Millington staves off the dread of going to prison by becoming someone else. At least, online.

While his former partners shrink from public view, Millington seems to crave attention. He frequently updates his overflowing social media feeds with facile inspirational quotes: "Our lives are just a living, breathing manifestation of the conversations going on inside our heads," and "The more you realize who you really are, the less you are willing to be who you've been."

Millington posts photos, too, mainly of the covers of the library of self-help books he powers through. Millington has not just one, but two websites that proudly boast that he is a "Certified World Class Speaking Coach." When pressed what that means, Millington reveals he got the designation after taking a course over the summer. "I'm out there but I don't have any clients," he admits. The achievement seems even more uncertain when Millington says he can grant the status to anyone who completes the course he can now sell, because he has "an affiliate code" with the marketing company that took his money. The cop who didn't understand the words *abdicate* and *contemporaneous* when his life depended on it in the witness chair, is now a "world class speaking coach."

To be sure, Millington is a confident-sounding speaker. He has embraced with religious zeal his membership in Toastmasters, the global public-speaking club with chapters all over the world.

Millington uploads videos of his selfie-shot monologues, frequently made from the driver's seat of his car. He expounds on various aspects of public speaking, storytelling, and generating self-confidence.

"The last couple of years especially have been about a lot of self-development," he says while getting a pot of rice cooking in the kitchen of his Toronto home. Millington is meticulous about the food he eats.

He has revived his skills as a personal trainer and maintains a number of clients. "I'm not as anxious anymore about the way things might turn out. I think about it, yes, but I just have to roll with it."

It's a good speech. It would make an uplifting internet meme. Like many things you find online, it's not necessarily what it seems.

Some of Millington's video views are in the single digits. After a couple of years on Twitter, he has just over a hundred followers. Online, Millington glosses over the most powerful story he owns. On his website, he uses his RCMP graduation photo from Depot and refers to himself as a police officer. The truth is, Millington hasn't worn the iconic red serge and Mountie hat for years. He probably never will again. Millington does acknowledge that "I have to live with the fact that someone died on my watch," but pairs that with his "indignation of being accused of lying about it." Millington's few terse lines of biography reveal very little about the man who wrote them.

"I don't talk to Monty or Gerry that much," he says when asked about how he's different from his former partners. "They seem to be more kind of stuck in that past." Millington may not be stuck in the past, but the past is definitely stalking him. The mythical power of all the books and sayings to which he religiously clings are impotent against it.

His wife, Cindy Sztejner, sees what Millington hides from his YouTube and Twitter subscribers. "Of course that's part of his therapy. It weighs on him," she reveals. She suggests Millington has never really moved past his role in the death of Robert Dziekanski. "It weighed on him at the time very heavily. People don't see that side, and people don't understand that."

There is a tension in Sztejner's voice that comes from swallowing a bitter reality of her own: she wants to have children. "That's a sore spot for me," she says. "If the worst-case scenario happens, I don't want to be in the position where I'm going to be having to do something like that alone. I kind of feel like I don't want the courts to make the decision about whether I have a family or not and that's kind of what I feel like is happening. I'm thirty-nine, so I kind of need to make that decision now."

The justice system, however, is in no mood to be rushed for Sztejner's biological clock. While the federal government's approval to fund Millington's appeal will likely be rubber-stamped, it will take time to set a date for the hearing, which won't be until well into 2016. Until then, Millington will rely on his new-found passion for public speaking to salve his fears about the future.

"I'll be honest, the reaction that I get from people [at Toastmasters] is different than what I've read in the news over the years," he says about the warm and open-minded welcome he's received as a member of two Toronto-area speaking clubs.

"Every time I would speak, whether it was at my club or another club, I would have this thought in the back of my mind: *Do people know who I am? Do they know my whole story? Are they judging me? What are they thinking?* This internal process started to drive me crazy. So I decided one day I was going to give a speech at another club and I was going to say my story. So I did a speech at that club and told my story. I don't know if people have negative thoughts but nobody shared them with me. I just got nothing but positive. That's why I lead with it now because at the end of the day people are going to judge. You may as well lead with it and let people think what they're going to think."

But the very people on who Millington relied to reinvent himself are the first to tell him he's mistaken. When Millington approached his club to seek permission for a journalist to record one of his speeches for a documentary dealing with what the Mountie had been through, the club's president declined. Millington says he was told of "numerous concerns raised by members about the Toastmasters brand being associated" with the story.

Rather than consider the troubling possibility that the balm of public speaking is really a quack cure for his ruined reputation, Millington chooses to stay positive. The club has effectively rejected him, so Millington blames himself. He says it was just a bad idea to invite scrutiny of his public-speaking-as-therapy.

"Had I thought about it," he writes in an email, "I would have gone a different route from the beginning."

There are those who think Millington should have written those words years ago.

————————

The Crown prosecutors had been stern-faced and mute when they left Millington's and Robinson's sentencing hearings. They refused to say anything, declining to offer even a benign comment about the merit of such a significant, expensive — and from their point of view, successful — prosecution. No doubt the likelihood of appeals in both cases stilled their tongues. The case is still *sub judice*, under judicial consideration. True or not, it's the go-to response from lawyers who simply don't believe they have to explain anything they do in court, except to a judge.

So it is an odd surprise when, just a few months later, the chief architect of those convictions appears on a program for a conference on the Law of Policing to be held in Vancouver.

Special prosecutor Scott Fenton is slated to speak to a room full of lawyers and police officers and give "an in depth analysis" of the Millington and Robinson convictions. Fenton is expected to delve into "credibility, demeanour, and other considerations during testimony." Fenton will also discuss the broader implications of the convictions.

The conference at which Fenton is booked to speak is the creation of a Toronto-based organization called the Canadian Institute. It's the same organization that hosted Thomas Braidwood as a luncheon speaker in 2010. After authoring his damning indictment of the four Mounties involved in Robert Dziekanski's death, Braidwood came to the luncheon armed with the Pritchard video. Police officers in the audience walked out. Flustered, Braidwood played it anyway. The room cleared as he stumbled through a presentation, mixing up the officers' names and arguing that the whole incident could have been avoided if the cops had just pulled up a chair to talk to Dziekanski.

The Canadian Institute bills itself as a think tank, established to provide "the business intelligence that Canadian decision-makers need to respond to challenges here at home, and around the world." Practically,

however, the Canadian Institute hosts conferences geared to professionals who have access to budgets big enough to afford the attendance fees.
Some people going to the Law of Policing conference will pay upward
of two thousand dollars for two days of sitting in a hotel banquet hall to
hear people like Scott Fenton speak.

The conference organizers agree to permit a lone journalist, me,
to attend the sessions, following a vetting process that takes weeks
and requires the submission of examples of past work. An hour after
the signed media accreditation form is returned, the session Fenton is
scheduled to conduct is declared off limits. Not to the people who've
shelled out the fee. Just to me.

Lawyer Glen Orris, who represented Gerry Rundel at his criminal
trial, is supposed to speak alongside Fenton. Orris is surprised to hear
the conference has effectively closed its doors to the public. Orris insists
it's not his doing. A spokesperson for the Canadian Institute plays dumb
when I ask her if Fenton wants the media kicked out. "It is not our policy to disclose that information," the senior marketing manager replies.
I ask if I could attend as a delegate if the full conference fee were paid.
She responds, "Those sessions would still be closed to you."

An appeal to Scott Fenton for an explanation and reconsideration
yields a confusing and contradictory reply. Fenton doesn't directly
answer the question about whether he invoked the media ban. Instead,
he brandishes the *sub judice* law and writes that it would be "inappropriate to consent to the media attending. The court could conclude that
the public reporting of such remarks violated the well-known *sub judice*
rule." Fenton sidesteps the notion that his talk is of public interest by
insisting that he will speak in his "private capacity, not as a spokesman
for the Crown."

Fenton ignores another accepted principle: trial decisions are considered "good law" unless and until the Court of Appeal rules to the
contrary. There is no danger in speaking about a decision. If that weren't
the case, Fenton couldn't speak at all. It's pointed out to him that his
audience will be members of the public, none of whom have signed
any undertaking of confidentiality. His remarks can still be reported,

with or without a journalist present. In fact, the session will be webcast to participants who can't make it in person. He ignores that argument. Instead, Fenton makes one of the oddest claims: that the product of his paid speech is somehow private property. He is indisputably speaking about what he learned as the public's prosecutor. Parcelling out analysis that's been bankrolled by the public to paying customers behind closed doors is a hard case to make, even for a lawyer as smart as Scott Fenton.

A Vancouver lawyer familiar with Fenton and who knows about the perjury cases chuckles when he hears about the back-and-forth. "You know why, don't you? He doesn't like you. He doesn't like the reporting you did because it made the Crown look bad."

When Fenton is offered a compromise that his remarks will be withheld until the Court of Appeal has ruled in both cases, he says he'll consider it.

On the surface it appears Fenton is managing his responses by himself. In reality, Fenton shares every email he opens on his iPhone or personal computer in Ontario with his friend, mentor, and boss, special prosecutor Richard Peck. The emails are bounced back and forth several times between Fenton and Peck's offices before Fenton sends his replies. At no time does anyone in Peck's office reveal they have been brought in on the conversation.

Fenton never responds to the offer of confidentiality that would have satisfied the concern he insisted he had about not wanting to interfere with the appeals. On the day of the conference, he doesn't show. Fenton's co-panelist, Glen Orris, is left on his own to give a rambling and pedestrian talk about matters that anyone who paid casual attention to his client's trial would already know.

Afterward, a lawyer in the crowd offers that Fenton "was told not to come." When reached later that day about why he pulled out at the last minute, Fenton explains that several days before he was due to fly to Vancouver, he was prevented by "a serious disclosure issue" in a trial. Fenton gives no details about the case that kept him from speaking at an event he'd been booked at months in advance. "I hope you enjoyed it," he writes, before signing off.

29 | FIGHTING BACK

GERRY RUNDEL IS A free man. His reputation, however, remains locked away. His acquittal was sound. No question. Toward the end of Rundel's criminal trial even the special prosecutor acted as if the case against Rundel was hopeless. For Rundel, however, acquittal does not equal vindication. Justice William Ehrcke, in his decision to convict Kwesi Millington, convicted Rundel as well, at least on paper. Ehrcke concluded that *all four* Mounties lied and colluded to mislead the Braidwood Inquiry. Justice Nathan Smith did essentially the same thing when he found Monty Robinson guilty. Unless both of those decisions are overturned, Rundel remains under a cloud of suspicion. He feels beat up. He's reluctant to leave his house. He's drinking more. It's not unusual for Rundel to become startled when his home phone rings, as it does months after his hollow victory in court.

"It's Inspector Cam Miller," the caller says. Rundel wracks his brain to put a face to the name but he can't. Miller says he's from Rundel's detachment in Nanaimo. Can Rundel meet to discuss getting back to work? Rundel is confused. He asks why Miller wants to meet, given he's still on a medical leave. "Yes, but you are still a member of the RCMP," Miller replies. Feeling pressured, Rundel agrees to meet the next day at a local restaurant.

The day dawns and Rundel has a headache. Headaches are frequent. It's also not surprising given it's early October and the eighth anniversary

298 | BLAMED AND BROKEN

of Dziekanski's death is just days away. If you ask anyone who's suffered from PTSD they'll tell you that anniversaries of traumatic events can trigger unexpected and involuntary physical reactions. When Rundel calls Miller to reschedule their meeting, the inspector's tone changes. He accuses Rundel of trying to "push off" the meeting. Miller sounds uninterested in Rundel's explanation that the YVR anniversary is playing havoc with his mental state. Miller says it's urgent that Rundel is medically cleared to get back to work. After some discussion, Rundel agrees to meet in a week. Miller assures him it's not a formal meeting. "I'm hoping to talk to you and see where you are at."

When Rundel arrives at the detachment, he walks into Inspector Miller's office with staff relations representative Brad Szewczok. Szewczok is the same staff sergeant who chided him for speaking publicly after Kwesi Millington's trial.

Miller is an imposing figure. He stands tall; his close-cut greying hair hints at his twenty-one years on the force. He considers himself to be fair and ethical. During the 2010 Olympics, Miller was in charge of Marine Security Operations for the RCMP. He has been a lead investigator in a corruption and stock market cases. He is a firearms instructor and a tactical troop leader. For all his experience as a police officer, however, it becomes clear he knows almost nothing about PTSD, and doesn't seem to care.

Miller is matter-of-fact, businesslike, and peppy as the meeting begins. He sounds as if he's trying to sell Rundel something. There's a what-do-I-have-to-do-to-put-you-in-this-car tone as he speaks.

"All the court matters are through. All the appeal periods are now over and closed. So there's no further action I believe coming from any of that. All internal stuff is spent, so there's nothing in that regard. That's my understanding. Is that your understanding as well?"

Rundel is tired and slow to respond.

"There's still two of the other officers. I've been accused in those courts of colluding with those other officers. Having my name fully cleared ... that's important to me. I mean, I've always been a person of integrity and that's why this has been so hard on me."

Miller doesn't follow up on how Rundel is doing. It's his job to get anyone back who's been off for more than thirty days.

"The work you did in the Intelligence sector was very, very highly regarded," Miller says. "People actually said pretty good things about you." Miller moves to close the sale. "Wondering what your thoughts are on returning to work."

Rundel struggles for an answer. "I just don't know if I can answer that right now. I'm still trying to deal with just getting better, and I don't want get into all my health issues. That's not really the purpose of this meeting."

Miller keeps talking. He compares Rundel to another member who injured a limb and is back on the job, doing desk work. Miller appeals to the police officer in Rundel, telling him that working behind a desk supports arrests of drug dealers and B&E artists.

"You've been off for … I think it's in excess of two years now?"

"I've been diagnosed with PTSD," Rundel begins to answer. "It's no secret or anything. I'm susceptible to triggers and I'm dealing with that —"

Miller cuts Rundel off and presses again for a return date.

Struggling, Rundel starts to repeat himself.

"I … I have no idea. I don't know. That's probably more of a discussion with my professionals that I'm talking to and dealing with —"

Miller interrupts again. "Well, actually, I'm going to respectfully disagree with you because your professionals cannot tell you when you can go back to work. You can get a diagnosis from them about your condition, but you're the one who can determine when you go back to work."

Szewczok, ostensibly there as Rundel's support, sides with Miller. "It can't go on forever though, Gerry. I mean that's what he's trying to say."

Miller suggests that if Rundel can't give him a timeline, the alternative is medical discharge.

"So …" Miller draws the one-syllable word out as if to make a point. "I just want to make sure I understand it then. You have no timeline?"

Rundel is feeling bullied. "I don't think I can give a timeline. I just can't. I'm in the process of working on things with my doctors."

Miller isn't about to take no for an answer. "What can we do from this end to assist?" he asks. "In addition to providing medical care, coverage, carrying on all your full benefits and that?"

Szewczok jumps in, repeating that the alternative to going back to work is expulsion from the force.

"This is not a threat, Gerry. I'm just telling you that."

Miller and Szewczok continue the tag-team approach to getting Rundel to commit to a return-to-work date, when Miller suggests Rundel's predicament is his own fault.

"You know, maybe you should have engaged more."

Something inside Rundel stirs.

"I'm just a little surprised that you wouldn't maybe just kind of look into me a little bit; see what I've been through."

"Well, I did. I pulled your file. I went through it."

"I mean google my name," Rundel retorts. "You'll see what I've been through. Pretty simple to do."

Miller makes it clear there's nothing special about the constable in front of him.

"I'm responsible for the health and well-being of 150 members right now and I'm focused on working with all of them. You're one of 150 members."

Almost as soon as the words come out of Miller's mouth, he tries to claw them back. "You're not a number, you're a name."

It has always been a sore spot with Rundel that the RCMP has never said anything in his defence. The force has been mute, even after Rundel was acquitted. When Rundel took it upon himself to publicly declare his own innocence, the RCMP threatened him with a code of conduct violation.

So, Miller doesn't seem to realize he's digging a deeper hole when he pulls out an internal memo written just the day before. The memo's subject is RCMP Constable Rick Drought. Three years earlier, Drought fired his gun at a speeding carjacker. No one died, but Drought was charged with careless use of a firearm. The note, written by E Division Commanding Officer Craig Callens, celebrates the Crown's decision to stay the charge. Callens expresses sympathy and support for Drought and what he went through. The missive was sent to every Mountie in British Columbia.

Miller gloats. "It fully states we stood behind the member the entire time."

"Yeah, Rick has gone through a terrible last three years," Szewczok adds.

Miller and Szewczok appear oblivious to their own tone-deafness. Three years under a cloud and you get a company-wide attaboy. Rundel has endured eight years of international scorn and suspicion. The charges weren't stayed. He went through a trial. A prison term hung in the balance. He was actually cleared by a court. Rundel didn't even get a handshake from a senior officer when it was over.

"Did they publicly support him?" is all Rundel can muster.

Now Miller is sounding peeved.

"What's your definition of publicly supporting? We cannot say anything. That is legislation." Miller claims the RCMP was gagged by legislation governing the Independent Investigations Office. The IIO is the civilian agency that handles all investigations of police-involved shootings in British Columbia.

Miller is adamant. "If the CO was to say anything, then that's contravening laws and there are severe consequences for that."

What was sold to Rundel as a meet-and-greet feels more like a high-pressure pitch to buy a time-share property. During the meeting, Miller presses Rundel no fewer than three times for an answer on when he is going to return to work. Rundel leaves Miller's office feeling bullied and harassed, but he agrees to meet again in a couple of weeks.

Later, Rundel emails Miller to ask for a reference to the section of the IIO Act that prohibits the RCMP from making public statements about members involved in investigations. Miller responds by telling Rundel to look it up himself.

He does. It turns out there is no such provision. Miller is wrong.

A week later, Rundel is face to face with Inspector Miller again, this time in his psychologist's office. Dr. Larry Waterman has invited Miller to educate him about PTSD and how he believes Rundel's return to work should be handled. After taking some notes, Miller cuts to the chase. "What's the prognosis and timeline?" he asks. Waterman is vague. He "hopes" the Mountie will be back at work sometime in the new year. Miller is agitated.

"It's not up to you when Gerry goes back to work. It's up to Gerry."

Waterman is having none of it.

"No, it *is* up to me, and if Gerry wants to go back and I don't think he's ready, he isn't going back."

Waterman doesn't back down. Miller's attitude and tactics, the doctor insists, have likely set Rundel's recovery back by a couple of months. Miller begins to argue. Waterman recites his credentials and his authority to declare whether Rundel is fit for duty.

Miller asks again when that will be. Waterman gives him the same answer: the new year.

Realizing he can't outmanoeuvre the doctor, Miller shifts his focus to Rundel. He tells Waterman that Rundel has "trust issues."

"Most members under the rank of management have 'trust issues' with the force," the doctor replies. Waterman says while it's true Rundel has been financially supported by the force during his illness, the RCMP has failed to support him publicly. It's starting to look as if Miller brought a water pistol to a firefight.

"How has the force failed to do that?" Miller asks incredulously, looking at Rundel.

"I'll address that in an email later today," Rundel replies.

"Why can't you address it now?"

Rundel is steadfast. He's overwhelmed with emotion. He repeats that he'll explain in an email.

"You can publish your email on the front page of the *Globe and Mail*," Miller suggests, derisively adding that if Rundel were employed by an American corporation and had been off work for two years, he wouldn't be enjoying the financial support doled out by the RCMP.

Rundel is feeling attacked. "What's your point?"

Miller suggests that he could have simply sent Rundel's file to the RCMP's Health Services department recommending a medical discharge. He didn't. Isn't that evidence of support?

Rundel shakes as the anger wells up to the surface and he lays in to Miller, questioning how the senior RCMP officer could sit and listen to a psychologist explain the effects, symptoms, and treatment for PTSD, and express "not one ounce of compassion. Not one."

"Your file is too large," Miller says, as a way to explain why he apparently knows so little about what Rundel has been through. "I wouldn't recognize you. The general public doesn't know who you are. In fact, I wouldn't recognize Monty Robinson if I met him on the street."

"We're not here to discuss Monty Robinson," is all Rundel can say before the tense meeting comes to an end.

Rundel's promised email to Miller later that day is scathing. "We have had a series of phone conversations, emails, and meetings in the last few weeks. As a result I've walked away feeling harassed, belittled, bullied, and my career threatened and do not feel fully supported."

While the tone of Miller's emails is scrupulously cordial, Rundel believes the inspector's style is different in person.

"It appears to me, from some of your comments and actions, that you have no understanding, or interest, of what I have been through in the last eight years and how it has affected me, my family, my career, and aspirations in life."

Rundel pours out his thoughts.

"The Force has never supported me publicly or within its membership. I feel my moral fibre and ethical values have been challenged and attacked by this organization. Despite my honest efforts to maintain the *esprit de corps* of this paramilitary organization, it has felt at times paralyzing."

Whether Rundel's allegations are true, they are serious and damning. Miller's response, however, is bizarre. He makes no mention of Rundel's allegations. He simply asks Rundel to correct an error when he mistyped the date on the email, "for good order sake." He misspells Rundel's name.

304 | BLAMED AND BROKEN

304 | BLAMED AND BROKEN

What Rundel doesn't know is that calling out Miller as a bully has hit a nerve. Privately, Miller gets in touch with the RCMP's relatively new department for dealing with internal intimidation.

Miller types "Indications of a Harassment Complaint" as the subject of his email. He mentions nothing of his role in raising Rundel's ire, or his dispute with Rundel's psychologist. Miller simply claims that all he's done is meet and speak with Rundel and the errant Mountie is now refusing to talk to him.

"I am seeking any suggestions, advice, or guidance you may have to help me deal with him," Miller writes.

When Miller does get back to Rundel, he mentions nothing of the complaint. Instead, he invites Rundel to look at RCMP policy about harassment, and offers to meet again.

"Thanks and have a wonderful weekend," Miller writes.

Rundel reads the line and feels like he's been slapped in the face.

Unsure of what to think, Rundel calls up retired Staff Sergeant Ken Ackles, the officer who was the watch commander in Richmond the night of the incident in 2007. Rundel runs it all by Ackles. The retired Mountie's opinion is blunt. "What an asshole."

Dr. Waterman also weighs in.

"Gerry did exactly what you asked him to do," Waterman writes to Miller. "You asked him what was wrong and what you could do to help. When he told you how he was feeling, you responded with policy and resolution options."

Miller says that all he was doing was making sure he wouldn't be accused of sweeping Rundel's harassment complaints under the rug. He admits he has continued behind the scenes to identify Rundel as a potential instigator of a harassment complaint, for his own good.

"While you may feel that I am using policy, I respectfully disagree. I take an interest in all 150 police officers at Nanaimo Detachment and regularly speak to different Members on various issues. Unfortunately I can't speak to every Member as often as I would like."

The anxiety from the back-and-forth exacerbates Rundel's physical symptoms. When his home phone rings, he jumps. His headaches are back. He's not sleeping. When Rundel does drift off, he is plagued by stressful nightmares of being back at work, losing his badge, and having to face Inspector Miller to explain.

Waterman is concerned.

"In my opinion, he is in what I would describe as experiencing the full impact of the trauma he has been living for the past eight plus years." Waterman advises that Miller keep his contact with Rundel to email only.

Miller appears unsympathetic when he contacts the RCMP's Health Services officer about the situation.

"Cst. Rundel has demonstrated a pattern involving long term periods of absenteeism since April of 2009," Miller pleads in an email. He appears to doubt Dr. Waterman's claim that he has set Rundel back.

"I am seeking clarification and your recommendation as Cst. Rundel's Health Services Officer on whether any contact limitations and restrictions are objectively supported and appropriate with his medical condition."

Miller then ratchets up the pressure with an email to Rundel that RCMP bureaucrats help him draft. It contains an implied threat. "As the commander of your substantive unit, I am responsible to approve, rescind or deny your sick leave."

Miller gives Rundel a two-week deadline to respond with his intention to return to work.

Dr. Waterman is unable to prevent the inevitable. When he meets with Rundel again, he advises that Rundel's "clock has run out" and he must either return to work or face a medical discharge.

"I may not be well," Rundel concludes, "but I'm well enough to sit at a desk."

Miller, still nursing his frustration that Rundel won't talk to him, complains privately to the RCMP's employment requirements officer that he will not negotiate Rundel's return through his doctor. Miller doesn't understand that Rundel is returning to work, not because of his efforts, but in spite of them.

As the detachment gears up to put Rundel to work again, there is an initial worry that his usefulness as a police officer may be compromised.

306 | BLAMED AND BROKEN

The concern is the 2009 Supreme Court of Canada decision, R. v. McNeil. The court ruled that prosecutors must disclose any misconduct or criminal convictions of police involved in any case they bring to trial. If Rundel finds himself once more in the witness chair, can defence lawyers bring down the prosecution simply by raising the spectre of the Braidwood Inquiry?

The matter is settled by Superintendent Mark Fisher, who writes Rundel "was found not guilty of perjury so there should not be a McNeill [*sic*] issue."

The plan is for Rundel to return to work a couple of days a week at first. Miller, oblivious to the hurt Rundel still feels about his treatment, types up a quick email after speaking with Rundel on the phone. "Gerry, great talking to you! You sounded awesome."

Miller attaches the 2015 year-end Christmas message from the head of E Division, Craig Callens. Callens fills his note with buzzwords like *pride* and *service*. He recalls the shooting of an RCMP constable that occurred more than a year earlier. He highlights routine police activities during wildfires and the recent federal election. There is no mention of Rundel's acquittal and vindication. An eight-year battle fought at the centre of one of the most embarrassing attacks on the RCMP's reputation ended in Rundel's favour. It doesn't make the note intended to boost morale. While the RCMP wants Rundel back, it seems the force would prefer his return was under the radar.

Rundel has something else in mind.

Ten years after Bentley sent those prideful emails home from Depot, the sentiments seem contrived and mawkish. After Dziekanski's death, Bentley began receiving email and telephone threats on his own life. He was shuffled into the Olympic security unit — a dumping ground where no one actually did anything. Bentley wanted to move to Serious Crimes to investigate violent robberies and attempted murders. He'd be plainclothes and out of the public eye, but still doing something meaningful. When he was transferred back to Ontario, the RCMP stuck him in Protective Services, seen largely as another of the RCMP's holes where cops who can't cut it are sent. Even there, Bentley was allowed to act only as support to other officers involved in the tedious job of babysitting VIPs. The RCMP never asked Bentley what he wanted. After YVR, the RCMP made the decisions for him.

Surely that would change now, Bentley thinks, now that he'd been acquitted both at trial and in a resounding decision by the Court of Appeal. Surely the RCMP would move quickly to welcome Bentley back so he could resume the pursuit of his childhood dream of being a police officer. Yet even as the RCMP tries to force a reluctant Gerry Rundel back to work, it appears to be working doubly hard to keep Bentley from returning.

Bentley's doctor clears him for duty in September, three months after the Court of Appeal upheld his acquittal. It takes nearly two more months of unanswered emails and phone calls before the bureaucrats who control Bentley's future invite him to a meeting to discuss his return to work.

Bentley has been off the job for more than six years. When he was side-lined by PTSD and depression, he only had eighteen months as a Mountie under his belt. He needs retraining in use of force, first aid, and a host of new workplace policies. As he enters the long-awaited meeting, Bentley hopes he'll be encouraged to begin upgrading his skills using the RCMP's internal online training programs. Bentley gets his first disappointment when he is told that will not happen. The encryption keys needed to access the training material online through an RCMP laptop are deemed too sensitive to give to Bentley. It's stated that, first, he needs to go through a security clearance, which could take another six months or more.

Bentley learns of a potentially bigger problem. He must not only submit to a complete examination by an RCMP doctor for what's known as a Periodic Health Assessment or PHA, he will have to convince the RCMP's psychologist he's fit for duty. At the long-awaited meeting, Bentley is introduced to psychologist Dr. David Fischman for the first time.

Bentley leaves the meeting frustrated but nonetheless anxious to meet every test the RCMP has set for him. In the meantime, staff relations representative Sergeant Peter Merrifield beseeches his superiors to deal with Bentley quickly.

"There are far more than medical assessments and profiles which need to be addressed if we as an organization are to salvage a very bright and capable member," Merrifield writes in an email. Merrifield's plea fails to light a fire under anyone. It may even have had the opposite effect and caused Bentley's overseers to resent him.

Bentley passes his physical, but his superiors give him the lowest rating in the RCMP's fitness-for-duty rating. On a scale from zero (best) to six (worst), Bentley is given a medical profile number of Oh-six: unfit for duty. When Bentley speaks with Corporal Cathie Glenn, the Gradual Return to Work coordinator for O Division in Ontario where Bentley is assigned, she has even worse news. When he does get back to work — eventually — he will not be doing investigative policing. Glenn tells him he will be put back in Protective Services because, she says, he needs a "controlled environment."

So, Bentley is already disappointed when he meets again with those handling his file. Nonetheless, Bentley expects to hear a plan when he walks into the boardroom at the detachment in Newmarket. Not only is there no return-to-work plan offered, the meeting appears to be little more than a meet-and-greet with a number of RCMP officers who may or may not have anything to do with Bentley's career.

Sergeant Merrifield, who sits with Bentley, becomes upset. He calls out everyone in the room for letting Bentley languish. The room is tense and Bentley is asked to leave while Merrifield embarrasses his superiors behind the boardroom door.

Corporal Glenn blithely omits any reference to what happened when she writes a follow-up email to Bentley a few days later. She asks if he has "any questions after … digesting all that was discussed in our meeting." Glenn then adds it will be well into the new year when they move forward on Bentley's case. It is an email written in the classic RCMP CYA (cover-your-ass) style.

Bentley barely contains his contempt in a reply. "To be forced back into the VIP unit feels punitive. I am not comfortable with being pushed into the VIP Unit with promises of future 'possibilities.'"

Bentley isn't alone in fearing the RCMP's autocratic decision. The psychologist who's been treating him for the past six years sternly warns the RCMP that assigning Bentley to Protective Services in the first place "in all likelihood may have contributed to the symptoms of depression and PTSD." Dr. Deborah Nixon says sending him back there "could trigger those memories and corresponding feelings. Why risk this negative outcome?" Nixon's letter might well have been written in Sanskrit for all the impact it has on those who read it.

A month later, Bentley is summoned to yet another meeting. He's told it's so he can give his informed consent to a series of documents from his file that will be passed on to the doctors chosen to conduct the psychological and psychiatric assessments. Once more, Bentley arrives at the meeting with Sergeant Merrifield at his side.

The meeting goes sideways immediately. Rather than receiving records from his file to review, Bentley is presented with two letters. One instructs a psychiatrist at Toronto's Centre for Addiction and Mental Health to evaluate Bentley's mental state. Is he capable of physical confrontations with violent offenders? Can he be trusted with guns and other weapons?

The other letter, addressed to a psychologist who will conduct a separate evaluation, is drafted by RCMP divisional psychologist Dr. David Fischman. Fischman hands Bentley a copy, tells him to read it over, and leaves the room. Bentley is bowled over.

It is a four-page narrative that bears only a passing resemblance to Bentley's understanding of what he went through. As he tries to comprehend what he's reading, the PTSD symptoms of panic and fear rear up and now threaten to smother him right where he sits.

Fischman begins by telling psychologist Dr. Percy Wright that if he isn't already familiar with Bentley's backstory "much information is available through open sources." Fischman himself has never had a conversation with Bentley, let alone conducted any interview with him. The letter Fischman now proffers as a factual dossier is cobbled together from websites like Wikipedia.

"The member's absence from work involved his attendance at an incident where questions were raised concerning the appropriate use of force." Fischman sets up a challenge for the evaluating psychologist: determine whether "Constable Bentley does in fact have the capacity and motivation to exercise the judgment and impulse control required to use the minimum amount of force necessary to stabilize a volatile situation and the capacity for integrity consistent with the core values of the RCMP."

Bentley is both stunned and angry. It was Bentley who had first calmly greeted Dziekanski with a casual "How's it goin', bud?" Bentley had nothing to do with the decision to use the Taser. It was Bentley who brought attention to Dziekanski's lips turning blue. Bentley upgraded the ambulance call. Bentley was not in charge that night. He was taking statements from witnesses when Dziekanski died. He did everything he'd been trained to do. B.C.'s highest court found Bentley's mistakes in reporting the sequence of events were honest ones. Now Fischman's letter could prejudice Bentley's critical psychological exam by implying the Mountie acted improperly and the RCMP can't be sure if Bentley can be trusted again.

It is made clear that if Bentley doesn't consent to the letters, the long, slow process of being cleared to return to work will come to a permanent halt and Bentley can say goodbye to any hope he had of salvaging his career.

Bentley flashes back to an encounter with Dr. Ron Clavier, an RCMP specialist he was ordered to see after testifying at Braidwood. Clavier had berated him for having single-handedly devastated the RCMP's reputation and suggested a stint in jail "wouldn't be so bad." Like Fischman, Clavier appeared to form his professional opinion of Bentley's state by reading the slurry of media headlines at the time. Bentley had left that meeting in 2009 in tears. Now he is angry.

Wrong, wrong, wrong, Bentley thinks to himself.

Bentley's understanding had been that he'd be signing off on forms about his medical history. Now he's confronted with a letter based on media reports that makes him sound like a soulless psychopath.

"Is there a risk that this member may act out with inappropriate aggression with members of the public?" Fischman asks in his letter.

Bentley turns to Merrifield for help. Merrifield warns that overreacting could delay the assessments Bentley needs to get back to work. The letter doesn't matter all that much, Merrifield tells him. When Fischman returns, Bentley reluctantly signs off on it. He second-guesses himself on the drive back to his house.

When he gets home, Bentley reads portions of the letter to his father over the phone. He also calls Mike Ingles and recites it. He phones up Gerry Rundel, too. They each tell him the same thing: the letter is awful.

Bentley crafts his own letter to Fischman, complaining that the doctor has written something full of "factual errors, misleading information" that depicts him "overall in a negative light."

Fischman responds in an email indicating that, indeed, he relied on "open sources." He admits he could have interviewed Bentley and didn't. Fischman says the constable is free to submit any corrections for his consideration.

"That being said," Fischman writes, "I remind you that your consent to … undergo the assessment is valid only if it is free and informed … withdrawal of consent will prevent us from proceeding with a recommendation." Translation: object to my letter, forget about getting back to work.

Bentley isn't sure if Fischman is the sole author of the damning letter or if it flows from an internal RCMP narrative intended to scuttle his chances at resuming his career.

Bentley contemplates a protest: he simply won't go to the assessments. If Fischman's letter could influence the doctors who are conducting them, the resulting thumbs-down could sewer his career for good. Challenging the RCMP now would be playing hardball and Merrifield urges him to reconsider. Together they'll speak to the doctors doing the evaluation about the errors in Fischman's letter. Merrifield urges Bentley to trust the system. It is a system that has until now been pointed at him like a weapon.

With the assessments just a few days away, Bentley's worry is that the tests are long. They demand a well-rested, clear-thinking mind. He doesn't have one after all he's been through. However, Bentley agrees to go if Fischman retracts the letter. When Merrifield calls Fischman to get his co-operation, Fischman not only refuses, he issues a not-so-veiled threat: Bentley must "own his actions" or Fischman won't change Bentley's medical profile number. If Fischman keeps Bentley as an 06, he'll never get back to work.

Bentley concludes he has no leverage. He's scared and nervous when he arrives at the Centre for Addiction and Mental Health for his psych evaluations. He and Merrifield do their best to put Fischman's letter in context to the doctors doing the exams. They try not to sound conspiratorial. In the end, psychologist Percy Wright doesn't seem interested in anything Fischman has to say. Wright seems more impressed with the fact Bentley wants to go back to work at all considering what he'd been through. Bentley answers hundreds of questions on paper. He submits to several hours of interviews with two specialists. He passes their assessments. Bentley also passes the point of believing the RCMP will ever do right by him.

"He's fucking delusional. He's toast." Monty Robinson's verdict in the case of Bentley versus the RCMP is swift and succinct. Robinson believes Bentley's dream of resuming an honourable career with the RCMP is a fiction. Robinson sounds as upset with Bentley as he does when he talks about the RCMP. Bentley is "damaged," Robinson says; Bentley has no stomach for confrontation, even when his own career is at stake.

The last time the two talked, Robinson lit in to Bentley about it. "They're keeping you at a six, you dumb shit, because they want to keep you where they can turf you. When I got retired, I went from a two to a four by the stroke of a fucking pen in a week."

Now he adds with resignation, "Bill couldn't fight his way out of a wet paper bag and I told him that before. That's the unfortunate part here because this stuff is not going away."

Robinson's penchant for quick, harsh, and personal criticism is one reason Bentley doesn't call very often. So Robinson learns many of the details of Bentley's predicament indirectly through people like Gerry Rundel. Bentley and Rundel share the fate of being acquitted. The two speak often.

Still, Robinson opines as if Bentley is sitting at his kitchen table in Delta, B.C., not thousands of kilometres away in Toronto. "They keep dicking you around, right? Why are they doing that? Why the delays? Why all these meetings? Why all the backtalk? Why the inconsistencies?"

Robinson is convinced the RCMP is setting Bentley up to get rid of him. The way Robinson sees it, Bentley has only one strategy left: strike first. Take the RCMP to court.

"You know damn well I'm suing."

It is a mark of how Robinson's brain works that he is planning a lawsuit against the RCMP while facing the imminent collapse of his appeal because of the non-payment of his legal bills. Robinson would rather think about what he can do about the future, than his fate if his appeal is struck.

"I have to accept the gravity of having been convicted for two years less a day. It's going to be wrong but has not the last eight years been wrong for me? What's another two years?"

As he speaks, Robinson glances at a single photo stuck to his fridge. The picture shows Robinson as a young father, holding his newborn infant son. Jail will rip him away from his boy, who's now a teenager.

"Is my life going to fall apart for two years less a day? I've got two pensions that they can't take away from me that I've secured. I look at people losing their jobs. Two years less a day is not going to affect my ability to pay for child support, or affect my dental plan. All these little things I have in place, which a lot of people don't. If I lose focus on that, I'll be angry and bitter every day."

Robinson adds with a casual ease that as a former police officer he'll be in protective custody. He says it as if that's a good thing.

While Robinson's future may be bleak, his present isn't going all that well, either. The complaints he and Gerry Rundel filed against the Vancouver Police Department, for how they investigated Janice Norgard's allegations of a secret meeting among the four YVR Mounties, have been dismissed.

In a letter from the Office of the Police Complaint Commissioner, Deputy Commissioner Rollie Woods — himself a former VPD detective — shuts down any hope that what happened will be examined. "It is clear that none of the presiding Justices [in the perjury trials] discounted Ms. Norgard's testimony," Woods writes. "Your assertion that 'Janice Norgard is guilty of Public Mischief' appears to be without merit."

Woods is guilty of the worst kind of parsing. While it is true no judge went so far as to call Norgard a liar, none accepted her evidence as fact.

Robinson and Rundel both accused the VPD of failing to do basic police work. The detectives involved never bothered to look at the Mounties' shift schedules, which could have ruled out a clandestine meeting. They didn't question Norgard's motives for coming forward with her story in the first place.

Woods says the commission won't even question how police went about their investigation unless it were to come up at Robinson's trial.

"Please provide transcript excerpts or evidence adduced from your trial that would provide a foundation of the allegations you raised."

Woods sets an entirely arbitrary and capricious bar that can't be met. The issue of the tunnel vision by VPD detectives never came up during the perjury trials because lawyers for Robinson and Rundel were focused on discrediting Norgard herself, not the police who put forward her shifting story as true.

"Following careful and serious consideration of your complaint," Woods writes, "your file with our office will remain closed."

Robinson sees it as a frustrating, if predictable, setback. It is his legal bill, however, that becomes his urgent focus as the calendar speeds toward 2016. Robinson's lawyer is sounding dire. "This is causing great distress to our operations," David Crossin writes. The RCMP says Robinson's bill will be paid, but Crossin is tired of waiting. "They have suggested that the technical obligation is for you to be reimbursed. Is it possible, Monte [sic], you could pay the accounts and then we send their cheque to you?"

Robinson is indignant when he replies. "The technical obligation the RCMP suggested is punitive and it exposes their continued harassment and persecution. I will not take on any more of their responsibilities."

In the new year, however, Crossin warns there's no time for debate. The factum — the written basis of Robinson's appeal — is due by Friday, February 5. If that deadline is missed, "the appeal could be struck."

Staff Sergeant Brad Szewczok, who guided Rundel through his return-to-work battle, steps in to find the source of the holdup. Szewczok speaks to Craig Callens, the commanding officer of E Division. It was Callens who vilified Robinson after his conviction for attempting to obstruct justice. It was Callens who publicly lamented that he wished he could have fired Robinson rather than sign his medical discharge papers. Now it is Callens Robinson he must trust to go up the chain on his behalf.

"Craig Callens checking on my perjury funding," he says with a smirk, "is like asking the person torturing you if can you help him out. Like Fuck!"

Callens does in fact check. Twice. Within days Szewczok reports that the public safety minister has signed off on paying for Robinson's unsuccessful defence: $192,000. There is bad news, however. The public safety minister has struck a board to look at whether to pay for Robinson's appeal. That bit of Ottawa bureaucracy will take time that Robinson doesn't have.

Szewczok turns to the Mounted Police Members Legal Fund — a pool of money all Mounties can apply to use when faced with crushing lawyers' fees. In short order, the non-profit fund grants Robinson an interim loan of fifty thousand dollars. It's enough to get his lawyer working again on the appeal. Robinson will not have to surrender himself to go to jail. Not yet, at least.

Robinson is emboldened by his reprieve and he fires off another rocket to his RCMP contacts. It is replete with his now familiar script about cover-ups and scapegoating. "The RCMP Heads knowingly agreed with reports that they knew were flawed, namely Thomas Braidwood and Paul Kennedy which contributed to my current circumstances. It is also troubling that Craig Callens who mislead the public on my retirement and went along with the scapegoating of the YVR members was the person who checked on my appeal funding just recently."

Szewczok is in no mood for Robinson's chest-thumping when he writes back. "Monty … Lay off on the emails would you. We are working hard for you here."

———————

Robinson isn't the only one with money troubles. Gerry Rundel is being squeezed by the RCMP, as well. In February 2016, Rundel's lawyer, Glen Orris, is still waiting to be paid nearly a year after he submitted his first bill to the RCMP. Orris is owed in excess of eighty-seven thousand dollars.

"If the accounts are not paid within 30 days," Orris writes to the RCMP in a letter devoid of any cordial politeness, "my only recourse will be to commence legal action against the RCMP."

The RCMP doesn't seem shaken by the threat. Betty Georgoulas, a claims analyst with the RCMP in British Columbia, insists "the matter is completely out of our hands." Georgoulas says the RCMP won't pay because the force has to wait for "approval from the Honourable Ralph Goodale, minister of public safety and emergency preparedness."

Georgoulas then turns Orris against his own client, suggesting he sue Rundel for the money. "The RCMP is not part of the contract between the Member and his/her lawyer."

As it turns out, this is only half true. While Treasury Board policy on legal assistance at public expense is intended to pay back employees who've already paid their own legal bills, the RCMP established a practice of covering the bills to prevent their members from going into severe debt.

Rundel is now worried that, on top of everything else, he's on the hook for his own defence while acting as a police officer. He is saved only when the RCMP's answer about the delay is revealed to be fiction. Georgoulas acknowledges the outstanding bills, one of which is eleven months old, could never have been approved by the public safety minister because they never left RCMP Commissioner Bob Paulson's desk.

"This morning I was informed by Ottawa that on February 26, 2016, the Commissioner signed the submission requesting the payment of the fees for Cst. Rundel," Georgoulas writes. "The submission package was delivered by hand this morning to the Minister's office."

There is no explanation as to why Paulson sat on the bills for close to a year without signing off on them. There is no apology for misleading Rundel and his lawyer about what was really going on.

All of this, of course, does nothing to ease the anxiety Rundel feels about being bullied back to work. He is buoyed by the few members at Nanaimo detachment who welcome him with a smile, or an enthusiastic handshake. These are the cops who never doubted him. These are the brothers and sisters who thank God it wasn't them on duty the night Robert Dziekanski died.

Rundel's return to work is indeed gradual. Yet even at just three half days a week, Rundel's PTSD symptoms are returning: headaches, anxiety, and sleeplessness. He can't shake the feeling of humiliation and powerlessness as he tries to work again for an organization that he feels betrayed him.

One saving grace is that Rundel is working across the street from the main detachment. He's away from the managers — the "white shirts." Rundel drives a desk, working for the federal Serious Organized Crimes section. It's plainclothes, and largely entails doing background checks. It's not glamorous. Rundel likes it that way.

When he's not supporting criminal investigations, Rundel is catching up on the training he's missed. One of the mandatory courses he has to take one day is called "Crisis Intervention and De-escalation." Rundel's PTSD symptoms return with a vengeance.

The course was created as a direct result of the recommendations of Thomas Braidwood, who, among other things, declared for all time that Rundel and his former partners were liars. Every Mountie who takes the training (and it is mandatory for all Mounties) learns that Gerry Rundel and his former partners fucked up the night Robert Dziekanski died. Rundel is so upset by having to complete a course that implicates him as a screw-up, he complains diplomatically to his superiors.

"The introduction of the course as it stands provides members with the perception that the 4 officers didn't respond appropriately," he writes.

Rundel isn't shy about claiming the course is based on the flawed conclusions of a biased former judge. "There have now been two Supreme Court Judges and three Appeal Courts Justices that have contradicted Braidwood thereby exposing the flaws in his recommendations and allegations made against myself and my fellow officers."

Rundel requests the force revise the course to recognize that, so far, two of the Mounties involved have been vindicated by the courts. Rundel's note is passed up the chain, finally landing on the desk of Superintendant Michel Legault, the officer in charge of training for the Pacific Region.

"I understand where Constable Rundel is coming from," he replies. However, Legault explains that the training course is owned by the Province of British Columbia, which is contracting police services from the RCMP. "The RCMP is not in a position to dictate changes," Legault says.

Once more the RCMP sends a message to the YVR four, that they should just suck it up. Their pain should stay in the past. Legault's reply is at best a bureaucratic shrug.

It is the last time Rundel asks his superiors for backup. Forbidden from speaking publicly, Rundel has only one avenue open to him to clear his name. It is a nuclear option that will surely annihilate what's left of his career. Rundel sues the RCMP.

The lawsuit Rundel files in B.C. court in March 2016 is technically against the attorney general of Canada and the minister of justice for

British Columbia. However, that is only because they are the authorities responsible for the RCMP.

Rundel's claim starts from the position that he was never involved in the use of the Taser or any decision to use the weapon the night Robert Dziekanski died. Yet, ever since he has been made to wear every criticism, valid or false, of what happened.

Commissioner Bill Elliott lumped all four Mounties together by publicly declaring all had "fallen short of their duties." Elliott also gave fuel to those tending a billowing fire of conspiracy, when he wrongly insisted the four inappropriately met in private after the incident. Elliott's successor, Bob Paulson, put Rundel and his former partners into the category of "rotten apples."

Rundel alleges that everyone who blocked the release of information that would have set the record straight is in breach of their duty. They ought to have known they were casting Rundel and the other three as "scapegoats" and leading them directly into a hailstorm of public criticism and contempt.

For this, Rundel alleges he's the victim of negligent and intentional infliction of mental suffering.

Rundel's lawsuit claims his career as a Mountie has been left in tatters after years of persistent national and international reporting. He's lost the trust of his fellow members, and can no longer trust that they will back him when he needs it.

His ordeal with Inspector Miller is detailed in full as an example of alleged harassment, and bullying.

Rundel also alleges the actions of other superior officers breached the RCMP's own administration manual, which defines harassment as "the improper use of power ... to interfere with an employee's job. It can include intimidation, threats, blackmail or coercion."

As a result, Rundel claims, he "suffered permanent and irreparable harm including extreme embarrassment, loss of reputation, extreme stress resulting in disabling psychological and physical injury, personal expense and financial loss."

The day the media learns the lawsuit has been filed, the coverage is pat and predictably shallow. While it is admittedly hard for any journalist to get to the bottom of unproven allegations in a statement of claim, few news agencies seem interested in trying. It is much easier to write a story simply by reporting it has been filed. Not surprisingly, TV news illustrates the story with visuals from the Pritchard video of Robert Dziekanski flailing on the airport floor. It is well known in TV journalism that viewers focus on the pictures, not the script. So it's no surprise on the day when Rundel alleges manifest bullying and harassment within the RCMP that the public turns on him, instead.

Most lob opinions anonymously in the comments sections online: "The plaintiff suffered extreme embarrassment; Robert Dziekanski suffered death, Not feeling much empathy here."

They are the same old arguments about conspiracy and cover-up, fuelled by the same falsehoods and flat-out lies about what really happened.

"One of the reasons these guys were charged with perjury is that they had talked about what they were going to do to this guy, before they even arrived on scene. Their actions, which resulted in his death, were pre-planned. They did not attempt to diffuse [sic] the situation … they were itching to hurt this guy."

Rundel is freely referred to as a murderer and a piece of shit by people whose memories for the truth have faded just as profoundly as their grasp of fiction tightened. The commenters are brave souls who post without names, like the person going simply by "E." "We have reached a new low. This piece of garbage should be in jail for murder. He was on salary for years instead of being indicted and now he is suing because he was made to 'look bad.' They killed an entirely innocent man and they have no guilt or shame. I hope something horrible happens to this garbage dressed as a human being."

Many posters hold up Braidwood's report as a talisman of truth, a shield in their crusade to avenge the death, nay, murder, of Robert Dziekanski. The trouble with these comments is that they make it clear that the people who've written them haven't bothered to read Braidwood's final report. If they had, they'd know that even the esteemed former judge went out of his way to make it clear none of the officers had any intention to harm Dziekanski, let alone kill him.

Rundel knows not to scroll inadvertently into the comments when he reads media coverage of his lawsuit, lest he catch sight of one of the pitchforks being wielded by the angry online mob.

The next day at work, a few members come up to him and give him a quiet pat on the shoulders. The White Shirts at Nanaimo detachment are silent.

If Bill Bentley's superiors in Ontario are worried that legal action is contagious, they don't appear concerned. Four months after Bentley passed all of the medical and psych tests to return to work, his medical profile number is moved to a 4, meaning he can return to work with restrictions. Yet Bentley is still sitting at home. That's when he files his own lawsuit. Bentley relies on the same lawyer who worked with Sheila Lemaitre and Gerry Rundel, so the language is very much boilerplate, though no less damning.

Bentley alleges the same culpable destruction of his reputation and career that Rundel does. Like Rundel, he argues the timing of the RCMP's apology and financial settlement to Dziekanski's mother just before Braidwood's report was released had the effect of implying that Bentley et al. were at fault.

While Bentley's lawsuit also details his experience with Dr. Fischman, Bentley takes the additional step of filing a complaint about Fischman directly to the College of Psychologists of Ontario.

"Based on Dr. Fischman's letter and his conduct," Bentley writes to the college, "I am also concerned that due to the position of power he holds, he may try to sabotage my career, as he has already threatened to do so."

An investigation by the college, however, refutes most of Bentley's claims and exonerates the doctor. A panel that examines the case concludes that while "this may have been a tense and difficult situation for both parties ... it does not appear that there is any independent evidence to corroborate Cst. Bentley's report that Dr. Fischman threatened Cst. Bentley's career." The panel decides to take no further action.

Even as Bentley struggles to rebuild his reputation and resurrect a career that has been practically mummified, he has the mental and emotional room to worry about his former partner Kwesi Millington.

Millington stoically insists that he feels no differently about his future, knowing his appeal hearing is just a couple of weeks away, than he did months ago.

Millington, whom Bentley firmly believes is innocent of perjury, is a bad liar.

"Kwesi's not doing good," Bentley confides on the eve of Millington's last attempt to avoid prison.

30 | JUSTICE

IT'S A BRIGHT, SUNNY day in June 2016 when Millington surrenders himself to the sheriffs at the Vancouver courthouse on the morning of his appeal hearing. Millington is made to sit alone in a holding cell while his lawyer, Ravi Hira, appears in a courtroom several floors above, alongside the special prosecutor's team. It is a seemingly prejudicial rule of the court that someone who's been convicted — even though free on bail — is not permitted to be present at such a critical point in their own defence. There isn't even any provision for Millington to listen or watch the proceedings of his own case. While he waits in isolation, a panel of three appeal court judges considers a central issue among several: whether Justice Ehrcke erred by concluding that the only inference he could draw from Millington's inquiry testimony was that the Mountie was lying.

The hearing ends after several hours. Hira is uncertain how the judges will hear his argument that at the very least Millington deserves a new trial. It could take them days, weeks, or months to decide. Millington will be released on bail while the judges deliberate. A coterie of Millington's supporters waits in the lobby of the court building for him to emerge from his cell. As minutes turn to hours, Mike Ingles looks nervously for Millington's appearance. One of the sheriffs who checked Millington into his cell is now leaving for the day. "Everything okay?" he says. Ingles cracks a smile in reply. "Waiting for him to get sprung.

Thanks for all your help this morning." As the sheriff reaches the door he smiles back, offering a word of sympathy. "Special consideration."

A month after Millington asked for another trial, he has been summoned back to Vancouver to hear the answer. Once more he surrenders himself to the sheriffs at the Vancouver courthouse, and is locked into a holding cell. Ravi Hira tells him that if someone doesn't come down in short order to release him, that means he's lost his appeal, and it will take some time to file a notice to the Supreme Court of Canada seeking an appeal there, and to arrange bail.

Several floors above him, the appeal court justices take their seats, and announce their decision in twenty seconds. Appeal dismissed. While there are reasons issued, they boil down to a simple principle: Millington's trial judge, in their opinion, didn't make any mistakes in law when he decided, on the basis of no direct evidence, that Millington committed perjury. Judge Ehrcke was entitled to do that, they said.

What virtually no one notices at first — not even Millington's own lawyer — is that one of the three appeal court judges who decided against him is David Harris. Harris was also part of the panel that dismissed the appeal brought by the Crown to overturn Bentley's acquittal. On the surface it appears irreconcilable. How can the same judge decide Bentley is not guilty yet Millington is? It's because the Court of Appeal was never looking at guilt or innocence. It cared only if Ehrcke could be shown to have made a mistake in law. The substance of his decision is almost entirely irrelevant.

Rundel is beside himself, questioning how Harris could seemingly believe two conflicting conclusions. "He agreed Bill didn't collude and then agreed Kwesi did," Rundel says. "Monty was physically not down at the subdetachment," he continues, "so who colluded with who?" Rundel is ashen-faced. "It seemed cold-hearted," he says, shaking his head. "I can't believe it. Just three words, 'Appeal is dismissed.' After nine years."

Staff Sergeant Mike Ingles, who has stood by all four officers since the night Dziekanski died, is dumbfounded when he writes to each of them. "I do not believe for a second he lied, attempted to be untruthful, or in any way obstruct any proceeding." Ingles is deeply disappointed. "As someone who believes it is better for 100 guilty men to go free than have one innocent person convicted it has shaken my faith in the system."

Married just a year, Cindy has taken Millington's last name, and everything that comes with it. "He's probably the most gracious, kind, thoughtful ... I'm gonna cry," she says, tears welling up. "It actually hurts him that people think anything worse or think anything wrong about him. They don't see that side of him that I do. People just think of him as that horrible guy that night that did that horrible thing. It's not who he is."

Millington says he would give anything not to have been working that night. To this day he is haunted by Dziekanski's death. In one sense, Millington died, too. His life stopped during those twenty-six seconds. "I feel everything is on hold. Everything's on hold and everything's uncertain. I feel like I'm being tested," Millington says. There will be no moving forward with their lives for the foreseeable future. Having children is out of the question.

As the case against Robinson enters its tenth year, the B.C. Court of Appeal announces it has come to a decision just eleven days into 2017. Robinson's goal to overturn his conviction is denied, but it is not a unanimous ruling. The appeal is rejected by two of the three judges on the panel. The third, Justice Peter Willcock, recognizes what has been obvious all along: there's a problem reconciling the finding of Robinson's judge that all four were involved in a conspiracy with the fact that two were acquitted. "The troubling fact in this case," Willcock writes in his dissenting opinion, "is that the differing outcomes followed careful consideration of substantially the same evidence." Willcock expresses his bewilderment that all of the judges looked at the same statements made to IHIT, the same eyewitness accounts, and the Pritchard video, yet came to different conclusions. At best, Willcock opines, the officers made just one common error describing what happened. "In light of these cases it cannot be said with any confidence that the trial judge would have concluded there had been collusion between the officers."

If it were up to Willcock, he would order a new trial. That isn't going to happen. However, the fact that an experienced jurist acknowledges what has been plain to anyone familiar with evidence gives Robinson hope. The fact that the appeal decision is not unanimous also means Robinson has an automatic right to have his case considered by the Supreme Court of Canada. It is also the first clear sign from the justice system that raises doubt about the reasons the Mounties were charged in the first place.

A much bigger issue at stake is that if the decisions convicting Robinson and Millington are allowed to stand, they will form an authority in law, a reference that can potentially be relied upon in other courts to convict police officers who make mistakes when describing an incident. It will send ripples through the law enforcement profession. Police officers will be reluctant to make any detailed statements immediately after a critical incident, as Robinson and his former fellow officers did. Who can blame them, after watching four Mounties lose their careers, their reputations and lives destroyed for a decade, because the man they tried to arrest using the skills they were taught died? For that reason alone, resolving the issues should be of critical public interest.

The federal minister of public safety had stalled Robinson's request for legal funding at public expense for close to a year. Robinson was forced to rely on the Mounted Police Members Legal Fund to pay for his appeal. It is a full two months after his case is already decided that the RCMP tells Robinson he's on his own. "Please be advised," an RCMP superintendent writes to Robinson, "the Minister found it would not be in the public interest to approve your request, under exceptional circumstances. Therefore your request for legal assistance is denied." There are no explanations for Goodale's decision. Given that Millington's funding is approved fairly quickly, it is tempting to conclude that what should have been a dispassionate evaluation, based strictly on the facts surrounding what happened at the airport ten years ago, was anything but in Robinson's case.

Robinson is emboldened by the court decision, not disheartened. In the months ahead, he steps up his letter-writing campaign, sending occasional emails directly to the federal justice minister and the prime minister himself, Justin Trudeau. "Crown's theory of similar mistakes are events that actually happened and not mistakes," he writes. "Striking similarities is not evidence of collusion but it is evidence of Crown laying charges for political reasons," Robinson rails. "How is the RCMP Brass not criminally responsible for accepting false facts that lead to charges on four of its members and convictions of two?"

It is long past the point at which Robinson might care whose toes he is stepping on. "It has been a Tsunami of corruption since 2007 that is so ingrained in the systems that one cannot hope to change Mother Nature, one just hopes to survive the storm."

Surviving will be difficult. Robinson and Millington will have to wait until the fall for their final shots at innocence.

On a cold, grey day in October, the great steel doors on the front of the Supreme Court of Canada building in Ottawa are reminiscent of the entrance to Dracula's castle. Surely, entering this building generates a similar fear for some, and carries the same risk that, once inside, an accused may never leave unmarked, able to walk freely in the sunlight.

On the day of the dual appeals of Robinson and Millington, the weather in Ottawa adds to a sense of foreboding. Winds from a terrific storm claw at the Canadian flags clinging to the masts in front of the building. The rain is blowing sideways. Traffic lights are out. Inside the court's cavernous lobby, towering polished stone pillars rise three storeys high to the ceiling, making anyone beneath feel small.

Despite the stakes for this hearing, there are no sad faces among the handful of people who have come in out of the rain on this day before Halloween, ten years since those twenty-six seconds swallowed so many lives. Millington and his wife and mother exchange handshakes and hugs with a small group of supporters, including Bentley and Rundel, who have both travelled to Ottawa to lend moral support. Lawyer Glen Orris, who successfully argued Rundel's innocence at his trial, is here as Millington's counsel, hoping to persuade the Supreme Court justices of the same truth.

Robinson has decided to stay home and watch the proceedings online. The lawyer who unsuccessfully defended him in both his criminal trials isn't here either. A few weeks ago, David Crossin surprised Robinson by telling him he would not be able to represent him, without explaining why. The next day it was announced that Crossin had been tapped to sit as a judge on the B.C. Supreme Court. Elizabeth France, Crossin's junior co-counsel who worked on the case, is now Robinson's last hope for vindication.

Up the stone stairs behind another set of doors, the wood-panelled hearing room waits. The lawyers sit at desks at the front of the room, heads down, pens in hand, writing as if they are students at a school exam and there's a minute left on the clock until the cry of "pens down." The smiles shared in the lobby now fade. The room goes quiet as seven justices enter through a door behind the bench and take their seats in seven red, high-backed chairs. A large digital timer set with thirty minutes on the clock begins to count.

France has half an hour to keep Robinson from serving a two-year prison sentence. She does her best to explain why, in Robinson's case, the B.C. Court of Appeal failed to catch the errors in Justice Nathan Smith's verdict to convict him. Smith had found Robinson lied when he told the Braidwood Inquiry he was mistaken when he told investigators he'd "wrestled" Dziekanski to the ground. The officers did wrestle with Dziekanski on the ground and Robinson testified he'd "blended the whole interaction" together. In order to conclude that was a lie and not just a mistake, Smith linked it to another mistake several officers made in describing Dziekanski as "swinging" the stapler before he was Tasered. Smith had said that not only showed that Robinson's explanation was perjury, but that there was in fact collusion.

"Seven civilian witnesses used swing or similar words," as Robinson did, France tells the justices. There's no suggestion the witnesses were colluding. Prosecutor Eric Gottardi twiddles his pen between his fingers as France tries to win Robinson's liberty. He stares off into space, puts his head in his hands as if bored, and occasionally makes a face expressing disagreement, shaking his head.

It's very soon clear that each of the Supreme Court justices has already formed an opinion about the evidence. Justice Michael Moldaver sounds annoyed with France's arguments. "The trial judge found your client perjured himself in respect of the wrestling, as well," Moldaver says from the bench. "Let's assume the collusion charge is not made out, where does that get you?"

France points out that collusion is the lynchpin of the Crown's case. It goes to the heart of what the Crown says was the motive to lie: to cover up excessive use of force. France reminds the justices that two other judges found there was no collusion, and two officers were acquitted.

"What if the convictions had come first?" Justice Andromache Karakatsanis asks. It is a purely hypothetical question that has no relevance to the facts at hand, but it is one of the many challenges the justices toss down from the bench, as if they are flexing some atrophied legal muscle.

France replies that of course it works both ways. Why wouldn't it? "You want to be certain of your analysis," France explains, "and you want to make sure that you've applied the appropriate legal principals and come to the correct conclusion."

When France's time is up, Orris rises and picks up on the point that the Court of Appeal should have seriously questioned why Millington was convicted yet Bentley and Rundel were not. "We've got a contrary finding here." Orris says the appeal court should have asked, "Why is that? Why is that?"

While this may seem like a commonsensical approach to justice, especially when someone's liberty and reputation is at stake, Orris's proposition is seen almost as legal blasphemy by Justice Michael Moldaver. "It could be that two judges look at something and both come to reasonable determinations and they come to different reasonable determinations on the basis of the evidence before them," Moldaver says with a chuckle, as if talking to a naive child. "This is a principle that is applied day in and day out that is applied by the courts, so to suggest somehow that this judge erred because a couple of others took a different view assumes there's only one reasonable answer in a particular case."

No one, it seems, not even Justice Moldaver, realizes they're essentially describing a system of justice that is, at its core, subjective, and ultimately dependent on the individual views of a particular judge.

"Go ahead," Moldaver says, shaking his head. "I don't see … explain the logic," he says to Orris.

Gottardi, watching the exchange, laughs from his seat.

"It's quite simple," Orris replies, explaining that it allowed an untenable result: the two judges who convicted Millington and Robinson of collusion effectively convicted Bentley and Rundel along with them even though they'd been acquitted. "It's a presumption of guilt. That's really what it comes down to," Orris says.

Moldaver has clearly made up his mind that the officers lied when they gave their statements, and they lied to cover up the lies. "For you to come, with respect, and say to us there is no reason in the world why they would try and embellish it a bit," Moldaver says forcefully, "they were concerned because someone has died. I guess they were concerned that they were going to have to justify the use of force … so they gilded the lily a bit. That's what this seems to me to come down to and here you are saying no motive whatsoever."

"Not true," Orris tells him. It's just that there's no evidence they were worried about it at all. "The Crown's theory," Orris reminds the court, "is, because somebody died, they must've believed they'd done something wrong." Orris concludes his time by saying that if Millington's conviction is allowed to stand, it is a miscarriage of justice.

"If Mr. Millington goes to jail for conspiring with the others … and he's asked why are you in jail and not the others, he's not able to explain it."

There is a brief break, during which the pained looks on Bentley's and Rundel's faces advertise their thoughts before they speak them. "I don't like it," Bentley says. "He's going to jail, and I'm not," Rundel adds.

When court resumes, Peck himself addresses the Supreme Court, in a casual, unhurried way, with long pauses between most words, that belies the wealth of legal acumen behind his rimless eyeglasses. He begins by explaining the reason why there were four separate trials and not one. He was worried about delays if the calendars of four separate lawyers for the police had to be coordinated. He tells the court that if it had been a jury trial, it would have been difficult for a jury to make sense of so many allegations. Of course, none of the trials was in front of a jury and there were plenty of delays in the trials themselves. Millington's spanned nearly a year.

Peck makes a point of describing why the officers were universally wrong about Dziekanski "swinging" the stapler. "The only time the stapler was up in the air as seen on the video was when Mr. Dziekanski had just been Tasered and was lurching to the right-hand side of the screen, convulsing and heading to the ground as fifty thousand volts were coursing through his body."

It is a gratuitous description that has little to do with the arguments. It is also a surprising description coming from the prosecutor, because it is factually wrong and Peck either does, or should, know that. A Taser does not deliver fifty thousand volts to a person's body. It's actually closer to twelve hundred, though fifty thousand sounds more dramatic. In any event, it's not the voltage that causes the debilitating contraction of muscles and pain; it is the unique way the current is pulsed when the Taser trigger is pulled.

Justice Suzanne Côté is the only one among her peers who seems interested in the troubling aspects of the Crown's theory. "I understand the Pritchard video was seized upon the instruction of Mr. Robinson, right?" she says to Peck.

"Yes," Peck tells her.

"And Mr. Robinson knew that the video was seized before giving his deposition or his statement to the investigators?"

"Yes," Peck concedes.

Peck then proceeds to recast what actually happened in terms more convenient to the Crown's case. "My friend Ms. France referred to this as a stressful and dynamic event," Peck says. "Stressful and dynamic event? Yes. Fast-moving? Not so much."

Peck's proof of this incredible characterization is that it took sixteen seconds from the time the Taser was first fired until the time Dziekanski was first touched on the ground. Ignoring that those sixteen seconds have been broken down frame by frame and played in slow motion by the Crown itself to illustrate the events that took place in that short space of time, Peck says now that "it's not exactly fast-moving."

Peck then misstates the evidence when he claims the mistakes made by witnesses can't be compared to the same mistakes made by the police. "It's one thing for an eyewitness to observe an event. It's quite another when you are directly involved in the activity. You wouldn't forget grappling with somebody."

It is an odd statement, given none of the officers "forgot" they grappled with somebody. They remembered clearly that they grappled with Dziekanski, and it is this intense struggle that was mentally superimposed on the whole incident.

Referring to the absurd result of having four people involved in a conspiracy but only one convicted of it, Peck says that's just the way the system works. "That's almost a hallowed understanding we have as trial lawyers as trial judges about our process."

When Gottardi gets up on his feet, he is asked by Justice Côté to explain the sense of why Robinson would lie, knowing there was a video.

With a smirk on his face, Gottardi implies the officers were just stupid. "Well, Justice Côté," Gottardi begins, caught off guard by the commonsensical question, "I don't know. We can speculate about what Corporal Robinson might have suspected about the video. What we know is this happened ten years ago, so video then isn't what it is today. You can shoot a feature movie on an iPhone now."

The Pritchard video, though shot with a digital camera in 2007, is fairly high quality, as anyone who's seen it, including Gottardi, knows. In fact, the Crown insisted the Pritchard video was remarkable. During Robinson's trial, Scott Fenton insisted it was "clear and high quality." Gottardi, however, implies something completely without evidence, namely that when the officers saw Pritchard's camera, they immediately assumed the video was poor.

"I've often been lamenting that my clients aren't always the smartest," Gottardi says, inviting the court to believe that the past ten years of pain and suffering for so many people can be traced to a miscalculation about whether Pritchard's video was any good. "I don't know that I can answer that one any better than that," Gottardi says, before adding ironically, "There's lots of unanswered questions in this case."

However, it is one of Gottardi's shortest sentences that comes across as the most outrageous. "Collusion was not a building block of each case," he says.

"My friends simply come to this court complaining that two got acquitted, two got convicted and it's not fair," Gottardi says, summing up.

Although it is apparent the justices who spoke during the hearing have formed opinions, it is nonetheless a surprise to Millington, Rundel, and Bentley, and their friends and family, when, instead of adjourning the hearing to consider a decision, the justices rise and announce they are "retiring." That can only mean they are intent on coming back in short order with a verdict. Fifteen minutes later they return. Millington shuts his eyes as Justice Rosalie Abella declares that both his and Robinson's appeals are dismissed by a majority of the court. Justice Côté dissented and indicated she would have ordered a new trial. But it is of little consequence.

In the end, the Supreme Court justices were as concerned with the guilt or innocence of Millington or Robinson as a bricklayer would be about what he builds. It doesn't matter what's being built — a garden terrace or a prison wall — as long as the bricks all fit together in straight, predictable rows. As much as the hearing held out the hope of liberty and vindication for the officers, the justices are interested only in whether it can be said the judges made mistakes in law.

"We're not dealing with presumption of innocence here anymore," Orris says, about the role of the Supreme Court of Canada.

Ten years after four Mounties were accused of killing Robert Dziekanski, it's an open question whether the presumption of innocence was ever part of the process.

"I'm sorry," Orris says as he walks back to where Millington is now standing, shakes his hand, and pats him on the shoulder. Out in the cold, stone lobby, tears are evidence of the sadness and frustration felt by Millington's wife and mother. Orris matter-of-factly runs through a going-to-prison to-do list for Millington, who seems in shock. He must surrender to the courthouse in Milton, Ontario, to begin serving thirty months in prison somewhere in Ontario. Orris advises him to take as little as possible with him. He tells Millington to work hard once he's in prison to show that he's a model prisoner so he'll be released as soon as possible, perhaps after serving just a third of his sentence. The many years that have passed since the Braidwood Inquiry could also factor in to his sentence being reduced.

In a case that ultimately came down to a handful of words the Mounties spoke a decade ago, and to the motive to mislead that some people believe was behind those words, it is telling what one of those allegedly manipulative masterminds now utters. "So I now have a criminal record?" Millington asks, sincerely uncertain.

"You now have a criminal record," Orris answers.

While Millington must walk away from his life in less than twenty-four hours, Rundel and Bentley go back to theirs, acquitted of any crime, yet still guilty.

"I always thought we'd win the war," Bentley says, the past ten years suddenly showing on his boyish face. There is a gloom in Rundel's eyes as he stares, disbelief that Millington will be behind bars by this time tomorrow. Both men now feel a kind of survivor's guilt. At the same time, the Supreme Court of Canada's decision means they will never be able to purge their names from the alleged conspiracy to lie, which will forever be seen as fact in the verdicts that damn Millington and Robinson.

Robinson is busy at home, saying his goodbyes to his partner, Louise, and his children, and making myriad phone calls to shutter his life for as much of his two-year sentence as he's required to serve. He also must report to a courthouse in the morning to surrender. Full of bravado and righteousness to the end, he says that he is not worried about going to jail as a former police officer.

Robinson is more worried about Millington. "For Kwesi, who did nothing wrong — he gave a statement to the best of his recollection and he's just getting fucked — done in for it," Robinson says about his former junior officer. "This isn't justice."

Zofia Cisowski learns of the high court decision while at home in Kamloops. She also finds the result imperfect and wishes all four of the men she routinely accused of murdering her son had been found guilty of more serious charges. This will have to do. "It's time to go to jail for them," Cisowski says, believing wrongly, as many people do, that it is only now the Mounties are facing consequences for what happened the night Robert Dziekanski died ten years ago.

AFTERWORD

MONTY ROBINSON WAS STOIC about the possibility of prison, back when he still had hope that the Supreme Court would see the absurdity of sending two men to jail while two others were acquitted of the same alleged conspiracy. "It's going to be wrong but has not the last eight years been wrong for me? What's another two years?"

Quite a bit, as it turns out. Robison surrendered himself the morning after the Supreme Court's ruling. He spent the next two days in a remand facility, where he was told that his safety couldn't be guaranteed where he was going. His hands and feet were shackled. He was loaded into a van and driven two hours east of Vancouver to Ford Mountain Correctional Centre.

A medium-security facility, it is surrounded by dense forest and snow-capped mountain peaks. The B.C. government's description of it makes it sound like a summer camp: "programs and activities are provided in work, recreation, education, life skills and personal development." Robinson's take is less positive. "It smells like ass," Robinson says of his dorm, where nineteen men share two showers.

The total inmate population fluctuates between seventy and ninety or so. Most are sexual offenders. "You throw a rock in the parade square," Robinson says, "you're going to hit a pedophile." It's eye-opening even for a police officer. "I've arrested them, but I haven't had conversations with them for months to see how sick they really are."

Robinson watches as some who he thinks are certain to reoffend get released before he does. He steels himself, determined not to come out with any bad habits. He chairs the weekly AA meetings in jail. He embraces a suspicion about everything.

Robinson sees stomach-churning unsanitary conditions. Fellow inmates don't wash. They handle the laundry. They work in the kitchen. "They fuck with your food," he says. "That's why sometimes guys won't touch soup."

Robinson drops weight and takes on the appearance of a heroin addict, despite working out and a steady routine of manual labour that involves grinding axe blades for the BC Forest Service. The reality that inmates — some of them serving time for violent crimes — are given access to axes and power tools adds to Robinson's anxiety. "I will have trauma from my first week in jail forever."

His only hope comes from the likelihood of early release. As is done with all offenders, Robinson is evaluated in detail for parole eligibility. Early in the new year, after serving two months, he's interviewed by a parole officer. It is yet another opportunity for the former Mountie to make the case that he's being punished for Robert Dziekanski's death.

"Mr. ROBINSON stated there was tremendous political interest as a result of the Dziekanski incident and media attention it received," parole officer Phil Smith writes in his report, adding that Robinson feels "he was 'scapegoated by both the RCMP and other high ranking officials in government.'"

Smith describes Robinson's behaviour in jail as "exceptional and without incident," and he notes Robinson has been compliant and respectful. "While Mr. ROBINSON maintains his innocence of this offence and that he never committed perjury, he has exhausted all forms of appeal and accepts that he will need to serve the sentence he received."

What that means, however, is release from custody after spending one-third of the sentence behind a barbed-wire fence. Robinson is released from custody in early July 2018. His partner, Louise, picks him up at a bus station and Robinson climbs into the driver's seat and heads straight home with a short list of priorities: "I want to reconnect with my kids, walk the dog, and Louise can hold me while I cry."

Release from jail doesn't mean complete freedom, however. For the remainder of his sentence, Robinson must regularly check with a parole officer and his local police department. He is also prohibited from going anywhere the parole office hasn't officially evaluated. So, while Robinson can drive from his home in Delta to Vancouver — about an hour away — he's not allowed to venture further by, say, driving over the Lions Gate Bridge into North Vancouver. He is also forbidden from making the three-hour drive to Merritt, where his sixteen-year-old son lives with the boy's mother.

It's hard to fathom why the travel restrictions are necessary. No one has suggested Robinson is a risk for reoffending, that he will embark on some kind of a perjury spree. The restriction is only a minor frustration, however, compared to incarceration. The constraint also becomes less pressing when the Department of Justice informs the lawyer handling Robinson's lawsuit against the RCMP that the government will seek to have his legal claim quashed. Government lawyers have dragged their heels for months, failing to produce documents Robinson believes will support his case. Now they say his lawsuit isn't valid because he waited too long to file it.

When Kwesi Millington learns of Robinson's release, he sends him a text. "Welcome home, man. Hope all is well."

Though Robinson and Millington have never been close, they share a brief exchange that transcends any differences. "I'm thin and built like a jacked up heroin addict," Robinson replies.

"Good. Good. Glad to hear you're out, my friend," comes the response.

———————

Millington tasted freedom before Robinson did, despite having a stiffer sentence. The man who pulled the trigger on the Taser has been out of prison for two months, albeit with a requirement to sleep each night at a halfway house until the end of August 2018, at which point Millington will have served a third of his thirty-month sentence. The condition allows Millington to spend a good part of the day with his wife, Cindy. It's not ideal, but it's better than being locked up in the minimum-security section of Joyceville Institution near Kingston, Ontario.

If Millington experienced anything comparable to Robinson's incarceration trauma, he doesn't let on, preferring, as he has for some time, to focus on the future.

It seems that the RCMP also wishes to forget the past and focus on the future. Indeed, the force moved swiftly to sever Millington's ties with it. Just two weeks after Millington entered prison, a superintendent of O Division signed a recommendation to discharge Millington. It was finalized and served on Millington with haste. He wasn't given the opportunity to respond or to see any documents, as is required by a standing order in the RCMP Act.

While Millington views his time in prison differently than does Robinson, it was, nonetheless, difficult. Initially, he and Cindy worried they would default on their mortgage. A campaign on GoFundMe was launched, then shut down for violating the crowdfunding site's terms that prohibit raising money to benefit those charged with serious violations of the law. Regardless of his parole conditions, Millington — ever the outward optimist — announces his return to semi-freedom with a post on Facebook: "New month, new beginnings. Happy and grateful for the next stage of life." He abandons an appeal he filed in B.C. Supreme Court to have his sentence overturned. He returns to posting on social media. His updates feature inspirational observations and biblical quotes.

While Robinson and Millington continue to pay their debt to society, a price is also exacted on their former partners acquitted of the so-called conspiracy.

Gerry Rundel and Bill Bentley live daily with the guilt. The beneficiaries of some fateful combination of defence lawyers and judges who looked at the evidence and knocked the stuffing out of Braidwood's conclusions about the Mounties, the pair, nevertheless, continue to serve their own kind of sentences. The verdicts in their criminal cases

aren't, by definition, declarations of innocence. Moreover, the findings of the two judges who issued convictions against Robinson and
Millington not only cast doubt on Rundel and Bentley, they essentially
named them as co-conspirators.

Bentley, anxious to resume his childhood dream of being a police
officer, tries to keep his head down, despite having filed his own lawsuit
alleging wrongdoing. By April 2018, Bentley is back at work, but yet
to be certified to the point he was at as a rookie a decade ago. He hasn't
shot a firearm in ten years. It's been a dozen years since he was trained in
use of force. His once boyish face now has a number of lines that hint at
his age and how much time has passed.

If the RCMP had a face, it might also reveal a network of wrinkles and
worry lines etched by a history of dysfunction and neglect, if not outright wanton mistreatment, of many of its thirty thousand members.
In order to put claims of systemic sexual harassment to rest, the RCMP
pledges one hundred million dollars to victims and their families. The
Merlo-Davidson settlement, named after two RCMP members among
the first to sue, opens a door that RCMP management never wanted to
open. In June 2018, two Mounties jointly apply to the Federal Court
of Canada to certify a one-billion-dollar class action against the RCMP
alleging a history of broad-based bullying, harassment, and corruption.
Ten years ago, the force could afford to keep silent while four officers
who thought they'd acted according to their training became the focus
of the public's animus. That strategy now seems quaint, by comparison.
The million-dollar settlement paid to Dziekanski's mother, a bargain.

The new RCMP commissioner, appointed in 2018, inherits it all.
Yet, in her formal remarks Brenda Lucki doesn't directly address the
litany of problems outlined by the minister of public safety in her mandate letter. Ralph Goodale instructs her to "prioritize that the RCMP is
free from bullying, harassment, and sexual violence." Goodale goes on
to tell her a prority must be to deal with clear mental health issues in

the force. Lucki, however, eschews allocuting the RCMP's failures, and instead refers obliquely to "challenges." "Throughout my career," she attests, "I can honestly say that I have been very lucky to have worked with so many great leaders who have made many positive differences in our organization."

Lucki's RCMP bears no resemblance to the organization described in any of the lawsuits, though she offers a vague promise "that no stone will be left unturned" to make things better. Whatever Lucki has in mind, it is too late for former constable Krista Carle. In Alberta, Carle endured dozens of incidents of sexual harassment and bullying before developing PTSD and receiving a medical discharge. She became a central figure, advocate, and witness decrying the abuse occurring in the ranks. The cost was high: she lost not only her career; she also lost her marriage and her family. Four months after Lucki became the first female commissioner of the RCMP, Carle committed suicide.

In July 2018, one day after Carle's death becomes public, the RCMP quietly settles a lawsuit brought by Pierre Lemaitre's widow, Sheila, and binds her to a nondisclosure agreement, assuring the best possible light for the RCMP at a coroner's inquest into Lemaitre's suicide scheduled for the following November.

———

Rundel has not given up shaking the tree. He writes to his new commissioner. After congratulating her on the appointment, Rundel lays out a synopsis of what he sees as the failure of the RCMP to back its members. "Shamefully, the RCMP ignored [the findings of B.C.'s Criminal Justice Branch], the Doust opinion, their own policies and procedures, and the facts of their own investigations." Instead, RCMP management threw the YVR Mounties to the wolves. "Why would the RCMP do this to its members?" he asks, before concluding that "it's never too late to right the wrongs of the past." Rundel asks for a full-blown criminal investigation.

Lucki eventually replies. It's not what Rundel wants to hear. "I acknowledge receipt of your requests," Lucki writes, "given the fact that there remains ongoing civil litigation regarding events related to this matter, it would not be appropriate for me to launch any investigations." It's not necessarily surprising, given Rundel, Robinson, and Bentley are suing the organization Lucki now runs. An argument could be made that the RCMP couldn't be relied upon to conduct an unbiased investigation into it's own actions that are the subject of lawsuits. It isn't the first, or the last, missive Rundel authors. In the fall of 2017, a New Brunswick provincial court judge found the RCMP guilty of failing to properly equip and train officers after a man shot and killed three of them. Testimony during the trial suggested that, years earlier, the RCMP had failed to do proper research before embracing the Taser as a go-to weapon. Rundel points out the revelation in an email to a long list of recipients from the prime minister of Canada on down.

Ralph Goodale sends a boilerplate reply about ensuring the safety of the "brave women and men who put themselves at risk." Goodale makes it clear, however, that he won't comment "on particular court decisions or matters before the courts."

It is a polite, but definite, way of closing the door in his face. Still, Rundel feels compelled to keep writing. He spends hours at his keyboard outlining his case, and bombarding the RCMP with freedom of information demands for documents the force is reluctant or slow to produce. Yet even if Rundel were to abandon the attempts to clear his name, he could never just walk away.

Early in 2018, Mounties in Chilliwack, British Columbia, use a Taser to subdue a man. He died. Before much of anything is known about what happened, a news story appears that references Dziekanski's death a decade earlier. It highlights the perjury charges, the prison sentences for the police involved, and little else.

"It's hard to heal when the bashing never stops," Rundel laments. "How do you heal when the bombs keep dropping? I guess that's why I head off into the woods fishing all alone and find my peace." As the calendar closes in on October 2018 and the eleventh anniversary of Dziekanski's death, there are some signs that the relentless stream of accusatory letters Rundel and Robinson have been firing at federal officials is having an effect. Commissioner Lucki, at first brusquely dismissive, emails Rundel that "there are many important components to both your messages as well as those from Mr. Robinson," adding, "I am further reviewing the questions you have raised." Through their lawyers, Rundel, Bentley, and Robinson are told the Department of Justice may be interested in settling their lawsuits rather than litigate them.

Whatever optimism they feel is quickly beaten down when Richard Peck formally ends his job as special prosecutor in the case in September 2018 and issues a promised "clear statement" to the public, explaining his rationale for charging the officers. For the first time Peck reveals he had considered indicting the Mounties for a whole list of crimes including manslaughter, assault, and failing to provide the necessities of life. For some offences — Peck doesn't specify which — he didn't think he had enough evidence to win in court. However, Peck expounds on why he felt prevented from going after the Mounties for Dziekanski's death. The officers were compelled by subpoena to testify at the inquiry. "The law protects the person from having such testimony used, either directly or indirectly, against that person at the person's subsequent criminal trial (except in the case of a perjury charge)," Peck writes. His assessment was that the officers' defence lawyers would successfully make their clients' right to a fair trial a "significant obstacle" to the prosecution. "My decision may not have been popular with some" Peck offers, presumably to those who wanted the Mounties charged with murder, "but I could not be swayed by emotion or public opinion." Still, Peck acknowledges he harboured his own feelings from the moment he wrote the indictments. "I was and remain mindful of the tragic consequences of that fateful confrontation at the Vancouver International Airport." Peck does not offer any analysis of the conflicting verdicts beyond simply listing them. A reasonable person reading his clear statement might very well conclude that despite two acquittals on the best evidence Peck's team could marshal, all four are not only guilty of perjury, but possibly much worse. For Bentley and Rundel in particular, Peck's final judgement amplifies that of Braidwood, condemning them with suspicion.

Branding four police officers as self-serving liars isn't the only legacy of Thomas Braidwood's inquiry. The retired appeal court judge's other achievement was to convince the provincial government to create an alternative to police investigating other police in cases of death or serious injury. Ostensibly, this was to avoid the perception of conflict and incompetence many believed tainted the investigation into Dziekanksi's death. Braidwood's idea — the Independent Investigations Office [IIO] — was to be a civilian-run organization untainted by scandal that would restore public confidence in the police.

In the years since its establishment in 2012, the IIO has arguably become known more for its own deficiencies and missteps than for ending cynicism about perceived police bias. Since its inception, a team of two dozen investigators — many of them former police officers — has been called in to more than a hundred cases. However, it has taken months, and in some cases years, to wrap up their findings. By the time Monty Robinson is released from jail, Crown prosecutors looking at the work of IIO investigators have found just fifteen cases in which evidence supports laying a charge. Just a handful of those actually result in convictions — for things like assault or careless driving, and usually because the officer pleads guilty. The rest are aquitted or the charges are stayed. In the same time period the IIO has suffered from its own crisis of public confidence. The organization's delays, fights with police and union officials, sloppy investigations that lacked discipline, and resignations amid allegations of internal bullying have all wound up as headlines. Most notably, it is simply impossible to objectively conclude the IIO has made police in British Columbia more accountable, or that it conducts investigations with any more integrity than the multiple probes carried out by trained police who examined the death of Robert Dziekanski. Perception, however, is often reality.

The unintended tragedy of Dziekanski's death cast a long and lasting shadow over many lives, including that of his mother. The police officers, who were the last to see him alive, also endure the separate punishment of forever carrying the indelible stain of guilt.

ACKNOWLEDGEMENTS

WHEN THE MANUSCRIPT for *Blamed and Broken* was finished, after months of writing and fine-tuning, my catharsis, which was more than a decade in the making, was short-lived. My editor wanted one more thing: the acknowledgements. I found myself more stymied by the terror of a blank page than at any other time telling this story. Perhaps it was because of the sheer volume of writing I'd just finished. I think it's more likely that this simple list of people (and cats) who helped me isn't as easy to finish because it's *my* story and not someone else's. So, thanks, Dominic Farrell, for pushing me on this extra step on top of polishing my prose.

There are many others at Dundurn Press without whom I wouldn't have attempted to construct a sentence using the word *whom*. From the editorial director, Kathryn Lane, who had faith in the importance of the story and my ability to write it, to Laura Boyle who designed the cover, and everyone else who touched this work in some way, thank you. Thanks to copy editor Laurie Miller for his fresh eyes and fine-tuning, which allows me to appear as if I can write good.

It's quite possible this book would not have been published were it not for my agent, Ron Eckel, and his colleagues at CookeMcDermid Agency, who championed my work and patiently helped me take an idea to a cohesive and compelling narrative.

I was introduced to Ron after publishers I'd approached on my own politely rejected the book as "old news." I was fortunate, then, when journalist and filmmaker Maureen Palmer put us in touch.

Maureen is business and creative partners with a woman I cannot thank enough for encouragement, support, sound judgment, and sage advice. Helen Slinger of Bountiful Films, thank you for the walks, the talks, and the tears. For his wisdom and counsel about this case, the law, and this book, I am grateful to Ravi Hira.

I feel secure enough to admit that the last few years have been the hardest and most difficult of my life, for reasons that have nothing to do with this book, per se. I developed PTSD as a result of my work as a journalist, reporting on natural disasters and human tragedy. On the one hand, I was traumatized. Relationships collapsed. On the other hand, I met psychiatrist Donna Dryer and her husband psychologist, Richard Yensen, who not only treated me, they encouraged me to write as therapy. So I took them up on it.

It should be obvious I could not have written authentically and reliably about people without having spoken to them and those who know them. It took years before the four men at the centre of *Blamed and Broken* cautiously agreed to submit to questions, doing so even though I could offer no guarantees or promises about where it would lead.

What Monty Robinson, Kwesi Millington, Bill Bentley, and Gerry Rundel wouldn't or couldn't tell me, I learned from a long list of others. Some are named in this book. Many are not. I thank them all.

My most humble gratitude and respect is reserved for two women linked by the tragic events of October 13 and October 14, 2007. Zofia Cisowski lost her son, and no apology or trial verdict can ever be seen as compensation. Sheila Lemaitre lost her husband after years of despicably false accusations.

As a journalist, first in radio, then TV, and eventually digital media, I felt writing a book was never a priority. There were too many stories happening every day to stop and take a long view. My mentor and dear departed friend David McLauchlin taught me many years ago why it's important to dig deeper into a story when others have decided there's nothing left to say. I dare say David has spoken to me most days since he died fifteen years ago. I see some of his spirit in those colleagues who also encouraged me as I pursued this story over the years.

While it might seem gratuitous to thank my family, I think it's imperative. I must, of course, thank my two brothers, John and Ed, for not having gone into journalism and writing books. This has allowed me to be the first author in my small family. I wonder sometimes what my mother would say. She died before I even had my first real job as a journalist. At one time she thought I might be a lawyer. Mom, this is as close as I got. My father has seen little of me as I've moved from one part of the country to another. Yet there's some of my father's honestly earned skepticism and critical thinking in me. Dad's regular "What's happening with the book?" during our infrequent phone calls was a source of motivation.

Finally, there are the people who've put up with every mood you can imagine having when you commit to writing a book like this. Yvette Brend, Eliana, and Daniel, I don't say thank you enough.

And when I could not read another document, type another word, or even speak, that was okay with Evie and Cheeks. Murr.

IMAGE CREDITS

Bill Bentley: 151
Braidwood Inquiry — screengrab from Pritchard video, Exhibit #32:
43, 44
Braidwood Inquiry — screengrab from Pritchard video, Exhibit #86:
42, 59, 160
Carolyn Hewitt: 159
Curt Petrovich: 77, 275, 276, 278, 279, 283, 286
Gerry Rundel: 146
Monty Robinson: 167
Sheila Lemaitre: 217
Yolande Cole: 231

INDEX

Italic page numbers indicate photos. Bold entries indicate chronological order of events.

Book Credits
Developmental Editor: Dominic Farrell
Project Editor: Elena Radic
Copy Editor: Laurie Miller
Proofreader: Ashley Hisson
Indexer: Siusan Moffat

Cover Designer: Laura Boyle
Interior Designer: B.J. Weckerle

Publicist: Tabassum Siddiqui

Dundurn
Publisher: J. Kirk Howard
Vice-President: Carl A. Brand
Editorial Director: Kathryn Lane
Artistic Director: Laura Boyle
Production Manager: Rudi Garcia
Director of Sales and Marketing: Synora Van Drine
Publicity Manager: Michelle Melski
Manager, Accounting and Technical Services: Livio Copetti

Editorial: Allison Hirst, Dominic Farrell, Jenny McWha,
Rachel Spence, Elena Radic, Melissa Kawaguchi
Marketing and Publicity: Kendra Martin, Kathryn Bassett,
Elham Ali, Tabassum Siddiqui, Heather McLeod
Design and Production: Sophie Paas-Lang

dundurn.com   dundurnpress
@dundurnpress   dundurnpress
dundurnpress   info@dundurn.com

FIND US ON NETGALLEY & GOODREADS TOO!

DUNDURN